T5-ANX-100

ZAGATSURVEY®

2007

PHILADELPHIA RESTAURANTS

Local Editor: Michael Klein

Local Coordinator: Marilyn Kleinberg

Staff Editor: Robert Seixas

Published and distributed by
ZAGAT SURVEY, LLC
4 Columbus Circle
New York, New York 10019
Tel: 212 977 6000
E-mail: philadelphia@zagat.com
Web site: www.zagat.com

Acknowledgments

We thank Fran and Joe Alberstadt; Charlotte Ann, Dick and Ann-Michelle Albertson; Carol Bedics and Ben Preston; Cindy and Richard Blum; Norman and Suzanne Cohn; Jennifer Dorazio; Marcia Gelbart; Ellen and Steve Goldman; Tom and Loretta Jordan; Alan and Jodi Klein; Rachel and Lindsay Klein; Sybil Rothstein; Doris and Joe Segel; Steven Shukow; Scott Soffen; and the *Philadelphia Inquirer*'s food crew: Maureen Fitzgerald, Craig LaBan, Marilynn Marter and Rick Nichols. We are also grateful to our editorial assistants, Jessica Grose and Kelly Stewart, as well as the following members of our staff: Maryanne Bertollo, Reni Chin, Larry Cohn, Andrew Eng, Schuyler Frazier, Jeff Freier, Natalie Lebert, Mike Liao, Dave Makulec, Emily Parsons, Becky Reimer, Thomas Sheehan, Joshua Siegel, Carla Spartos, Sharon Yates and Kyle Zolner.

Contents

About This Survey

Here are the results of our *2007 Philadelphia Restaurant Survey,* covering 872 establishments as tested, and tasted, by 5,035 local restaurant-goers. To help you find the area's best meals and best buys, we have prepared a number of lists. See Most Popular (page 9), Top Ratings (pages 10–16), Best Buys (page 17), Prix Fixe Bargains (page 18) and 49 handy indexes (pages 162–219).

This marks the 27th year that Zagat Survey has reported on the shared experiences of diners like you. What started in 1979 as a hobby involving 200 of our friends rating NYC restaurants has come a long way. Today we have over 250,000 active surveyors and now cover dining, entertaining, golf, hotels, resorts, spas, movies, music, nightlife, shopping, theater and tourist attractions. All of these guides are based on consumer surveys. They are also available by subscription at zagat.com, and for use on PDAs and cell phones.

By regularly surveying large numbers of avid customers, we hope to have achieved a uniquely current and reliable series of guides. More than a quarter-century of experience has verified this. If understood properly, these guides are the restaurant industry's report card, since each place's ratings and review are really a free market study of its own customers.

This year's participants dined out an average of 2.7 times per week, meaning this *Survey* is based on roughly 698,000 meals. Of these 5,000-plus surveyors, 49% are women, 51% men; the breakdown by age is 12% in their 20s; 26%, 30s; 19%, 40s; 25%, 50s; and 18%, 60s or above. Our editors have synopsized our surveyors' opinions, with their comments shown in quotation marks. We sincerely thank each of these people; this book is really "theirs."

We are especially grateful to our editor, Michael Klein, a features columnist at the *Philadelphia Inquirer,* who has written its restaurant-news column, "Table Talk," since 1993 – his first year as Zagat Survey's Philadelphia editor, and our coordinator, Marilyn Kleinberg, local franchise operator of CruiseOne in Cherry Hill, NJ.

Finally, we invite you to join any of our upcoming *Surveys* – to do so, just register at zagat.com. Each participant will receive a free copy of the resulting guide when it is published. Your comments and even criticisms of this guide are also solicited. There is always room for improvement with your help. Just contact us at philadelphia@zagat.com.

New York, NY
August 23, 2006

Nina and Tim Zagat

What's New

If you like to dine out in Philadelphia, these are happy days, and not just because openings easily exceeded closings in the past year (as they have every year we've published this book). Mayor John F. Street has a City Council smoking ban awaiting his signature and scheduled to take effect in January 2007. It's a move 89% of our surveyors are looking forward to.

Bring It In: Couple the rising numbers of entrepreneurial chef-owners with the soaring cost of liquor licenses, and you have the recipe for America's most bustling BYO scene. Newcomers such as Bistro 7, Divan Turkish Kitchen, Majolica and Taste have joined the long list of Philly's BYO standouts. As evidence of the flourishing market, 46% of respondents report bringing their own as frequently as they did last year, while 37% say they are doing so more often.

The High Life: Since 65% of Philadelphians say they're spending more per meal than they did two years ago, it's no surprise that high-end dining is thriving. Consider a few of the latest expense-account entries: Amada, Jose Garces' Spaniard (and this year's top-rated newcomer); Estia, a Greek seafooder opposite the Academy of Music; Blush, a New American that has replaced Bianca; Pond, the French-Med in Passerelle's former space; Nineteen in the Park Hyatt at the Bellevue; and Gayle, a tiny New American from Le Bec-Fin alum Daniel Stern, who also plans to debut Rae, a New American. And for those who thought the days of haute were gone, Fountain has again captured the Triple Crown this year, placing No. 1 for Food, Decor and Service.

More in Store: Rolling out at press time is Water Works, a Museum of Art–area New American to be situated by the Schuylkill. A branch of the luxury chain Oceanaire Seafood Room is slated for Washington Square this fall, while the renowned Georges Perrier and his protégé, Chris Scarduzio (Le Bec-Fin, Brasserie Perrier, et al.), are cooking up a New American for the Comcast Center, with a 2007 date in mind.

Check-out Counter: It's certainly news that Philadelphians are the nation's highest tippers (leaving 19.4% on top of every check). But it's also worth noting that the $32.81 average cost of a Philly meal is mere pennies above the nation's ($32.40), dollars less than New Jersey's ($35.03) and NYC's ($37.61), and about half of what you'll pay in London ($70) and Paris ($66) – all the better to understand why gourmets, from cheese steak enthusiasts to fine-dining fans, enjoy eating here.

Philadelphia, PA
August 23, 2006

Michael Klein

Ratings & Symbols

Name, Address, Phone Number & Web Site

Zagat Ratings

Hours & Credit Cards

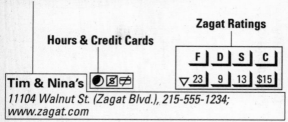

	F	D	S	C
	▽23	9	13	$15

Tim & Nina's ◑ 🗓 ⇹

11104 Walnut St. (Zagat Blvd.), 215-555-1234; www.zagat.com

"Yo!" – join all the Iggles and Phils fans who flock to this "run-down" 24-hour joint for its "belly-busting" cheese steaks and "five-pound" hoagies served up proudly with a side of "sass" by "Port Richmond girls" dripping with "attitude"; though your cardiologist surely thinks of this "classic" Philly grub as a "heart attack on a plate", you'll probably find him in line here, possibly looking for patients.

Review, with surveyors' comments in quotes

Top Spots: Places with the highest overall ratings, popularity and importance are listed in BLOCK CAPITAL LETTERS.

Hours: ◑ serves after 11 PM
🗓 closed on Sunday

Credit Cards: ⇹ no credit cards accepted

Ratings are on a scale of **0** to **30**.

F	Food	D	Decor	S	Service	C	Cost
23		9		13		$15	

0–9 poor to fair	**20–25** very good to excellent
10–15 fair to good	**26–30** extraordinary to perfection
16–19 good to very good	▽ low response/less reliable

Cost (C): Reflects our surveyors' average estimate of the price of a dinner with one drink and tip and is a benchmark only. Lunch is usually 25% less.

For newcomers or survey write-ins listed without ratings, the price range is indicated as follows:

I	$25 and below	**E**	$41 to $65
M	$26 to $40	**VE**	$66 or more

Most Popular

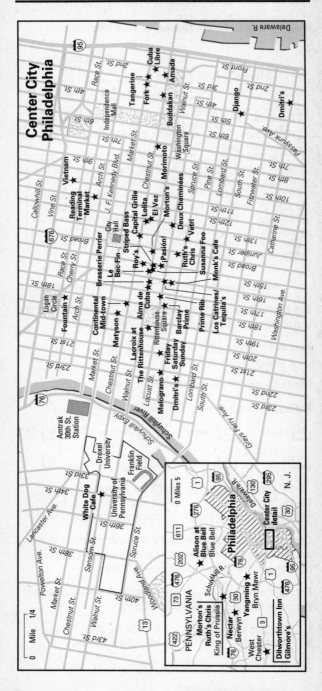

Center City Philadelphia

Delaware R.

Cuba Libre
Amada
Tangerine
Fork
Buddakan
Django
Dmitri's
Vietnam
Reading Terminal Market
Morimoto
Washington Square
Capital Grille
Lolita
El Vez
Morton's
Deux Cheminées
Vetri
Striped Bass
Brasserie Perrier
Le Bec-Fin
Roy's
¡Pasión!
Ruth's Chris
Susanna Foo
Monk's Cafe
Fountain
Continental Mid-town
Matyson
Alma de Cuba
Los Catrines/Tequila's
Lacroix at The Rittenhouse
Friday Saturday Sunday
Barclay Prime
Prime Rib
Melograno
Dmitri's
Amtrak 30th St. Station
Drexel University
Franklin Field
White Dog Cafe
University of Pennsylvania

Independence Mall
City Hall

PENNSYLVANIA
Morton's
Ruth's Chris
King of Prussia
Alison at Blue Bell
Blue Bell
Philadelphia
Center City detail
N. J.
Nectar
Berwyn
Yangming
Bryn Mawr
West Chester
Dilworthtown Inn
Gilmore's
Schuylkill R.

0 Miles 5
0   Mile   1/4

Most Popular

Each surveyor has been asked to name his or her five favorite places. This list reflects their choices.

1. Buddakan	21. Gilmore's
2. Le Bec-Fin	22. Prime Rib
3. Fountain	23. El Vez
4. Lacroix/Rittenhouse	24. Cuba Libre
5. Brasserie Perrier	25. Continental Mid-town
6. Alma de Cuba	26. Monk's Cafe
7. Susanna Foo	27. Melograno
8. Morimoto	28. Lolita
9. Striped Bass	29. Alison/Blue Bell
10. Vetri	30. Barclay Prime
11. Capital Grille	31. Morton's
12. ¡Pasión!	32. Yangming
13. Matyson	33. Deux Cheminées*
14. Dmitri's	34. Reading Term. Mkt.
15. Tangerine	35. Dilworthtown Inn
16. Fork	36. Roy's
17. Amada	37. Ruth's Chris
18. Nectar	38. Vietnam
19. Django	39. Friday Sat. Sun.
20. White Dog Cafe	40. Los Catrines

It's obvious that many of the restaurants on the above list are among Philadelphia's most expensive, but if popularity were calibrated to price, we suspect that a number of other restaurants would join the above ranks. Given the fact that both our surveyors and readers love to discover dining bargains, we have added a list of 80 Best Buys and restaurants offering prix fixe bargains on pages 17–18. These are restaurants that give real quality at extremely reasonable prices.

* Indicates a tie with restaurant above

Top Ratings

Excluding places with low voting, unless indicated.
Top places outside Philadelphia appear on pages 13–14.

Food

28 Fountain	EverMay/Delaware
Le Bar Lyonnais	Alison/Blue Bell
Birchrunville Store	Totaro's
Le Bec-Fin	Nan
Vetri	Bridgetown Mill
27 Lacroix/Rittenhouse	L'Angolo
Gilmore's	Rest. Alba
Morimoto	Pif
Savona	Shank's & Evelyn's*
Amada	Brasserie Perrier
Buddakan	**25** Capital Grille
Bluefin	Majolica
Deux Cheminées	Susanna Foo
26 Paloma	Lolita
Gayle	Barclay Prime
Mainland Inn	High St. Caffé
Striped Bass	Bitar's
Blue Sage	Umbria
La Bonne Auberge	Dilworthtown Inn
Swann Lounge	Kimberton Inn

By Cuisine

American (New)
26 Gayle
Mainland Inn
Swann Lounge
EverMay/Delaware
Alison/Blue Bell

American (Traditional)
25 Kimberton Inn
24 Mercato
Standard Tap
Rose Tree Inn
General Warren

Barbecue
23 Rib Crib
22 Sweet Lucy's
20 Bomb Bomb BBQ
19 Abner's BBQ

Cheese Steaks
24 Tony Luke's
Dalessandro's
22 Jim's Steaks
21 Campo's Deli
20 Pat's Steaks

Chinese
25 Susanna Foo
Shiao Lan Kung
24 CinCin
Yangming
Lakeside Chinese

Continental
26 Bridgetown Mill
23 William Penn Inn
22 Avalon
21 Vickers Tavern
20 Seven Stars Inn

Eclectic
26 Totaro's
25 Umbria
Sabrina's Café
Citrus
24 Sola

French
28 Birchrunville Store
27 Lacroix/Rittenhouse
Gilmore's
Savona
Deux Cheminées

French (Bistro)
28 Le Bar Lyonnais
26 Pif
22 Spring Mill Café
    Brasserie 73
20 Bistro St. Tropez

French (New)
28 Fountain
    Le Bec-Fin
26 Swann Lounge
    Brasserie Perrier
24 Bunha Faun

Greek
24 Dmitri's
23 Estia
21 Effie's
    South St. Souvlaki
20 Zesty's

Indian
24 Karma
22 Khajuraho
20 Cafe Spice
    Palace of Asia
19 Tandoor India

Italian
28 Vetri
26 L'Angolo
    Shank's & Evelyn's
25 Melograno
    Sovalo

Japanese
27 Morimoto
    Bluefin
24 Margaret Kuo's Peking
    Margaret Kuo's Media
23 Shiroi Hana

Latin/South American
25 ¡Pasión!
24 Alma de Cuba
23 Tierra Colombiana
22 Cuba Libre
21 Mixto

Malaysian/Vietnamese
24 Vietnam
    Nam Phuong
23 Vietnam Palace
21 Penang
20 Pho 75

Mediterranean
24 Overtures
    Tangerine
23 Valanni
    Arpeggio
22 Figs

Mexican
26 Paloma
25 Lolita
24 Los Catrines
23 Las Cazuelas
    La Cava

Pizza
24 Tacconelli's Pizzeria
23 Mama Palma's
    Arpeggio
22 Celebre's
21 Marra's

Pub Food
24 Standard Tap
22 N. 3rd
    Monk's Cafe
20 Abbaye
18 America B&G

Seafood
26 Striped Bass
24 Dmitri's
    Little Fish
23 Bridgets
    Radicchio

Southern/Soul Food
24 Honey's Sit 'n Eat
22 Carversville Inn
21 Marsha Brown
19 Abner's BBQ
18 Jack's Firehse.

Steakhouses
25 Capital Grille
    Barclay Prime
    Prime Rib
24 Morton's
23 Bridgets

Thai
26 Nan
23 Cafe de Laos
    Teikoku
    Thai Orchid
    Vientiane Café

Top Food

By Special Feature

Breakfast

25 Sabrina's Café
24 Honey's Sit 'n Eat
22 Morning Glory
   Famous 4th St. Deli
21 Carman's Country

Brunch

28 Fountain
27 Lacroix/Rittenhouse
26 Mainland Inn
   Swann Lounge
25 Kimberton Inn

BYO

28 Birchrunville Store
27 Gilmore's
26 Blue Sage
   Alison/Blue Bell
25 Chlöe

Child-Friendly

23 Mama Palma's
20 Winnie's Le Bus
19 Nifty Fifty's
18 California Pizza
15 Christopher's

Classic Philly

20 Pat's Steaks
19 Geno's Steaks
18 Old Orig. Bookbinder's
   City Tavern
17 Melrose Diner

Hotel Dining

28 Fountain
   Four Seasons
27 Lacroix/Rittenhouse
   Rittenhouse Hotel
26 Swann Lounge
   Four Seasons
   EverMay/Delaware
   EverMay on the Delaware
25 Prime Rib
   Radisson Warwick

Late Dining

25 Shiao Lan Kung
24 Tony Luke's
   Standard Tap
   Dalessandro's
21 Dahlak

Meet for a Drink

26 Brasserie Perrier
25 Capital Grille
   Prime Rib
24 Standard Tap
23 Beau Monde

Newcomers/Rated

27 Amada
26 Gayle
25 Ansill▽
24 Horizons▽
23 Estia

Newcomers/Unrated

Bar Ferdinand
Blush
Divan Turkish Kitchen
Nineteen
Pond/Bistro Cassis

Offbeat

27 Morimoto
24 Tacconelli's Pizzeria
   Honey's Sit 'n Eat
22 Pod
21 Carman's Country

People-Watching

27 Lacroix/Rittenhouse
   Morimoto
   Amada
   Buddakan
26 Striped Bass

Power Lunch

28 Fountain
   Le Bec-Fin
27 Lacroix/Rittenhouse
   Morimoto
   Buddakan

Private Rooms for Parties

27 Lacroix/Rittenhouse
   Savona
   Amada
26 La Bonne Auberge
24 Alma de Cuba

Quick Bites

25 Bitar's
24 Tony Luke's
   Reading Term. Mkt.
23 Tierra Colombiana
22 Jim's Steaks

Top Food

Quiet Conversation
28 Birchrunville Store
27 Lacroix/Rittenhouse
Gilmore's
Deux Cheminées
22 Le Castagne

Sleepers▽
25 Pho Xe Lua
Sovana Bistro
Bona Cucina
Golden Pheasant*
Jong Ka Jib*

Small Plates
27 Lacroix/Rittenhouse (French)
Amada (Spanish)
23 Teca (Italian)▽
22 Continental (Eclectic)
21 Derek's (New American)

Transporting Experience
28 Birchrunville Store
Le Bec-Fin
Vetri
27 Lacroix/Rittenhouse
Gilmore's

Trendy
27 Morimoto
Amada
Buddakan
25 Capital Grille
Ansill▽

Winning Wine Lists
28 Le Bec-Fin
Vetri
27 Lacroix/Rittenhouse
Savona
23 La Famiglia

By Location

Art Museum/Fairmount
22 Rose Tattoo
Figs
20 Bridgid's
19 Rembrandt's
Museum Restaurant

Avenue of the Arts
25 Capital Grille
23 Grill
Bliss
22 Palm
20 Sotto Varalli

Bucks County
26 Blue Sage
La Bonne Auberge
EverMay/Delaware
Bridgetown Mill
25 Knight House

Center City (east of Broad St.)
28 Vetri
27 Deux Cheminées
25 Lolita
24 Mercato
Reading Term. Mkt.

Center City (west of Broad St.)
28 Fountain
Le Bar Lyonnais
Le Bec-Fin
27 Lacroix/Rittenhouse
26 Striped Bass
Swann Lounge
Brasserie Perrier
25 Susanna Foo
Barclay Prime
Melograno

Chester County
28 Birchrunville Store
27 Gilmore's
25 Majolica
High St. Caffé
Dilworthtown Inn

Chestnut Hill
25 Citrus
24 CinCin
23 Osaka
21 Roller's/Flying Fish
20 Melting Pot

Top Food

Chinatown
25 Shiao Lan Kung
24 Vietnam
Lakeside Chinese
23 Lee How Fook
Sang Kee Duck Hse.

Delaware County
24 Margaret Kuo's Peking
Rose Tree Inn
Margaret Kuo's Media
23 Teikoku
Roux 3

Lancaster/Berks Counties
28 Gibraltar
27 Gracie's
25 Rest. at Doneckers
24 Green Hills Inn
Haydn Zug's

Main Line
27 Savona
26 Rest. Alba
25 Carmine's Creole
24 Nectar
Sola

Manayunk
25 Jake's
22 La Colombe
Il Tartufo
21 Derek's
Hikaru

Montgomery County
27 Bluefin
26 Mainland Inn
Alison/Blue Bell
Totaro's
25 Zakes Cafe

Northeast Philly
26 Paloma
22 Sweet Lucy's
Jim's Steaks
21 Moonstruck
20 Pho 75

Old City/Northern Liberties
27 Amada
Buddakan
25 Sovalo
Chlöe
24 Bistro 7

South Philly
26 L'Angolo
Pif
Shank's & Evelyn's*
25 Bitar's
Sabrina's Café

South St./Queen Village
26 Gayle
25 Django
24 Overtures
Dmitri's
Little Fish

Washington Square West
27 Morimoto
22 Rist. La Buca
Kibitz in City
20 Jones
17 El Azteca

West Village/University City
26 Nan
25 Marigold Kitchen
23 Rx
Vientiane Café
22 Pod

New Jersey
26 Sagami
Ritz Seafood
Laceno Italian
25 Giumarello's
Mélange Café

Delaware
26 Rest. 821
25 Green Room
Krazy Kat's
Moro
Culinaria

Top Decor

28 Fountain	Amada
27 Le Bec-Fin	Prime Rib
Lacroix/Rittenhouse	Alma de Cuba
Swann Lounge	**24** Inn at Phillips Mill
Buddakan	Barclay Prime
Tangerine	Susanna Foo
La Bonne Auberge	Washington Square
Morimoto	Duling-Kurtz Hse.
26 Deux Cheminées	Georges'
Nectar	Brasserie Perrier
Savona	Pod
Striped Bass	Kimberton Inn
Bridgetown Mill	Simon Pearce
Marsha Brown	Earl's Prime*
Dilworthtown Inn	Marrakesh
25 Estia	**23** ¡Pasión!
EverMay/Delaware	Los Catrines
Teikoku	Beau Monde
Cuba Libre	General Warren*
Moshulu	City Tavern
Grill	William Penn Inn

Outdoors

Bliss	Moshulu
Centre Bridge Inn	Pond Restaurant
Cresheim Cottage	Positano Coast
Coyote Crossing	Rouge
Golden Pheasant	333 Belrose
Le Jardin	Washington Square

Romance

Astral Plane	Pond Restaurant
Birchrunville Store	Striped Bass
Deux Cheminées	Susanna Foo
Gilmore's	Tangerine
Le Bec-Fin	Vetri

Rooms

Barclay Prime	Le Bec-Fin
Bliss	Nectar
Brasserie Perrier	Nineteen
Buddakan	Pond Restaurant
Continental Mid-town	Striped Bass
Lacroix/Rittenhouse	Teikoku

Views

Azalea	EverMay/Delaware
Bistro St. Tropez	King George II
Black Bass Hotel	Lacroix/Rittenhouse
Chart House	La Veranda
Cuttalossa Inn	Nineteen

Top Service

29 Fountain	Capital Grille
27 Le Bec-Fin	Striped Bass
Vetri	Prime Rib
Swann Lounge	Barclay Prime
Gilmore's	Brasserie Perrier
Lacroix/Rittenhouse	Gayle
26 Birchrunville Store	**23** Buddakan
Deux Cheminées	William Penn Inn
EverMay/Delaware	Overtures
La Bonne Auberge	Bridgetown Mill
25 Dilworthtown Inn	Jake's
Le Bar Lyonnais	Twin Bays
Mainland Inn	Restaurant Alba
Savona	General Warren
Grill	Amada
Morimoto	Abacus
Susanna Foo	Knight House*
Kimberton Inn	Inn at Phillips Mill
Paloma	Morton's
24 Majolica	Duling-Kurtz Hse.

Best Buys

Top Bangs for the Buck

1. La Colombe
2. Bonte
3. Brew HaHa!
4. Dalessandro's
5. Jim's Steaks
6. Nifty Fifty's
7. Pink Rose
8. Honey's Sit 'n Eat
9. Bitar's
10. Tony Luke's
11. Campo's Deli
12. Geno's Steaks
13. Reading Term. Mkt.
14. Pho 75
15. Pat's Steaks
16. Baja Fresh Mex.
17. Shank's & Evelyn's
18. Izzy & Zoe's
19. Celebre's
20. Isaac's
21. Hank's Place
22. Taco House
23. Qdoba Mex.
24. Vientiane Café
25. Taq. La Veracruzana
26. Lakeside Chinese
27. Morning Glory
28. Mayfair Diner
29. Melrose Diner
30. Sweet Lucy's
31. Ardmore Station
32. New Delhi
33. La Lupe
34. Beijing
35. More Than Ice Cream
36. Kibitz in City
37. Fergie's Pub
38. McGillin's
39. Vietnam Palace
40. Sabrina's Café

Other Good Values

Abbaye
Abner's BBQ
Abyssinia
Alyan's
An Indian Affair
Ben & Irv Deli
Carman's Country
Cheeseburger/Paradise
Cherry St. Veg.
Chun Hing
Dahlak
Day by Day
Dessert
Down Home
Famous 4th St. Deli.
Geechee Girl
Grace Tavern
Harmony Veg.
Johnny Brenda's
Jong Ka Jib

Kabobeesh
Kingdom of Veg.
Lee How Fook
Mama Palma's
Nam Phuong
Nan Zhou
Pepper's Cafe
Pho Xe Lua
Ray's Cafe
Ruby's
Singapore Kosher Veg.
South St. Souvlaki
Standard Tap
Tacconelli's Pizzeria
Tampopo
Tandoor India
Taq. La Michoacana
Tenth St. Pour Hse.
Trolley Car
Vietnam

Prix Fixe Bargains

Lunch

Bay Pony Inn	$15	Karma	$10
Bistro Cassis	18	Lacroix/Rittenhouse	26
Bliss	20	Lemon Grass Thai	9
Caribou Cafe	15	Ly Michael's	13
Cassatt Tea Room	20	Mamma Maria	20
Cedars	25	Paradigm	12
Dahlak	14	Pattaya Grill	8
Estia	17	Peacock/Parkway	10
Fountain	43	Susanna Foo	25
Hikaru	12	Thai Orchid	8
Indonesia	7	Thai Singha House	8
Kabobeesh	7	Zocalo	10

Dinner

Bay Pony Inn	$25	My Thai	$16
Caribou Cafe	29	Old Orig. Bookbinder's	35
Casablanca	25	Overtures	25
Casablanca/Warrington	28	Paradigm	30
Cedars	25	Pattaya Grill	10
Chun Hing	26	Peacock/Parkway	16
Dahlak	14	Pompeii Cucina	25
Devon Seafood	33	Prime Rib	30
Estia	30	Ravenna	28
Fayette Street	31	Roller's/Flying Fish	12
Fez Moroccan	25	Roux 3	20
Fioravanti	20	Roy's	33
Franco's Pastaria	30	Rx	25
Gnocchi	30	Sansom St. Oyster	25
Hikaru	27	Slate Bleu	32
Kabobeesh	7	Summer Kitchen	18
La Belle Epoque	25	Tratt. San Nicola/Berwyn	16
La Locanda/Ghiottone	35	Twenty Manning	30
Le Jardin	30	Twenty21	35
Little Marakesh	25	Valanni	30
Marrakesh	25	William Penn Inn	22
Moonstruck	27	Zocalo	26

Restaurant Directory

Philadelphia

F	D	S	C

Abacus
₂₃ **23** **18** **23** **$26**

North Penn Mktpl., 1551 S. Valley Forge Rd. (Sumneytown Pike), Lansdale, 215-362-2010

Host Joe Chen's "shtick" ("jokes that never change") makes you "feel like family" at this "crowded" Chinese BYO "in the woods" of Montco; beyond punch lines and a "strip-mall" setting, adherents find food that's a "cut above" and specials that are "even better than they sound"; in all, the pluses count up quickly here.

Abbaye ☻
20 **18** **17** **$21**

637 N. Third St. (Fairmount Ave.), 215-627-6711

Northern Libertarians think of this "laid-back" corner Belgian pub as the "answer" to their "prayers", especially at "weekday lunch" when many competitors are closed; it's "comforting" to sit with "friends" (including the four-legged variety) over "reliable" food ("lots of vegetarian choices") and "wonderful" beers.

Abbraccio
15 **19** **18** **$24**

820 S. 47th St. (Warrington Ave.), 215-727-8247;
www.abbracciorestaurant.com

"Homey" vibes and a separate dining room built "for kids" are reasons to embrace this "welcoming" West Philly Italian; while detractors deride "so-so" fare that "misses the mark", "friendly" service and a fireplace that's "nice on cold winter nights" help make amends.

Abner's Authentic Bar-B-Que
19 **9** **17** **$17**

Ogontz Plaza, 7155 Ogontz Ave. (71st Ave.), 215-224-8600
Jenkintown Square Shopping Ctr., 505 Old York Rd.
(Hillside Ave.), Jenkintown, 215-885-8600
www.abnersbbq.com

"Construction workers" and "lawyers" "get napkins" and satisfy their fix at these "serious" sibs vending barbecue that "perfectly walks the line between juicy and guaranteed-to-clog-arteries"; never mind that "plain" environs are as "charming as a church meeting hall", since the "dry-rub" ribs are "delicious" and service is "quick"; N.B. Jenkintown has tables, while Mount Airy is takeout only.

Abyssinia ☻
▽ **22** **11** **14** **$15**

229 S. 45th St. (Locust St.), 215-387-2424

Don't let "gloomy" looks or "patchy" service keep you away from this West Philly Ethiopian BYO that's a magnet for those craving a "wonderful" "bargain" meal with the bonus of a "real social occasion" (who knew "eating with your hands would be so sexy"?); thrill seekers'll be-seein-ya at the "loud and lively" upstairs bar.

Adobe Cafe   18 13 16 $23
4550 Mitchell St. (Leverington Ave.), 215-483-3947
Manayunkers have *dos* ways of looking at this "casual" Southwesterner in an "old" house up the "hill": most insist it "deserves more credit than it gets" as they praise food that's "pretty good" for the price (and that includes "creative" vegetarian options); naysayers, however, aren't impressed with the "painfully slow" service.

Agave Grille & Cantina   15 18 18 $28
110 E. Butler Ave. (York St.), Ambler, 215-641-1420;
www.agavegrille.com
Margarita mavens are "pleased as punch" that this "crowded" Southwestern "hangout" has joined the Ambler scene; despite its "ambitious" premise (it "tries to be upscale") and "imaginative" dishes, some dub it a "hit-or-miss" experience with sometimes "clueless" service.

Alberto's   21 20 19 $42
191 S. Newtown Street Rd. (½ mi. south of West Chester Pike),
Newtown Square, 610-356-9700; www.italiansteakhouse.com
You may think you're in a *Sopranos* episode" at this "expensive", "old-world" Italian steakhouse in Main Line; fans know it's easy to feel "special" while grooving to "live jazz" on weekends and lapping up "consistently fine" steaks, pastas and fish.

Al Dar Bistro   17 15 16 $30
281 Montgomery Ave. (Levering Mill Rd.), Bala Cynwyd,
610-667-1245; www.aldarbistro.com
Opinions of this "informal" Med "local haunt" in Bala vary, with many digging the "grottolike" environs along with falafel sandwiches and other fare on an "interesting" menu that's hard to turn down; others, however, resist "overpricing" and "servers who occasionally serve."

Alex Long New Asian Cuisine   16 14 16 $27
50 E. Wynewood Rd. (Lancaster Ave.), Wynnewood,
610-896-8892
Habitués of this Asian fusion Wynnewood BYO appreciate a menu with "variety" and call the food "a cut above" the norm; still, foes offer that it "needs to get the snap back", and add that "high prices" and "ok" fare disappoint in the face of "competition."

ALISON AT BLUE BELL ⊠⊄   26 16 22 $44
721 Skippack Pike (Penllyn-Blue Bell Pike), Blue Bell,
215-641-2660; www.alisonatbluebell.com
There's "no need to schlep to Center City" since "skilled" chef-owner Alison Barshak is "on top of every detail" at her cash-only New American BYO in the Montco burbs;

her fan club calls it a "foodie's delight" with "innovative", "Manhattan-quality" eats served in a "warm", "simple" space – just don't mind "being squashed" ("get used to sitting in your neighbor's lap").

ALMA DE CUBA　　　　| 24 | 25 | 22 | $48 |

1623 Walnut St. (bet. 16th & 17th Sts.), 215-988-1799; www.almadecubarestaurant.com

Wear something "sexy" to Stephen Starr and celebrity-chef Douglas Rodriguez's "lively", "sleek" split-level "gastronomic getaway" off Rittenhouse Square, where you "and the girls" or a "special date" can go "on a trip to Cuba" for "authentic-ish" Latin fare "with a vengeance"; while the "terrific" food and "fascinating" drinks vie for attention with the "spectacular scenery" (i.e. "beautiful people") and "hanging-out-in-Havana" decor, "dim" lighting helps to hide a "high" bill that'll send a chill through your wallet.

Alyan's　　　　| ▽ 21 | 9 | 16 | $13 |

603 S. Fourth St. (South St.), 215-922-3553

"You could easily walk by" this BYO "hole-in-the-wall" off South Street, but then you'd miss one of Philly's "best cheap-eats" spots known for "fantastic" Middle Eastern "yummies" including "outstanding" kebabs and hummus "beyond compare"; P.S. couples often opt for the garden-like "back room."

AMADA　　　　| 27 | 25 | 23 | $47 |

217 Chestnut St. (bet. 2nd & 3rd Sts.), 215-625-2450; www.amadarestaurant.com

Spanish-loving surveyors dip into their bag of superlatives over Jose Garces' Old City venue (this *Survey*'s top new-comer), where "magical" justly describes the tapas that are accompanied by "fantastic" sangria, "phenomenal" flamenco dancers (some nights) and "attentive" service; it's the "best thing to happen to Philadelphia in a long time", but it's advised to go early before "noise" rises "above the pain threshold."

America Bar & Grill　　　　| 18 | 18 | 18 | $34 |

Shops at Lionville Station, 499 E. Uwchlan Ave. (bet. Llonville Station Rd. & Rte. 113), Chester Springs, 610-280-0800
Shoppes at Brinton Lake, 981 Baltimore Pike (Brinton Lake Rd.), Glen Mills, 610-558-9900
www.americabargrill.com

For "dining with no surprises" in the western 'burbs, these aspiring-to-be "upscale" New American "strip-mall" twins deliver "consistent", "steady but not spectacular" food from a menu that's "less about innovation than about straightforward enjoyment"; "busy" bars make them just right as neighborhood "hangouts."

Anastasi Seafood
21 | 11 | 17 | $28 |

Italian Mkt., 1101 S. Ninth St. (Washington Ave.), 215-462-0550

"You know things are fresh" at this "dinerlike" South Philly seafooder smack in the middle of the Italian Market, where "friendly" waitresses sling "crab cakes" and "you see your meal before it's cooked"; though a few object to "fish store odor", others have smelt worse.

An Indian Affair
∇ 21 | 18 | 19 | $22 |

4425 Main St. (Carson St.), 215-482-8300

All of Manayunk is talking about this "elegant", "romantic" East Indian BYO affair, where gossip is fueled by a "fireplace in the cozy back room" and "tasty" food ("some like it hot"); the "friendly" staff helps keep the nearby Penn community coming.

Anjou
20 | 19 | 18 | $35 |

206-208 Market St. (bet. 2nd & 3rd Sts.), 215-923-1600; www.anjouphilly.net

This "hip" French-Asian fusionist in an "overhyped", "sceney" stretch of Old City is praised for its "interesting", "assorted" menu that includes sushi, Korean and Gallic dishes; while the upstairs room is more "understated", the downstairs lounge is totally "too-cool-for-school."

Ansill
∇ 25 | 21 | 23 | $40 |

627 S. Third St. (Bainbridge St.), 215-627-2485; www.ansillfoodandwine.com

Queen Village tongues are wagging over David (Pif) Ansill's Eclectic small-plate specialist/wine bar offering "comfort" and "sophistication" in wood-filled quarters; an "excellent" staff walks you through "sublime" though "unusual" nibbles – but those who've been say expect to order "a lot to make a meal."

Aoi
16 | 10 | 15 | $26 |

1210 Walnut St. (bet. 12th & 13th Sts.), 215-985-1838

"Competitive" sushi eaters stuff their faces with the all-you-can-eat deal at this "overlooked" Japanese in Center City; "black", "old-dance-club" decor has a few unwilling to "break out the chopsticks", and some say "Aoi-vey" – "don't leave even the rice behind because they'll actually charge you for it."

Apamate ⌷
– | – | – | I |

1620 South St. (17th St.), 215-790-1620

The burgeoning Graduate Hospital neighborhood shouts *sí!* for this warmly decorated, casual Spaniard dishing out affordable fare (with an emphasis on tapas) at breakfast, lunch and dinner; though the place is BYO, the back patio and flamenco nights help intoxicate; N.B. they also sell a number of products from Spain.

Ardmore Station Cafe
| 18 | 10 | 19 | $15 |

6 Station Ave. (bet. Lancaster & Montgomery Aves.), Ardmore, 610-642-2683

For the "best pancakes this side of the tracks", locals station themselves at this "family-friendly" "treasure" of a diner in the Ardmore train stop; patrons find the "broad" menu and "pleasant" service expressly convincing.

Ariana
| 21 | 14 | 19 | $23 |

134 Chestnut St. (bet. Front & 2nd Sts.), 215-922-1535

"Fragrant and flavorful" food and "reasonable" prices are the hooks at this "quiet" Old City Afghan BYO that attracts more than a few to its "small" yet "relaxing" space; P.S. ask for the table in the "front window where you sit on pillows."

Arpeggio
| 23 | 16 | 20 | $24 |

542 Spring House Village Ctr. (bet. Bethlehem Pike & Norristown Rd.), Spring House, 215-646-5055;
www.arpeggiobyob.com

"Delicious" wood-oven pizzas and hummus account for the "overcrowding" at this "homey" central Montco Italian-Med pumping out "terrific" dishes served by a "young", "capable" staff; "arrive early" or "late" to avoid the "waits", but rest assured if you "go hungry, you'll leave stuffed."

Astral Plane
| 17 | 21 | 18 | $35 |

1708 Lombard St. (bet. 17th & 18th Sts.), 215-546-6230;
www.theastralplane.com

For nearly 35 years, this "funky", "spunky" Center City Eclectic has epitomized "kitsch" and "keeps rolling along" for those seeking nights of "romance" or "entertainment for the in-laws" amid a "cluttered" setting complete with "mismatched table settings"; while some "forgive slips in cooking and service", others say they "need to come back to earth" to see "what's going on" in the 21st century.

Athena ⊅
| 18 | 14 | 16 | $25 |

264 N. Keswick Ave. (Easton Rd.), Glenside, 215-884-1777

If you're headed to a show at the Keswick Theater in the heart of Glenside and crave something "good", this "rustic", strip-center Greek BYO fills the bill with "savory", "home-made" fare, albeit "without surprises"; insiders tend to get most "comfortable" with a seat on the outdoor patio on warm evenings.

Audrey Claire ⊅
| 21 | 15 | 19 | $33 |

276 S. 20th St. (Spruce St.), 215-731-1222;
www.audreyclaire.com

"Bump elbows" with Rittenhouse Square "cell-phone-toting professionals" at Audrey Claire Taichman's "chic" and "spare" cash-only BYO, where "yummy" "twists" on Med cuisine "make up for the noise" and window seats allow for a view of passersby; it's as "cozy" as a "pair of fuzzy bunny slippers", so don't be surprised if "nice", "chatty" service comes with the territory.

August 🈲🚭   22 | 20 | 22 | $35
1247 S. 13th St. (Wharton St.), 215-468-5926;
www.augustbyob.com
"Any month is perfect for August" is the line on this snug, quintessentially "neighborhood" BYO "off the beaten path" in South Philly; "everything about it works", from the "surprisingly sophisticated" "feel-good" Italian food to "welcoming" service; N.B. cash only.

August Moon   22 | 15 | 19 | $31
300 E. Main St. (Arch St.), Norristown, 610-277-4008
"Some of the best sushi around" and other fare comes from this "hidden" Japanese-Korean run by a "friendly" staff in a Norristown storefront; supporters point out the offerings "expand" their culinary "horizons" and are so "good" that it's "worth the trip" to the "dingy" neighborhood.

Ava   21 | 16 | 19 | $34
518 S. Third St. (bet. Lombard & South Sts.), 215-922-3282;
www.avarestaurant.com
Although this "family-run", "true" Italian BYO off South Street might be "one of Philly's best-kept secrets", word's trickling out about Michael Campagna's "first-rate" fare that's enjoyed in a "serene", albeit "plain" room; the staff "never makes you feel rushed", which makes sense since "this kind of food should be savored."

Avalon   22 | 20 | 20 | $42
312 S. High St. (Union St.), West Chester, 610-436-4100;
www.avalonrestaurant.org
New chef Steve Ferdinand turns out "consistently solid" European-inspired American food at this "romantic", "unpretentious" BYO run by an "attentive couple" in West Chester; it's a toss-up whether it's best to sit by the fountain in the middle of the dining room or out on the "lovely" patio.

Azalea   ▽ 20 | 24 | 20 | $51
Omni Hotel at Independence Park, 401 Chestnut St. (4th St.),
215-931-4260; www.omnihotels.com
"A step above typical hotel dining", this "well-decorated" Traditional American in the Omni has "excellent" brunches and a "lovely" view of Independence National Historic Park; "slower-than-snails" service, though, threatens to undermine an otherwise "tasteful" experience here.

Azure   22 | 18 | 21 | $26
931 N. Second St. (Laurel St.), 215-629-0500;
www.azurerestaurant.net
"Foodies" and "picky eaters" find much to share on the menu at this "dependable" Northern Liberties Eclectic offering "exciting" Caribbean-focused dishes accompanied

by suitably "island"-esque decor; factor in a "friendly" staff, and there's little to feel blue about.

Bahama Breeze ◐　　　16 | 19 | 16 | $26
320 Goddard Blvd. (Mall Blvd.), King of Prussia, 610-491-9822;
www.bahamabreeze.com

To its fans, these "festive" Caribbean chainsters in Cherry Hill and King of Prussia deliver an "islandy" experience that includes "tropical" decor, "gargantuan" portions of "good", "reasonably" priced food and "marvelous" cocktails; still, detractors don't like "average" fare, "long waits" ("have *War and Peace* ready") and "slow" service that makes some want to "breeze on out."

Baja Fresh Mexican Grill　　　17 | 10 | 13 | $11
Abington Shopping Ctr., 1437 Old York Rd. (London Rd.),
Abington, 215-885-4296
Plymouth Square Shopping Ctr., 200 W. Ridge Pike (Butler Pike),
Conshohocken, 610-828-4524
340 DeKalb Pike (I-276), King of Prussia, 610-337-2050
1138 Baltimore Pike (Rte. 320), Springfield, 610-690-1064
www.bajafresh.com

If you crave "fresh", "made-to-order" Cal-Mex and need it "fast", this Wendy's-owned "fast-food" chain puts "Taco Bell to shame"; while the "cafeteria-style" settings won't win awards, "cheap" tabs and "cheerful" service put many on the *camino* in; P.S. the salsa bar is a "plus."

Bamboo Club　　　17 | 19 | 16 | $30
Pavilion at King of Prussia Mall, 640 W. DeKalb Pike
(bet. Allendale & Long Rds.), King of Prussia, 610-265-0660;
www.thebambooclub.com

A "Zen-like" atmosphere at this "trendy" Pan-Asian fusionist provides an "oasis" to shoppers in the King of Prussia mall including those who can't get into the "Cheesecake Factory"; despite an "interesting" menu, however, some skewer "hide-and-seek" service and "inconsistencies" from a kitchen that sends out food in "fits and starts."

Banana Leaf ◐⊭　　　– | – | – | I
1009 Arch St. (bet. 10th & 11th Sts.), 215-592-8288

Some crew members from Penang have traveled around the corner to open this lively, cash-only tropical-themed Malaysian BYO in Chinatown; though the menu is almost identical to its popular inspiration, the sushi bar supplies an interesting (albeit not authentic) addition.

BARCLAY PRIME　　　25 | 24 | 24 | $69
Barclay Hotel, 237 S. 18th St. (Locust St.), 215-732-7560

It's "best to be on someone's expense account" (think $100 cheese steaks) when dining at Stephen Starr's "elegant" Rittenhouse Square meatery, whose "retro" "library" motif makes it the most "unsteakhouselike steakhouse in the city"; count on "melt-in-your-mouth" Kobe beef sliders that arrive via "extra-good" servers and, for added cachet, a steak knife presentation, where you choose your own from a tray presented tableside.

Bar Ferdinand ●   – – – M
1030 N. Second St. (Girard Ave.), 215-923-1313
Restaurant designer Owen Kamihira (Buddakan, The Continental) has taken the plunge into ownership with this handsome, brand-new Northern Liberties tapas bar, where chef Blake Joffe (who apprenticed at two of Spain's top spots) whips up modestly priced dishes matched by an Iberian wine list.

Basil Bistro & Bar   17 16 18 $34
522 King Rd. (Lancaster Ave.), Paoli, 610-647-1500; www.basilbistro.com
Main Line "moms" "duck out" for a "civilized lunch" at this "upbeat" New American, whose ambiance may "not be for romantic nights" but still offers a "great variety" of food that "pleases the masses" and a "kid-friendly" staff; those who deride "so-so" fare are overruled.

Bay Pony Inn   19 19 20 $38
508 Old Skippack Rd. (Salfordville Rd.), Lederach, 215-256-6565; www.bayponyinnpa.com
"Take your grandmother" to the "splendid" brunch buffet at this "consistent" Traditional American in Montco, where there's "nothing out of the ordinary", but nothing ordinary about the "elegant", "country" setting; while modernists believe both menu and decor could use an "update", "an older crowd" says the mare's "worth the ride" from all points.

Beau Monde   23 23 19 $28
624 S. Sixth St. (Bainbridge St.), 215-592-0656; www.creperie-beaumonde.com
You'd swear you were on a "Breton holiday" at this "sexy" yet "family-friendly" Queen Village crêperie, where "endless" combinations of fillings all lead to "mouthwatering" results; service disputes aside ("flaky" vs. "excellent"), all agree the "slice-of-Paris" cafe setting and "romantic" fireplace "knock your socks off"; P.S. "leave room" for the dessert crêpes and you can always "dance" it off at the upstairs bar, L'Etage.

Beige & Beige   20 21 16 $42
2501 Huntingdon Pike (bet. Red Lion & Welsh Rds.), Huntingdon Valley, 215-938-8600; www.beigebeige.com
"Haute cuisine meets the steppes of Russia" at this "cosmopolitan" Eclectic BYO in Huntingdon Valley, where "beige" means anything but "bland" in that fans find the fare "flavorful"; while opinions are shaded by the attempts at the diverse offerings that include French dishes and sushi ("all they need next is Indian"), most maintain that it deserves "more recognition."

Beijing
18 | 7 | 16 | $14

3714 Spruce St. (bet. 37th & 38th Sts.), 215-222-5242
"Hospital workers" can be heard saying if only HUP "were run as efficiently" as this college-catering BYO near the Quad at Penn, a Chinese "staple" where Quakers "cram" in for "cheap", "delicious" food served by "comically swift" servers; in fact, speed is no surprise given the staff's "hurry-up-you-go-now" hospitality.

Bella Trattoria
19 | 16 | 18 | $28

4258 Main St. (bet. Cotton & Rector Sts.), 215-482-5556; www.bellatrattoriapa.com
Main Street "people-watching" seems to be the strong suit of this "relaxing" Manayunk Italian dishing out "good", "simple" pizzas and pastas to families and "bargain" seekers who drop in for "impromptu" dinners; it's "without pretense", and overall "solid."

Bellini Grill
19 | 13 | 19 | $29

220 S. 16th St. (bet. Locust & Walnut Sts.), 215-545-1191; www.bellinigrill.com
To cure an Italian fix, try this "dependable" BYO around the corner from the Kimmel Center; given the affordable tabs, it's an "insurance salesman's Palm", with "good", albeit "basic" food and a "quaint" setting warmed by the presence of an "affable" owner.

Ben & Irv Deli Restaurant
19 | 9 | 16 | $16

1962 County Line Rd. (Davisville Rd.), Huntingdon Valley, 215-355-2000; www.benandirvs.com
Take a trip with the "tribe" to this "old-style" Jewish deli in a Montco strip mall, where you "can't beat" the mushroom barley soup and bagels and lox on Sunday morning while waitresses "kvetch" down the aisles; what a few call a "redecoration" was more like a "redreckoration", and some say it's safe to wear "warmup suits" and to accessorize with "diamond bracelets."

Bertolini's
18 | 17 | 16 | $30

Plaza at King of Prussia Mall, 160 N. Gulph Rd. (bet. DeKalb Pike & Mall Blvd.), King of Prussia, 610-265-2965; www.mortons.com
"If you're shopping" in King of Prussia "and don't want to move the car", this Italian from the Morton's chain may be "worth" your time for fare that's a "step above" typical food court options; while the "inconsistent" service chafes, the "contemporary" setting "pleases."

BIRCHRUNVILLE STORE CAFE ⏏✄
28 | 23 | 26 | $50

1403 Hollow Rd. (Flowing Springs Rd.), Birchrunville, 610-827-9002; www.birchrunvillestorecafe.com
Bring cash along with your GPS to Francis Trzeciak's "remote", "bare-bones" BYO in an old Chester County "coun-

try" store; diehards know to "reserve" a spot "well in advance" for the "sophisticated" Franco-Italian cuisine prepared with "thought and care", "romantic" atmosphere and servers so "gracious" you "want them as your friends"; N.B. closed Sundays–Tuesdays.

Bistro La Baia ⊘   21 | 13 | 19 | $27
1700 Lombard St. (17th St.), 215-546-0496
The "smiling owner" keeps a "watchful eye" on his "dependable" cash-only Italian "shoebox" of a BYO in Center City where locals enjoy "yummy", "carb lover's'" cooking and "charming" service; most admit the food is "good enough" to compensate for the "incredibly cramped", "awfully crowded" conditions.

Bistro La Viola ⊘   23 | 13 | 21 | $29
253 S. 16th St. (bet. Locust & Spruce Sts.), 215-735-8630
Kimmel Center–goers know a "bargain" when they see one, and this Center City BYO is "ridiculously cheap" for "terrific" Italian "dishes" that make you think "were designed especially for you"; patrons are amazed that "courteous", "acrobatic" waiters can maneuver through a "crowded room" that makes "sardine" cans seem roomier; P.S. forget lingering, since they effectively "shut down after-dinner conversations by clearing tables" quickly.

Bistro Romano   21 | 22 | 22 | $36
120 Lombard St. (bet. Front & 2nd Sts.), 215-925-8880;
www.bistroromano.com
The setting alone of this "grottolike" Society Hill Italian "bistro" in a noteworthy early-18th-century building is "something to experience at least once"; candlelit, exposed-brick quarters conducive to "romance" charm, as does the "excellent" food (props to the "best" Caesar salad prepared tableside) and service; P.S. for extra "intimacy", reserve a table in the basement wine cellar.

Bistro 7   24 | 17 | 21 | $35
7 N. Third St. (Market St.), 215-931-1560
"Grab a spot at the counter" at this "small", "simply" decorated New American BYO and "watch the magic happen" as the chef converts "oh-so-fresh" ingredients into "sublime" dishes backed by "engaging" service; it's also "one of the few" places in Old City where "you can eat for less than a monthly BMW payment."

Bistro St. Tropez ⊠   20 | 18 | 18 | $42
2400 Market St., 4th fl. (23rd St.), 215-569-9269;
www.bistrosttropez.com
Window tables supply "spectacular views of the Schuylkill" from this "obscurely" situated Marketplace Design Center French bistro that "brightens up the nearby landscape"; "compelling" and at times "innovative" food helps redeem "outdated" interiors and "inconsistent" service.

BITAR'S ⊠   25 8 18 $13

947 Federal St. (10th St.), 215-755-1121; www.bitars.com
Middle Eastern fans trek to this affordable Lebanese
"fast"-foodery, whose original, "typical-store" South Philly
location has spun off a satellite in Mount Airy and stands
at Penn; the fare is "incomparably" good and includes the
"best" falafel around and "fresh" pita that's much bitar
than what you get at "the supermarkets."

Black Bass Hotel   21 22 21 $49

Black Bass Hotel, 3774 River Rd. (north of Greenhill Rd.),
Lumberville, 215-297-5770; www.blackbasshotel.com
"Even George would have been a turncoat" had he
camped out at this "romantic" Bucks New American getaway in a "picture-perfect", "veddy British" setting by the
Delaware in "the middle of nowhere"; though a few have
trouble with "fusty" decor "in need of a face-lift", most sign
on for the "consistently" good fare and Sunday brunch
where "quantity, quality and variety are in abundance."

Black Door ◐   ▽ 17 19 16 $26

629 S. Second St. (Banbridge St.), 215-574-2958
Now occupying a "quaint" tri-level Queen Village corner
space is this latest resident boasting a "great" beer selection and an early rep as a neighborhood "meeting place"; the
"upscale" American pub food seems "more expensive"
for the norm, so it's no surprise if patrons opt for the bar.

Black Sheep Pub ◐   16 15 15 $22

247 S. 17th St. (Latimer St.), 215-545-9473;
www.theblacksheeppub.com
This "comfy" Irish pub off Rittenhouse Square can become
"your favorite hangout" if you like "slumming" over TV
"soccer matches", "darts", "Guinness" and burgers; the
cookin's "pretty good", and most report "you can really
feel the back-home Irish airs."

Bliss ⊠   23 21 22 $49

220-224 S. Broad St. (bet. Locust & Walnut Sts.), 215-731-1100;
www.bliss-restaurant.com
Francesco Martorella's "chichi" New American in the
Bellevue has become a "beautiful people's" "power-lunch
alternative" to "the Palm" next door and a "handy" dinner
bet before the Kimmel Center thanks to "inventive" cuisine
and the "Zen-like" vibe of the "minimalist" decor; as for
the service, it's blessedly "attentive."

Blue Bell Inn ⊠   20 17 20 $42

601 Skippack Pike (Penllyn-Blue Bell Pike), Blue Bell,
215-646-2010; www.bluebellinn.com
It's "not jazzy by any means", but this 60-year-old, family-
operated Traditional American in Montco has had a long
run at delivering "good" food to generations of fans; the

"sizzling", "swinging septuagenarian bar scene" on Friday nights and $20 early-bird specials, though, reinforce perceptions that it's a "blue-hair" hang.

BLUEFIN 🚭   27 | 14 | 20 | $34

1017 Germantown Pike (Virginia Rd.), Plymouth Meeting, 610-277-3917; www.sushibluefin.com

Sushi-philes swear "if you aren't going to Morimoto", this "tiny" Japanese BYO in a "slightly dated" Plymouth Meeting strip center is an "excellent" alternative, where the "phenomenal", "amazingly fresh" fare includes rolls that are a "treat for the eyes and taste buds"; a "pleasant" staff helps make up for the "modest" decor.

Blue Horse Restaurant & Tavern   16 | 20 | 16 | $37

602 Skippack Pike (Penllyn-Blue Bell Pike), Blue Bell, 215-641-9100; www.thebluehorse.net

Fans of this "casual" New American in Montco "pop in" for Kobe beef burgers and bask in the "chic", "downtown" setting; but many get on their high horse and cite a "confused" concept offering "inconsistent" food, "unacceptable noise levels" and "slow", "subpar" service.

Blue Pacific   19 | 14 | 17 | $30

Plaza at King of Prussia Mall, 160 N. Gulph Rd. (bet. DeKalb Pike & Mall Blvd.), King of Prussia, 610-337-3078; www.bluepacificrestaurant.com

This Pan-Asian is a "diamond in the rough" of the King of Prussia Mall and serves "good" fare to adherents who savor sushi and Japanese beers; despite detractors who "skip it" and its "tacky" decor for "better places Downtown", the consensus is it has a fin up on "other food court options."

BLUE SAGE VEGETARIAN GRILLE 🚭   26 | 14 | 22 | $26

772 Second Street Pike (Street Rd.), Southampton, 215-942-8888; www.bluesagegrille.com

Come "prepared to wait" – even with "reservations" – for the "ridiculously good" fare at Mike and Holly Jackson's "tiny", Bucks strip-mall vegetarian BYO, where fans forget about "mock" ingredients, "substitutes" and meat, since what they taste is an "amazing creativity with veggies"; who cares if the setting "isn't fancy-schmancy" when "huge" portions can supply you with a "tantalizing" meal the next day?

bluezette 🚭   ▽ 18 | 19 | 16 | $38

246 Market St. (bet. 2nd & 3rd Sts.), 215-627-3866

Delilah Winder's Old City Caribbean-soul fooder is "the place to go" for "good", "down-home" comfort food with "flair"; while it's reliable for its "sophisticated" ambiance, "beautiful-people" people-watching and "bar scene", some find a "menu that reads better than it delivers" and ask "where's the soul?"

Blush   – | – | – | E
24 N. Merion Ave. (bet. Montgomery & W. Lancaster Aves.),
Bryn Mawr, 610-527-7700; www.dineatblush.com
At first blush, this upscale burgundy-hued newcomer in
Bryn Mawr looks much like Bianca, the sumptuous yearling it replaced, but the giveaway that things are different
is Nicholas Farina's menu, which focuses on New
American rather than French; the veranda is likely to turn
into a scene suited to pre- or postprandial cocktails.

Bomb Bomb Bar-be-que Grill ☒ 20 | 9 | 19 | $26
1026 Wolf St. (Warnock St.), 215-463-1311
This "old-school" South Philly Italian/BBQ corner spot's
got "heart" and is considered "da bomb" for "melt-in-
your-mouth" ribs and "great" veal parm; its "time-warp"
digs could still use an upgrade, but who cares when waitresses "nicer than my mom" call you "'hon' and 'doll'"?

Bona Cucina ⊄   ▽ 25 | 12 | 22 | $23
66 Sherbrook Blvd. (Marshall Rd.), Upper Darby, 610-623-8811
The "great smell hits you" as soon as you walk into this
"unpretentious" Delco BYO known for "delicious", "gen-
erously portioned" Italian food in an "ordinary", rustic
setting that seems right for the neighborhood; that you'll
feel "at home" makes it a *cucina* worth considering.

Bonefish Grill   20 | 19 | 19 | $33
460 W. Lincoln Hwy. (Whitford Rd.), Exton, 610-524-1010
Regency Sq., 1015 Easton Rd. (Fitzwatertown Rd.), Willow Grove,
215-659-5854
www.bonefishgrill.com
"Bang bang shrimp" and other fish "done right" pleases
the "young", "hip" "masses" at Outback's "upmarket"
seafood chain duo that "succeeds in not being catego-
rized as a chain"; expect servers with "megawatt smiles"
and a "happy hour" that draws crowds for apps and
drinks – the latter compensation for "long waits."

Bonte   19 | 12 | 15 | $10
130 S. 17th St. (bet. Sansom & Walnut Sts.), 215-557-8510
922 Walnut St. (bet. 9th & 10th Sts.), 215-238-7407
www.bontewaffles.com
The "spectacular" Belgian waffles at these Euro-style
Center City twins will "ruin your diet", but you'll be "going
back for more" (or maybe for a "top-quality" sandwich);
relax over a cuppa joe and a selection of papers and mag-
azines, and though they're smack in the middle of the "land
of a thousand coffee shops", the duo attracts a "following."

Bourbon Blue   19 | 19 | 19 | $32
2 Rector St. (Main St.), 215-508-3360; www.bourbonblue.com
An "awesome" bar scene and live music may be the main
attractions at this "trendy" Cajun-Creole in a renovated

stable by the Manayunk Canal; a few fuddy duddies find the fare "misses the mark", but many focus on that "taste of Mardi Gras without the beads", with "good" food to boot.

Branzino
         22 | 17 | 20 | $38

261 S. 17th St. (bet. Locust & Spruce Sts.), 215-790-0103
"Deferential" service and tableside flourishes (i.e. filleted fin fare) distinguish this "old-world" Italian BYO seafooder near Rittenhouse Square; those who visit feel like "aristocrats" dining over "delicious" preparations at a "laid-back" pace, and, what's more, the "reasonable" bill is money in the bank.

BRASSERIE PERRIER
         26 | 24 | 24 | $57

1619 Walnut St. (bet. 16th & 17th Sts.), 215-568-3000;
www.brasserieperrier.com
Philly's "established boomer crowd" keeps "coming back" to Le Bec-Fin's nearby, "scaled-down" Center City brother "for the rest of us", an art deco–designed destination where Georges Perrier and Chris Scarduzio join forces to deliver "divine" New French cuisine; though the fare's "not cheap", a "professional" staff helps – overall, this one "hits all the right notes"; insider's dish: check out the bar area before "a night on the town."

Brasserie 73
         22 | 23 | 18 | $46

4024 Skippack Pike (Mench Rd.), Skippack, 610-584-7880
"Interesting" fare and a "nice" wine list help attract fans including "ladies who lunch" to this "expensive" French bistro in "small-town" Skippack; while the service is "not up to the food" and Route 73 "isn't exactly the Champs-Elysées", the "excellent" alfresco dining and "upscale" decor make many report it's a "delight."

Brew HaHa!
         16 | 13 | 18 | $10

1967 Norristown Rd. (Welsh Rd.), Maple Glen,
215-619-9950
9 W. Gay St. (High St.), West Chester, 610-429-9335
www.brew-haha.com
"Oversized" sofas and a "wide range" of pastries and lunch fare make this local coffee mini-chain a "welcome alternative to Starbucks' hegemony"; it's a "terrific place to get some work done", and though sometimes "slow" service needs to perc up, at least everyone there is "friendly."

Brick Hotel, The
         19 | 20 | 18 | $40

The Brick Hotel, 1 E. Washington Ave. (State St.), Newtown,
215-860-8313; www.brickhotel.com
This "historic" Newtown New American "tries really hard" to please, offering an ambiance made "charming" by a "wonderful" wraparound porch and garden seating; enthusiasts extol the "hopping" bar that's a good bet for an "after-dinner cocktail", along with an "excellent" Sunday brunch, but others would just as soon hit the bricks over "inconsistent" food and "high prices."

Bridget Foy's ◐   19 | 16 | 17 | $31
200 South St. (2nd St.), 215-922-1813; www.bridgetfoys.com
Grab a table on the deck and stare at the "crazy" South
Street scene before you at this "lively", "strategically located" corner standby where, "more often than not", you'll
get "no-nonsense" New American "comfort food" and
"personable", "down-to-earth" service; P.S. as far as watering holes come, the bar is "first-rate."

BRIDGETOWN MILL HOUSE ⊠   26 | 26 | 23 | $58
*760 Langhorne-Newtown Rd. (Bridgetown Pike), Langhorne,
215-752-8996; www.bridgetownmillhouse.com*
The "countryside" setting in a "historic" inn along the
Neshaminy Creek seems "perfect" for this "quiet" New
American–Continental tailor-made for "romantic tête-à-
têtes"; "marvelous" food served on "exquisite" Limoges
china lends an unmistakably air of "elegance", so even if
some disagree about service ("attentive" or "not up to par
with the prices"), no one denies that the place is "lovely to
look at, and lovely to eat at."

Bridgets   23 | 21 | 22 | $42
*8 W. Butler Pike (Main St.), Ambler, 267-465-2000;
www.bridgets8west.com*
This "welcome addition" to Ambler delivers "incredibly interesting" Hawaiian-influenced steakhouse specialties
(from Big Island–trained Scott Simmers) and supplies a
"terrific" experience abetted by a "great" staff and "generous" martinis; N.B. they're offering wine tastings on
Tuesday nights at press time.

Bridgid's   20 | 16 | 20 | $24
*726 N. 24th St. (Meredith St.), 215-232-3232;
www.bridgids.com*
"When you want to get close to your date", it's worth
"squeezing" into this "dark" Fairmount Euro-Eclectic "bistro" for "homestyle" chow off a "chalkboard" menu and an
"incredible" beer selection; in sum, you'll feel as comfortable
as if "your best friend invited you over for dinner", especially when you see the "unbelievably reasonable" prices.

Buca di Beppo   14 | 17 | 17 | $26
*1 W. Germantown Pike (DeKalb Pike), East Norriton,
610-272-2822
300 Main St. (Bartlett Ave.), Exton, 610-524-9939
www.bucadibeppo.com*
It can be "fun" to "bring the family" to *mangia* at this
"goofy" Italian chain for "amusement-park" decor "tacky"
enough to "induce seizures", a "cheery" staff that em-
braces the "cheesy" charm and stereotypically "gargantuan" portions of dishes including "meatballs as big as
your head"; while fans consider them "guilty pleasures",
many dis the eats as "an insult to Italians everywhere."

BUDDAKAN 27 | 27 | 23 | $53 |
325 Chestnut St. (bet. 3rd & 4th Sts.), 215-574-9440;
www.buddakan.com
If you want to "impress someone" who's "hard to impress",
join the "wait list" for Stephen Starr's "swank", "theatrical"
Asian in Old City, a fave of "fashionistas" and "celebs"; it's
Philly's Most Popular restaurant thanks to "memorable",
"groundbreaking" food served by "solicitous" servers and
a "gorgeous" setting that "makes you feel beautiful, even
if you think you're not"; as far as scoring a reservation in
prime time, try rubbing the "giant" Buddha's belly inside.

Bunha Faun 24 | 11 | 21 | $31 |
152 Lancaster Pike (¼ mi. east of Morehall Rd.), Malvern,
610-651-2836; www.bunhafaun.com
A transformed Dairy Queen now houses this Malvern BYO,
a French-Asian "treasure" full of "locals" who've discovered its "incredible" food and "attentive" service that
"never let you down"; "dull", "minimal" digs, though, take
some of the faun out of things.

Butcher's Cafe 19 | 14 | 17 | $30 |
Italian Mkt., 901 Christian St. (9th St.), 215-925-6200
"Super" brunches have surveyors lining up for this Italian
Market BYO in a former butcher shop that's been upgraded
slightly (e.g. with modern art), but still keeps the meat
hooks; the "good" Italian fare is complemented by servers
that may be "spotty" at times, but at least are "warm."

Byblos ● 18 | 16 | 17 | $29 |
114 S. 18th St. (bet. Chestnut & Sansom Sts.), 215-568-3050;
www.byblosphilly.com
This "sultry" Center City Mediterranean has two vibes: at
lunch and dinner, a "disinterested" staff serve "faithful",
"flavorful" renditions of "reasonably priced" Lebanese
food; after hours, the "techno is turned up to 10" while the
"groovy", "meet market" crowd puffs on hookahs.

Cafe de Laos 23 | 19 | 19 | $25 |
1117 S. 11th St. (bet. Ellsworth St. & Washington Ave.),
215-467-1546
"Adventurous" Asia-philes are pleasantly "surprised" to
find "real", "superb" Laotian and Thai cuisine at this
"pretty" BYO in an "otherwise unappealing stretch" near
South Philly's Italian Market; the "calming" interior is "like
stepping into another world", and servers in "traditional
garb" "know the food and take pride in it, as they should."

Cafe Fresko ⌧⌿ 21 | 16 | 18 | $38 |
1003 W. Lancaster Ave. (Warner Ave.), Bryn Mawr,
610-581-7070; www.cafefresko.com
Plan on bumping into "someone you know" at the Pappas
family's snug, "homey" BYO, whose "Greek-diner friendli-

ness and efficiency" and "rich", "delish" French-Med fare add up to a "welcome change for the Main Line"; some say it's best to "go on a weeknight" when it's not nearly as "hectic" and you can "hear yourself think."

Café Habana
| 21 | 21 | 21 | $32 |

102 S. 21st St. (bet. Chestnut & Sansom Sts.), 215-561-2822; www.cafehabana.com

This "low-key" "little piece of Cuban heaven" in Center City wows the neighborhood with "true" cooking, mojitos and a "friendly" floor crew, and further "spices it up" with live bands and dancing on weekends; though a bit "expensive", it manages to stay "hip" and "cosmopolitan" while not succumbing to the "annoying, sceney" thing, à la some of its competitors.

Cafe Preeya ⊠
| 22 | 15 | 19 | $34 |

Village Ctr., 2651 Huntingdon Pike (Red Lion Rd.), Huntingdon Valley, 215-947-6195

Here are three good reasons this "quiet" Thai-influenced International BYO in a Huntingdon Valley strip center is a longtime "favorite": "consistently excellent" food, "wonderful" service and plenty of parking; if a few preeya that they "update" the decor, many more maintain they "can't wait to go back."

Cafe San Pietro
| ▽ 16 | 16 | 16 | $32 |

41 W. Lancaster Ave. (Ardmore Ave.), Ardmore, 610-896-4740

Ristorante Positano's "little brother" in Ardmore seems "underappreciated" ("why is it empty?"), and is regarded as a "quiet place to meet up with friends" over drinks or for a "quick" Med meal; despite so-so scores, the consensus is the "well-prepared" fare comes in a "notch above" the stuff from the joints who peddle more "corporate"-style eats.

Cafe Spice
| 20 | 20 | 18 | $31 |

35 S. Second St. (bet. Chestnut & Market Sts.), 215-627-6273

Cafe Spice Express ⋈
Liberty Pl., 1625 Chestnut St. (S. 16th St.), 215-496-9580 www.cafespice.com

"Young" and "beautiful" "hipsters" favor this "chic", "urban" Indian, an NYC import in Old City's "party district" known for its "helpful" staff serving "delicious", affordable fare and for late-night "dance club" action; the Liberty Place venue is more suited to quick meals.

Cafe Sud
| ▽ 23 | 17 | 21 | $24 |

801 E. Passyunk Ave. (Catharine St.), 215-592-0499; www.sudcakes.com

A "sweet couple" (Deborah Kaplan Mouhib and Mostapha Mouhib) runs this "adorable" Moroccan BYO "nook" in South Philly, turning out "sublime" tagines and "amazing" pastries; "don't go if you're in a hurry", but "how often do you get served tea by someone with the Royal Palace at

Fez on his résumé?"; N.B. open for dinner Wednesdays–
Saturdays, and brunch on weekends.

Cafette
20 | 13 | 18 | $23

8136 Ardleigh St. (Hartwell Ln.), 215-242-4220;
www.cafette.com
The "Friday night fried chicken" special and "fresh",
"delicious" sandwiches and vegetarian specialties any
time make this "low-key", "kitschy" Eclectic BYO on "the
wrong side of the tracks" in Chestnut Hill a "wonderful"
drop-in spot for the neighborhood; the "patio is the place
to be" on a warm evening, even if "grouchy" servers tend
to leave some cold.

Caffe Casta Diva 🍴🚭
23 | 16 | 20 | $37

227 S. 20th St. (Locust St.), 215-496-9677
Among the multitude of Italian BYOs, this "jewel" in a
"converted" apartment near Rittenhouse Square "stands
out" with "beautiful" food and "friendly" service; it
attracts a crowd, and bear in mind that "close", "intimate"
quarters can mean "you hear everything your dinner
neighbors have to say."

Caffe Valentino
▽ 23 | 18 | 23 | $32

1245 S. Third St. (Wharton St.), 215-336-3033;
www.valentinoonthesquare.com
An example of what a South Philly "neighborhood" Italian
is, this "cute" and casual BYO where you're "likely to hear
Italian at the next table" is deemed ideal for "pre-theater"
or "quiet" lunches on account of its "wonderful" cooking;
"costly" specials aside, the place is still a "favorite", albeit
a relatively obscure one.

California Cafe
20 | 20 | 19 | $33

Plaza at King of Prussia Mall, 160 N. Gulph Rd. (bet. DeKalb Pike &
Mall Blvd.), King of Prussia, 610-354-8686;
www.californiacafe.com
"When you need a civilized break from shopping", try
this King of Prussia "safe house" vending "serious"
Californian food and "liquid therapy" amid the Plaza's
"madhouse" setting; it's a natural choice for those who
also want "quality" in a sea of food court choices, though
it is a "little pricey."

California Pizza Kitchen
18 | 13 | 16 | $21

Court at King of Prussia Mall, 470 Mall Blvd. (DeKalb Pike),
King of Prussia, 610-337-1500; www.cpk.com
"Surprisingly good" food suits frazzled moods at this King
of Prussia mall chain pizzeria providing an "escape from
the crowds" in the food court; the "'80s" environs "sag a
bit", but "tasty", "trendy" pizzas and salads "fortify" shoppers for the "traffic they'll face inside and outside";
P.S. fellow diners "don't mind your kids acting up because
they brought theirs too."

Campo's Deli ⊄   21 12 16 $12
214 Market St. (Strawberry St.), 215-923-1000;
www.phillyhoagie.com
Take "out-of-towners" or drop in on your own to the Campo
family's "affordable" Old City hoagiery for "great" sandwiches loaded with "first-rate" fillings; they offer "arguably
some of the best" goods around, and "fast", yet "friendly"
"whaddya-want" service helps keep things moving.

Cantina Los Caballitos ●   _ _ _ I
1651 E. Passyunk Ave. (bet. Morris & 12th Sts.), 215-755-3550
This hipper-than-*tú*, late-night South Philly Mexican, an
early fave of the tattooed and multiply pierced, stocks a
roster of tequilas (40) for margarita mavens or for those
who like their chasers (or starters) shot-style; Alma de
Cuba alum Miguel Aguilar's moderately priced menu gets
its due in the rustic barroom setting.

CAPITAL GRILLE, THE   25 22 24 $58
1338 Chestnut St. (Broad St.), 215-545-9588;
www.thecapitalgrille.com
You have to "pay to play" to hobnob with the "power
brokers" at this "testosterone"-heavy meatery near City
Hall attracting a "rich", "sexy" crowd including plenty of
"women in heels"; it registers high both "on the suit
meter" and on the palates of steak fans who praise "out-
of-this-world" beef accompanied by "engaging" service,
all in typically "clubby" decor replete with marble and
wood; in short: "this many people can't be wrong."

Carambola   24 14 17 $33
Dreshertown Plaza, 1650 Limekiln Pike (Dreshertown Rd.),
Dresher, 215-542-0900; www.carambolabyo.com
This "grown-up" New American BYO in a Montco strip
mall makes its mark with "stylish" presentations of
"amazing" food that rivals what's offered at "some of
Philly's finest"; while critics condemn "noise", "attitude" and
"no reservations" (dinner), the majority reasons that the
"consistently excellent" kitchen atones for any negatives.

Caribou Cafe   20 19 17 $33
1126 Walnut St. (bet. 11th & 12th Sts.), 215-625-9535
"Edith Piaf would feel right at home" at this "charming"
French bistro, a "sleeper" in Center City dishing up a "real
taste of Paris" on Walnut Street and "interesting", "well-
done" cooking for cravers of cassoulet and the like; even if
you bou sometimes "slow" service, you'll enjoy the "trans-
porting", "inviting" indoor setting and "perfect" outdoor dining.

Carman's Country Kitchen ⊄   21 13 18 $19
1301 S. 11th St. (Wharton St.), 215-339-9613
"Prudes" need not apply to Carman Luntzel's "quirky",
"raunchy" Eclectic breakfast-luncher (open Mondays, and

Fridays–Sundays) in South Philly serving "comfort-food" concoctions that show a "knack for combining flavors"; though some may want to "close their eyes", overall, many find things here inphallible.

Carmine's Creole Cafe   25 | 17 | 20 | $37
232 Woodbine Ave. (bet. Hampden & Iona Aves.), Narberth, 610-660-0160; www.carminescreole.com
"Arrive early or be prepared to wait" at this "N'Awlins" BYO in Narberth where "everyone's talking" about John Mims' "knockout" Cajun-Creole food; the "intimate" space is a "big upgrade from the old location – though the new spot tends to generate "noise" and the restaurant has now adopted a "no-reservations" policy.

Carversville Inn   22 | 21 | 20 | $45
6205 Fleecydale Rd. (Aquetong Rd.), Carversville, 215-297-0900
"Authentically Colonial" is this "cozy" historic Bucks inn by the Delaware in Carversville warming souls with a "lovely" fireplace for "cold nights"; most feel rewarded with "reliable" Southern food and "charming" service, and if you "need a bloodhound" to find it, many agree it's "well worth" sniffing out.

Casablanca   ▽ 20 | 20 | 22 | $29
7557 Haverford Ave. (City Ave.), 215-878-1900
Warrington Mews Plaza, 1111 Easton Rd. (Bristol Rd.), Warrington, 215-343-7715; www.casablancaone.com
"Finger-licking good" food and a "full night of entertainment" featuring "exotic" belly dancing (weekends) are the draws for "large parties" at these "diverting" Moroccan twins; it's advised to "set aside time" for a multicourse, "family-style" feast fit for a "sultan."

Cassatt Tea Room & Garden   ▽ 24 | 26 | 23 | $37
Rittenhouse Hotel, 210 W. Rittenhouse Sq. (bet. Locust & Walnut Sts.), 215-546-9000; www.rittenhousehotel.com
The "precious" atmosphere alone makes this "feminine" tearoom (open 2–5 PM) just off the lobby of the "tony" Rittenhouse Hotel an "amazing find" for fans craving "delightful" mini-sandwiches and "decadent" scones, pastries and whatnot, all for a tuppence; "add champagne" to the mix and "before you know it", you'll be in such a swoon that you'll need to "rent a suite upstairs."

Catherine's ☒   ▽ 20 | 19 | 21 | $41
General Store, 1701 W. Doe Run Rd. (Rte. 82), Unionville, 610-347-2227; www.catherinesrestaurant.com
You may "need a road map" to find this "quaint" New American BYO in the woods of Chester County, but when you do, the payoff is a "soft", candlelit (read: "very dark") setting and New American–Southwestern cooking with "flair"; what's more, the "efficient" service lacks

any "highbrow nonsense often found at other city-meets-the-suburbs spots."

Cedar Hollow Inn   ▽ 20 | 20 | 20 | $34
2455 Yellow Springs Rd. (Rte. 29), Malvern, 610-296-9006;
www.cedarhollowinn.com
Locals know all about this Malvern New American for a "quiet lunch" "hidden away" near "corporate America"; many applaud "good" eats, while others opt to deal with "smoke" and "noise" from the bar that attracts an "after-work" following.

Cedars   ▽ 22 | 13 | 18 | $22
616 S. Second St. (bet. Bainbridge & South Sts.), 215-925-4950;
www.cedarsrestaurant.com
Fez and Byblos' "inexpensive" Lebanese sibling has been a "staple" in Queen Village for years, turning out "mouth-watering" fare in "relaxing" surroundings (and there's "never a wait for a table"); if the only complaint is decor in "need of sprucing up, "nice", "fast" service compensates.

Celebre's Pizzeria ●   22 | 10 | 18 | $14
Packer Park Shopping Ctr., 1536 Packer Ave. (Broad St.),
215-467-3255
If you need a pizza "fix" with "the family" before a game at the sports complex, this "standby" purveying "tasty" pies is an obvious choice; you're assured of "friendly", "South Philly"–style service – and "strip-mall" decor that some may not celebrate, but many overlook.

Centre Bridge Inn, The   ▽ 19 | 23 | 21 | $44
The Centre Bridge Inn, 2998 N. River Rd. (Upper York Rd.),
New Hope, 215-862-9139; www.centrebridgeinn.com
"What's not to like?" ask habitués of this "delightful" New American New Hope inn, what with a "great" location and overall setting suited to "romantic trysts" beside the fireplace or on the patio "watching the Delaware flow"; it's perfect for "weddings" and "parties", even if, foodwise, some find "high" and "low" points.

Chabaa Thai Bistro   ▽ 25 | 22 | 20 | $26
4371 Main St. (Grape St.), 215-483-1979;
www.chabaathai.com
Make room in your calendar for this "pretty", relatively new Manayunk "mecca", a Thai "keeper" of a BYO marketing "exceptional" cuisine to admirers in "chic", "comforting" environs on two floors (the upstairs a showcase for works of art); P.S. "reservations are a must."

Chaleo Thai   ▽ 22 | 12 | 20 | $21
700 S. Fifth St. (Bainbridge St.), 215-592-4622
You'll wish you had a "Thai mother" who could cook up curries and noodle dishes as "superb" as at this modest, "unassuming" BYO off South Street; "bargain" prices and

a "friendly" staff help it add up to "everything you could ask for" in a meal.

Charles Plaza   21 | 14 | 22 | $23
234-236 N. 10th St. (Vine St.), 215-829-4383
"Cheerful" Charles Chen is "the man" and meets, greets and treats everyone like a "long-lost friend" at his Chinese "favorite" in Chinatown; aside from being "fresh" and "tasty", the Mandarin fare's the "healthiest" in the hood, and a "wonderful value" too; P.S. some say you can have Charles and the crew "customize the food to your liking."

Chart House   19 | 21 | 18 | $47
Penn's Landing, 555 S. Columbus Blvd. (Lombard Circle), 215-625-8383; www.chart-house.com
This large, casual Penn's Landing surf 'n' turfer, part of a national chain, sports a view so "spectacular" that "even Camden looks good across the river"; even though some dissenters deem it a leaky house with "overpriced", "routine" offerings, many point to the "great" brunch and can't forget the "beautiful" appeal of looking out at the Delaware flowing by.

Cheeseburger in Paradise   16 | 18 | 16 | $18
750 Middletown Blvd. (Lincoln Hwy.), Langhorne, 215-757-3179; www.cheeseburgerinparadise.com
"Take the kids" for some "fun" at this brand-new Jimmy Buffett–inspired American hamburger specialist outside of the Oxford Valley Mall; most parrot the line it's also a "great place to hang at happy hour" amid island-esque digs, though some disagree whether the reasonably priced eats are "good" or "standard" enough to make you conclude "if this is paradise, I'm giving up religion."

Cheesecake Factory   19 | 17 | 17 | $27
Pavilion at King of Prussia Mall, 570 Mall Blvd. (Allendale Rd.), King of Prussia, 610-337-2200; www.thecheesecakefactory.com
"Bring an army" to feast on "enormous" portions ("even for Americans") at this KoP mall chain supplying fans with an "overwhelming" American menu that's "as long as a Tom Clancy novel" and "surprisingly good" food served by a "rushed" yet "perky" staff reminiscent of "overwhelmed" factory workers; the noise is "out of control" and, as the "mobs" waiting to get in attest, the "ridiculous waits" can run into the "hours"; P.S. there's "never any room" for their "delicious" signature cheesecakes, "so bring some home."

Chef Charin   19 | 9 | 19 | $32
126 Bala Ave. (bet. City & Montgomery Aves.), Bala Cynwyd, 610-667-8680; www.chefcharin.com
Those on their way to the flicks fuel up at this "tiny" Continental BYO in a Bala storefront for "good" (if "acceptable" to some) dinners and service that "tries to please

and often succeeds"; "lack of frills" in decor strikes fans as "low-key" and others as a call to "freshen things up."

Cherry Street Vegetarian   20 | 11 | 18 | $19

1010 Cherry St. (bet. 10th & 11th Sts.), 215-923-3663
"Sure, no one's fooled" by the meat substitutes (i.e. gluten, seitan and tofu) at this Chinatown kosher vegetarian BYO, but the food still can be "great" for "diehards" and beef eaters too; "plentiful" portions and a staff that's "eager to please" help soothe those who mock "tired", "shabby" digs.

Chestnut Grill & Sidewalk Cafe   18 | 15 | 17 | $25

Chestnut Hill Hotel, 8229 Germantown Ave. (Southampton Ave.), 215-247-7570; www.chestnuthillhotel.com
You'll "fit right in" if you "dress preppy" and sit outside on the patio to watch "the scene" at this "family-friendly" Traditional American in the Chestnut Hill Hotel; they employ "some of the friendliest and attentive" servers around (especially when "smaller children" are present), and the "good", "consistent" comfort food is "affordable."

Chez Colette   19 | 19 | 18 | $46

Sofitel Philadelphia, 120 S. 17th St. (Sansom St.), 215-569-8300; www.sofitel.com
The few who've been talk up this "quiet", "unknown" New French in the Sofitel that's an "easy place to linger and talk" over "tasty" fare at "power breakfasts" or dinners amid a scene of "French travel posters"; if it's just "ok" and "boring" to some, *la majorité* disagree.

Chickie's & Pete's Cafe ●   17 | 15 | 16 | $22

1526 Packer Ave. (15th St.), 215-218-0500
4010 Robbins Ave. (Frankford Ave.), 215-338-3060 ⊟
Roosevelt Plaza, 11000 Roosevelt Blvd. (bet. Red Lion & Woodhaven Rds.), 215-856-9890
www.chickiesandpetes.com
Sports nuts "don't wear their best clothes" to suck down "awesome" crab fries, wings and mussels at Pete Ciarrocchi's "crabby-chic" pubs (including a new outpost in Bordentown) that are all good "fun", especially when the game is on one of the "large-screen" TVs ("it's like sitting in the 700 level"); count on a staff "full of Philly 'tude", and you better be cool with "beer-swilling" and "noise."

Chlöe ⊠⊟   25 | 17 | 22 | $34

232 Arch St. (bet. 2nd & 3rd Sts.), 215-629-2337; www.chloebyob.com
Mary Ann Ferrie and Dan Grimes' 32-seat, cash-only New American BYO opposite the Betsy Ross House in Old City is so "intimate", you'll think you've been seated at a "dinner party"; though the no-reservations policy "irritates" and makes it next to "impossible to get in" on weekends, the "delicious", "innovative" fare and "down-to-earth" vibe are bound to leave you glowing.

Chops   19 18 19 $50

401 City Ave. (Monument Rd.), Bala Cynwyd, 610-668-3400;
www.chops.us

"Power-lunching" Bala businessmen on "expense ac-
counts" and Main Line "families" at dinner wear extra
large pants to get their steak on at this "airy" meatery,
where "flashy cars outside" betray the "lively" scene inside;
the staff's pleasant, but disagreements over the food have
some calling it "good" and foes labeling it "inconsistent."

Christopher's ◐   15 13 15 $25

108 N. Wayne Ave. (Lancaster Ave.), Wayne, 610-687-6558;
www.christophersaneighborhoodplace.com

"Rowdy" kids run amok at this "super-kid-friendly" Wayne
New American known as a "hangout for Main Line moms";
the location "is key", the food "inexpensive" and "reliable", and the floor crew "pleasant" (if "slow"), and to
avoid the "screamers" who rule at lunch, it's advised to
come later for a "more relaxing" setting at dinner or join
the bar scene dominated by college students.

Chun Hing   ▽ 24   9 22 $20

Pathmark Shopping Ctr., 4160 Monument Rd. (City Ave.),
215-879-6270

This steady, 28-year-old Chinese BYO in a Wynnefield
shopping center "surprises", especially "if you know what to
order" (though the menu is filled with "very good" dishes);
figure in "easy parking", "nice" prices and a "lovely" staff,
and you've "saved yourself a trip to Chinatown."

CinCin   24 18 20 $32

7838 Germantown Ave. (Springfield Ave.), 215-242-8800

Chestnut Hill's "answer to Yangming" is "deservedly popular" with a "packed" house of diners craving "top-drawer"
French-tinged Chinese fare that's served amid "acoustically
unsettling" din; it may be "so good they named it twice",
and while there's no "Zen" in an "overbooked" wait list,
most agree it would be a SinSin to pass this one up.

Citron Bistro   17 18 17 $37

818 W. Lancaster Ave. (Bryn Mawr Ave.), Bryn Mawr,
610-520-9100

Main Liner opinion is split on this Spanish bistro next to the
Bryn Mawr art theater: proponents propose it's "underrated", with a "comfortable" setting, "diverse" menu and
food that shows "real care" on the part of the kitchen; but it's
"overpriced" to some who also sour on "unoriginal" eats.

Citrus ⊠⊅   25 12 18 $33

8136 Germantown Ave. (bet. Abington Ave. & Hartwell Ln.),
215-247-8188

"Cooking artistry and fresh ingredients combine" to create
"fabulous" food at this meat-and-poultry-free Chestnut Hill

Eclectic as tight as a "shoebox", a BYO that also caters to vegetarians; still, despite the "outstanding" menu and "fair" prices, cons cringe at a "militant" attitude that manifests itself in service and in the "overbearing" "politics" (you can't wear fur in the restaurant).

City Tavern | 18 | 23 | 20 | $40 |
138 S. Second St. (Walnut St.), 215-413-1443; www.citytavern.com
Old Cityites and their "out-of-town guests" like to "step back in time" for some Revolutionary "shtick" at this "period" piece in Old City specializing in "solid", really old-school American fare (as in the same recipes used in Colonial times) served by a costumed staff; Tories, however, cite "mediocre" fare and prefer to surrender this tavern to "tourists."

Clam Tavern | ▽ 19 | 16 | 19 | $24 |
339 E. Broadway Ave. (Edgemont Ave.), Clifton Heights, 610-623-9537
Few need fancy when there's "homey" in the form of this affordable Delco seafooder (around since JFK was in the White House) turning out "surprisingly well-made" items in a "residential neighborhood"; to the bewilderment of some, it's "either forgotten" or "undiscovered."

Cock 'n Bull | 16 | 17 | 17 | $31 |
Peddler's Village, Rte. 202 & Street Rd., Lahaska, 215-794-4010; www.peddlersvillage.com
This Traditional American comfort-fooder "still holds up" as an ideal spot to "unwind after shopping" in the Peddler's Village and the "proper place to take auntie" for a "terrific" "bargain" brunch; while "fun" seekers enjoy "murder mystery" theater on weekends, negativists nix the operation as "average" 'n' "touristy."

Coleman Restaurant | 19 | 23 | 19 | $49 |
Normandy Farm, 1431 Morris Rd. (DeKalb Pike), Blue Bell, 215-616-8300; www.normandyfarm.com
The "picturesque" setting of Blue Bell's Normandy Farm gives admirers reason to visit "celeb-chef" Jim Coleman's "rustically elegant" New American, and once there, his followers consider the "innovative" meals "calories well spent"; though some look past the "expense", a number see "lost potential", with "uneven execution" in dishes and "spotty" service as evidence.

Continental, The | 22 | 19 | 18 | $33 |
138 Market St. (2nd St.), 215-923-6069
"Crowds", "smoke" and "noise" are to be expected at Stephen Starr's "original", his "retro" diner-style Old City Eclectic that helped build the brand and is still a "star"; "sexy" servers, "glamour girls" and boys share the stage here, as does the "magnificent" martini list and "really good" small-plate fare; P.S. whether the Mid-Town offspring is more "sceney" is a source of much debate.

CONTINENTAL MID-TOWN | 20 | 23 | 18 | $34 |
1801 Chestnut St. (18th St.), 215-567-1800
"What's not to love"? ask the smitten about Stephen Starr's "flashy", "electrifying" Eclectic small-plater in Center City replete with "hip" crowds slurping "Buzz Aldrin" martinis, and pals nibbling on "tasty" tapas served by "affable", "Abercrombie"-like servers who are "morsels in themselves"; word is the roof deck is the "coolest" bar scene in town, but just beware the "swinging" seats on the balcony.

Copabanana ◐ | 16 | 12 | 14 | $20 |
Grant Plaza, 1619 Grant Ave. (Welsh Rd.), 215-969-1712
344 South St. (4th St.), 215-923-6180
4001 Spruce St. (40th St.), 215-382-1330
Copa Miami ◐
1716 Chestnut St. (bet. 17th & 18th Sts.), 215-568-8282
www.copabanana.com
The "holy trinity" of margaritas, burgers and Spanish fries keeps this "upbeat" Mexican-American bar mini-chain in business; it's "the place to be whether it's noon or midnight" on account of its "good" grub, and for those who think the original's digs "look and smell like a frat house", the newer outposts (Grant Avenue, Spruce Street and the most recent, Chestnut Street) may address decor shortcomings.

Copa Too ◐ | 16 | 10 | 14 | $20 |
263 S. 15th St. (bet. Locust & Spruce Sts.), 215-735-0848
Around the corner from the Kimmel Center is this "down 'n' dirty" Center City relative of Copabanana thriving on its reputation as a "hopping" late-night "college bar" and "cheap-date" joint selling "scrumptious" burgers and "killer" margaritas; the "good" beer selection puts "weak" service in perspective.

Core De Roma | – | – | – | M |
214 South St. (2nd St.), 215-592-9777
Friends and their countrymen have a soft spot for this warm, "friendly" and informal South Street Italian newcomer that replaced Ristorante San Carlo; at its core, the simple, reasonably priced menu looks to Rome for inspiration, while the BYO policy also allows wine lovers to tote their own.

Coyote Crossing | 20 | 20 | 17 | $33 |
800 Spring Mill Ave. (8th Ave.), Conshohocken, 610-825-3000
102 E. Market St. (Church St.), West Chester, 610-429-8900
www.coyotecrossing.com
"Go for the scenery" (as in "singles" scene) is the line on these "friendly", "festive" 'burb *hermanos* hooking amigos with "modern" south-of-the-border specialties that are "worth every peso"; many go "loco" over "satisfying" sangrias, margaritas and prices that rank among the more "expensive north of the border"; N.B. the Food score may not reflect a post-*Survey* chef change.

Creed's Seafood & Steaks ☒　　23　20　21　$48
*499 N. Gulph Rd. (Pennsylvania Tpke.), King of Prussia,
610-265-2550; www.creedskop.com*
It's "always a tough choice" choosing between the surf or
turf at this "pricey", "white-tablecloth" KoP carnivorium,
which maintains its "special-occasion" vibe in the "hushed"
dining room and draws backers who bask in "attentive"
service while settling in to "perfect" fish and "great"
steaks; P.S. weekend live music is an "after-dinner treat."

Crescent City ●　　　　　—　—　—　M
*600-602 S. Ninth St. (South St.), 215-627-6780;
www.crescentcityphilly.com*
Southern hospitality and cooking show up in this handsome
newcomer in a refurbed pool hall on an up-and-coming
South Street stretch; chef-owner Michael Duplantis is behind the burners, turning out regional dishes while a welcoming bar is enlivened by beautiful people every night.

Cresheim Cottage Cafe　　18　20　17　$32
*7402 Germantown Ave. (bet. Allens Ln. & Cresheim Valley Dr.),
215-248-4365; www.cresheimcottage.com*
For "dependable" food and a "charming" setting, partisans
of all persuasions pick this New American housed in a circa-
1706 building in Mount Airy; the setting may upstage the fare,
but the consensus is that the "oldie's" "potential is being re-
alized" with the addition of a "modernized" menu.

Criniti　　　　　　19　16　17　$26
2611 S. Broad St. (W. Moyamensing Ave.), 215-465-7750
"Big plates, big portions" and "savory" homestyle Italian
fare are the hallmarks of this "venerable" South Philly spot
in a converted church; it's a "nonna's-kitchen" kind of place
(ok, with "stained-glass windows"), and how can you ignore
"reasonable" prices and service that "tries to please"?

CUBA LIBRE　　　　22　25　20　$40
*10 S. Second St. (bet. Chestnut & Market Sts.), 215-627-0666;
www.cubalibrerestaurant.com*
Take a "date" or find one amid the "palm trees" at this
"lively" "street scene" on Old City's Second Street strip;
"even the most gringo" among us feel like they've "died and
gone to Havana" considering Guillermo Veloso's "playful"
takes on Cuban cuisine that provide a "gastronomic voy-
age", and once you factor in "dangerous" mojitos and salsa
dancers, you'll think it's Cuba "without the dictator."

Cucina Forte　　　　22　14　18　$34
768 S. Eighth St. (Catharine St.), 215-238-0778
"Divine" gnocchi and the house dream soup are the fortes of
this "dependable" South Philly Italian BYO; the "grandma"-
style menu is enhanced by daily specials, a welcome compensation for "cramped" conditions.

Cuttalossa Inn, The ⬛   ▽ 16 23 18 $41
3487 River Rd. (Cuttalossa Rd.), Lumberville, 215-297-5082;
www.cuttalossainn.com
It's "all about the view" at this (circa 1758) Traditional
American inn with an "idyllic" location in Upper Bucks, so
"eat with your eyes" and take in the 30-ft. waterfall from
the tables on the patio; many who keep in mind "you're
paying for the scenery" cut loose "mediocre" comestibles
and "pricey" tabs.

Dahlak ◖   21 14 18 $19
4708 Baltimore Ave. (bet. 47th & 48th Sts.), 215-726-6464;
www.dahlakrestaurant.com
East African enthusiasts "eat with their hands" at this
West Philly Eritrean "institution" dishing out "family-style"
food; sit at "low tables" and soak up "fantastic", fairly
priced eats and an ambiance warmed by "courteous" service, then hang with a "diverse" crowd at the bar in back.

Dalessandro's Steaks ◖⬛⊄   24   5 16 $9
600 Wendover St. (Henry Ave.), 215-482-5407
"Worth the schlep to Roxborough" is this standby far from
"Ninth Street's cheese steak wars"; "wear a bib", settle in
then suck down "properly greasy", "sinful" sandwiches in
a setting filled with "pot bellies and attitude"; fans appreciate "fast" service, but note that the digs seem "dumpy."

D'Angelo's   18 13 17 $42
Ristorante Italiano ◖⬛
256 S. 20th St. (bet. Locust & Spruce Sts.), 215-546-3935;
www.dangeloristorante.com
"Have dinner with the locals" over "good", "simple" cooking
at this Italian red-saucer off Rittenhouse Square; it holds
special appeal for those who marvel at "older guys and the
young things on their arms"; P.S. the music's "good" when
the late-night DJ starts spinning (Thursdays–Saturdays).

Dante & Luigi's ⊄   21 15 20 $36
762 S. 10th St. (Catharine St.), 215-922-9501;
www.danteandluigis.com
This "red-gravy", cash-only Italian is still strong after more
than 100 years, serving "delicious" veal among a "reliable" lineup of classics; yeah, the setting is *"Godfather"*-
esque and it may get flak from some who think it "lives on
reputation", but for the majority, it's "great" because it's
"what South Philly is all about."

Dark Horse Pub ◖   16 16 16 $25
421 S. Second St. (Pine St.), 215-928-9307;
www.darkhorsepub.com
Chef changes are part of the sport at this "homey" British
pub on Head House Square; despite the revolving door of
toques , it's "holding its own" claim Englishmen who go for

the soccer on the telly, pints and, sometimes, the "varied" New American menu.

Dave & Buster's　　　13 | 15 | 13 | $25
Pier 19 N., 325 N. Columbus Blvd. (bet. Callowhill & Spring Garden Sts.), 215-413-1951; www.daveandbusters.com
"Stay in your kids' good graces" and "bring a bundle of money" for all the video games and other entertainment to this behemoth chain of a playground-cum-eatery on the Delaware Riverfront; sure, since it's the "Chuck E. Cheese's for adults", the American fare is "a passing thought", and if the "sensory overload" starts to kick in, there's beer just in case.

Davio's　　　22 | 21 | 23 | $53
111 S. 17th St. (bet. Chestnut & Sansom Sts.), 215-563-4810; www.davios.com
"Power-lunchers" and "romantics" convene at this "upscale" Northern Italian steakhouse oozing "men's club" and offering a "respite" from Center City's hubbub with a "high-ceilinged" space like a "bank vault"; "you can't go wrong" with "satisfying" meals and service that's been "perfected", though habitués hedge it's an "expense-account" investment.

Day by Day　　　20 | 10 | 17 | $17
2101 Sansom St. (21st St.), 215-564-5540; www.daybydayinc.com
Vending "affordable", somewhat "exotic" lunches and "great" brunches that are a "cut above the norm" is this "pleasant", "low-key" Rittenhouse Square American-Eclectic in business for 25 years; the decor could use some "renovations" to pull it out of a "time warp", but this one's such a "gem" folks "wish they'd stay open for dinner."

Delmonico's Steakhouse　　　▽ 24 | 20 | 20 | $54
Hilton Philadelphia City Ave., 4200 City Ave. (Stout St.), 215-879-4000
It may not be the busiest chophouse in town, but this "elegant" Hilton steakhouse in Wynnefield does a grade A job of serving "wonderful" meat that ranks "alongside what you get at the top steakhouses" amid "relaxing", mahogany-filled quarters; even those who say it's "too much buck for the bang" are keen on "return visits."

Derek's　　　21 | 20 | 19 | $36
(fka Sonoma)
4411 Main St. (bet. Gay & Levering Sts.), 215-483-9400; www.dereksrestaurant.com
We "love the makeover!" aver admirers of Derek Davis' "reinvented" Manayunk New American (formerly the home of his Sonoma), a showcase for "tasty" "small plates of goodness"; the split-level digs feature bars on each floor, where fans of fancy drinks sample over 100 kinds of

"trendy" martinis and vodkas; in sum, it's a "nice turn-around" for an "old pro."

Dessert ⊟　　　　　　　▽ 21 22 19 $13
806 S. Sixth St. (E. Passyunk Ave.), 215-923-9733;
www.dessertphilly.com
"Every neighborhood needs a place" like this South Philly dessertery, whose deliciously "warm, comforting" atmosphere makes it a good bet for those who want to "indulge" in "glorious" sweets with coffee or tea; plus, it's "cheaper than visiting a cafe in Paris."

Deuce ●　　　　　　　　▽ 17 17 17 $25
1040 N. Second St. (George St.), 215-413-3822;
www.deucerestaurant.com
This "dark-red", "hip" yearling in the middle of "cool" Northern Liberties makes a "good alternative" to other bar/restaurants in the area; no, it's "not outstanding", but considering the "interesting" takes on Americana that give comfort food "a kick", it "trumps several" nearby competitors; N.B. the Food score may not reflect a post-*Survey* chef change.

DEUX CHEMINÉES ⌧　　　　27 26 26 $80
1221 Locust St. (bet. 12th & 13th Sts.), 215-790-0200;
www.deuxchem.com
Fit for a "17th-century king" is Fritz Blank's "utterly *romantique*" Classic French mainstay in an "elegant" 1875 Center City townhouse; "hedonists" sit down and partake of the "superior", "richly prepared" "haute cuisine" served by an "impeccable" staff "devoid of pretense"; the "seamless experience" is, no doubt, "memorably" expensive; N.B. closed July–August.

Devon Seafood Grill　　　21 19 20 $41
225 S. 18th St. (bet. Locust & Walnut Sts.), 215-546-5940;
www.devonseafood.com
This "upmarket" Rittenhouse Square "unchainlike" chain seafooder "as noisy as a construction site" draws a "professional" clientele for dinner featuring the "world's best" crab cakes and biscuits and a happy-hour/late-night crowd of the town's "youngest and hottest" at the bar; as far as service, it's "prompt" and "courteous", but it still's got nothing on the first-rate "people-watching."

DILWORTHTOWN INN　　　25 26 25 $57
1390 Old Wilmington Pike (bet. Pleasant Grove & Street Rds.),
West Chester, 610-399-1390; www.dilworthtown.com
"Bring your sweetie" and your "Amex" to this "romantic" circa-1758 "Colonial" New American near West Chester for "well-orchestrated" "candlelit" meals; while a few casual contrarians peg it as a bit "stuffy" (jackets recommended), far, far more insist if your dining partner isn't pleased with the "wonderful" food and "accomplished"

service (not to mention the "fabulous" 1,000-label wine list), "maybe you need a different companion."

DiNardo's Famous Seafood 19 | 10 | 17 | $35 |

312 Race St. (bet. 3rd & 4th Sts.), 215-925-5115;
www.dinardos.com
Crabs good enough "to dive for" is the hook at this "kitschy" "family favorite" of a seafooder in a "nondescript" Old City building, where fans hit the "awesome" hard shells and servers "give you a lesson in cracking"; in sum, it's "the best you're going to get this side of Baltimore."

Divan Turkish Kitchen – | – | – | I |

918 S. 22nd St. (Carpenter St.), 215-545-5790
The fresh pita bread from the oven helps warm this sunny family-owned Turkish in Center City; complementing the colorful decor are familiar treats (shish kebabs and various lamb dishes) and a BYO policy, with a $5 corkage fee.

DJANGO 25 | 17 | 23 | $45 |

526 S. Fourth St. (South St.), 215-922-7151
"It's still worth waiting for a reservation" at this "bohemian" Queen Village BYO commended for Ross Essner's "sublime" European food, servers that pay "attention to detail" and "charming touches" (bread served in flower pots); some who lament the recent departure of Bryan Sikora and Aimee Oxley say the ship's "slipped somewhat", but the majority maintains it remains "heaven in a storefront."

DMITRI'S 24 | 13 | 18 | $30 |

2227 Pine St. (23rd St.), 215-985-3680
795 S. Third St. (Catharine St.), 215-625-0556 ✆
"A shark couldn't get better seafood" than at Dmitri Chimes' "bustling", "no-frills" Greek twins serving the "freshest" grilled calamari, octopus and other bounty of the sea there is; the Queen Village BYO isn't for "claustrophobes", and if you want to "hear your companion" or avoid the "crush", arrive early at both locations.

Dolce ☒ 17 | 19 | 16 | $39 |

241 Chestnut St. (3rd St.), 215-238-9983;
www.dolcerestaurant.com
As "dark" as a "cave" is this Old City Italian near the Ritz specializing in a "great" vibe that makes the place perfect as a "nightspot"; while critics note there's "something missing here" and the food is "nothing spectacular", it's "cool to watch the lights change color under the glass floors."

Don Pablo's 16 | 15 | 14 | $22 |

Oxford Valley Mall, 2763 E. Lincoln Hwy. (N. Oxford Valley Rd.),
Langhorne, 215-269-4976; www.donpablos.com
"Endless" batches of chips and salsa, and "reliably good" food and margaritas mean this "cavernous" Mexican chain spot near Langhorne's Oxford Valley Mall is, "as far as such

places go", a "cut above" the competition; "*mañana*-type"
service, though, makes it "the TGI Friday's" of cantinas.

Down Home Diner ☒⇗   17 11 15 $17
Reading Terminal Mkt., 51 N. 12th St. (Filbert St.), 215-627-1955;
www.downhomediner.com
"When you miss that truck stop in Georgia", Jack
McDavid's "Philly classic" in the "buzzing" Reading
Terminal Market comes a callin' with "stick-to-your-ribs"
Southern goods and "excellent"breakfasts; as with the
chow, the name aptly describes the "what-can-I-get-you,
dear" service and "plain" decor.

Drafting Room   17 13 18 $27
Colonial 100 Shops, 635 N. Pottstown Pike (Ship Rd.),
Exton, 610-363-0521
900 N. Bethlehem Pike (Norristown Rd.), Spring House,
215-646-6116
www.draftingroom.com
An "amazing" collection of beers on tap brings
brewhounds to these suburban twins, though the "gut-
bustin'" pubby, yet "creative" New American vittles have
a similar effect; no one's bothered if they get "loud" and
"fratty", but the decor's "dated" and pros pronounce it's
wise to carry a "gas mask" at peak hours or get smoked out.

Duck Sauce   23 16 19 $25
127 S. State St. (bet. Mercer & Penn Sts.), Newtown,
215-860-8873
The Huang family's "popular" BYO in Downtown Newtown
is "not your usual Chinese", and you know it when you see
fans eagerly braving "waits" to tuck into "lighter-than-air"
dumplings along with "fusion" fare that "treats the taste
buds"; add in a "friendly" staff and "reasonable" prices,
and it's even more than it's quacked up to be.

Duling-Kurtz House & Country Inn   23 24 23 $49
Duling-Kurtz House & Country Inn, 146 S. Whitford Rd.
(Lincoln Hwy.), Exton, 610-524-1830; www.dulingkurtz.com
Unless someone decides to "pop the question", there are
"no surprises" at this Exton inn eatery, an "old standby"
decked out in enough fireplaces to keep "romantics" interested; the "good" Continental comestibles and "fine" service please, though Casanovas counsel the experience
can be "wallet deflating."

Earl's Prime   22 24 21 $58
Peddler's Village, Rte. 202 & Street Rd., Lahaska, 215-794-4020;
www.peddlersvillage.com
This modern steakhouse in Peddler's Village offers a
"break" from Bucks County's "touristy, countrified spots",
offering a "chic", brown-and-teal setting and jazz on
weekends; but the prices are "outrageous", and the consensus is the "food's prime but the service only select."

Effie's 🚭   21   15   20 $25

1127 Pine St. (Quince St.), 215-592-8333;
www.effiesrestaurant.com

"Get the sampler platter" because "you'll want to try everything" at the Boukidis family's "quaint" and "cute" cash-only Greek BYO in Wash West; "unbelievably low" tabs accompany the "hands-down delicious" fare served "with love" by people who "take pride" in what they do; P.S. the "waits are worthwhile", especially if you secure a seat in the "lovely" courtyard.

El Azteca   17   9   16 $18

1710 Grant Ave. (Bustleton Ave.), 215-969-3422
El Azteca II 🅂

714 Chestnut St. (bet. 7th & 8th Sts.), 215-733-0895;
www.elazteca2.com

For "straightforward" Mexican, it's hard to top these three cantinas dishing out "overflowing" helpings that "guarantee full tummies"; those who can abide decor and food "heavy on the cheese" are in the money, since the trio is "cheap"; N.B. the Grant Avenue location serves alcohol.

Elephant & Castle ◕   10   11   12 $24

Crowne Plaza Philadelphia Center City, 1800 Market St.
(18th St.), 215-751-9977; www.elephantcastle.com

"Think London 1972 and the rest will make sense" at these Philly and Jersey links in a "faux" "English Empire"–themed chain; charitable blokes find the fish 'n' chips "acceptable" and the beer list "large", but many are "unimpressed" with "stale" decor, "spotty" service and "mediocre" grub ("don't just send it back to the kitchen, send it back to England!").

El Sarape   21   16   19 $30

1380 Skippack Pike (Dekalb Pike), Blue Bell, 610-239-8667;
www.elsarapebluebell.com
Los Sarapes 🅂

Horsham Center Sq., 1116 Horsham Rd. (Limekiln Pike),
Horsham, 215-654-5002; www.lossarapeshorsham.com
17 Moyer Rd. (E. Butler Ave.), Chalfont, 215-822-8858;
www.lossarapes.com

A "genuine" south-of-the-border experience is the reason folks favor these "warm" Mex triplets marketing "good" Mexicana and margaritas (thanks to their extensive tequila lists) to suburbanites; though a "little expensive" for what they offer, most make "multiple visits."

El Sombrero   21   11   19 $20

Pleasant Valley Shopping Ctr., 295 Buck Rd. (bet. Holland &
Rocksville Rds.), Holland, 215-357-3337

Holy "mole" – though there's "nothing fancy" about this "mom-and-pop" Mexican BYO in a Bucks strip center, the cooking is "hard to beat" and the "virgin" margaritas may even be "better than" the real thing; the "very good" food, though, can come with enough "'tude" to "send you to the nearest Taco Bell."

EL VEZ　　　　　　　　　　21　23　19　$37
121 S. 13th St. (Sansom St.), 215-928-9800;
www.elvezrestaurant.com
"Beneath the glitter" of Stephen Starr's "sexy" Center City Mex, a "whimsical"/"hit" made to look like the lovechild of a "Tijuana"/"Vegas" union, is "serious" food and "many" margaritas for the "young" "scenester" crowd (along with a "photo booth" to capture magic moments); sure, the digs can "deafen" and the service ranges from "fast" to "slow", but overall, it's clear "Elvis hasn't left the building."

Epicurean, The　　　　　　19　15　18　$31
Village at Eland, 902-8 Village at Eland (Kimberton Rd.),
Phoenixville, 610-933-1336; www.americabargrill.com
New American fare prepared with "flair" and a "great" beer selection are to be savored at this Phoenixville venue in the Village at Eland; if it "tries to be upscale without making it", many rely on it as a "sports bar" and find it more useful as a place to "meet" over drinks.

Ernesto's 1521 Cafe　　　　　21　17　22　$37
1521 Spruce St. (bet. 15th & 16th Sts.), 215-546-1521;
www.ernestos1521.com
"They know how to get you to the concert on time" at this "serene", "warm" and "welcoming" Italian favored by both Kimmel-Center "orchestra members and goers"; hats off to the "fine", "reasonably" priced food that's paired with a small but "good" wine list (though patrons can also bring their own without a corkage fee) and "attentive" service – overall, "bravo!"

ESTIA　　　　　　　　　　23　25　21　$53
1405-7 Locust St. (Broad St.), 215-735-7700;
www.estiarestaurant.com
This "upscale" Greek newcomer near the Academy of Music features "beautiful" wood-filled quarters that successfully evoke the Mediterranean and has early acolytes choosing from a "stunning", "sparkling" array of seafood that's priced by the pound and destined for the plate; if the budget-conscious bemoan "steep" tabs, others reply that's the cost for the "freshest stuff this side of the Atlantic."

Eulogy Belgian Tavern ●　　　17　14　17　$24
136 Chestnut St. (2nd St.), 215-413-1918;
www.eulogybar.com
"You could drink your way to Belgium" (though the "fab" mussels here aren't from Brussels) at this small, "Gothic" Old City tavern where beerheads come alive over a list so "outstanding" it should be "studied"; mavens of the macabre kick back in the upstairs coffin room, "one of Philly's more unusual drinking spots."

EVERMAY ON THE DELAWARE   26   25   26 $67
EverMay On The Delaware, 889 River Rd. (Headquarters Rd.), Erwinna, 610-294-9100; www.evermay.com
"Take your wife or girlfriend" on a "scenic" drive through Upper Bucks and arrive at this "decadently romantic" and pricey New American in a B&B by the Delaware; though many revel in the "dreamlike experience" and fare, be advised the Food rating may not reflect a recent chef change; closed Mondays–Thursdays, and jackets suggested.

Fadó Irish Pub ●   16   17   15 $23
1500 Locust St. (15th St.), 215-893-9700; www.fadoirishpub.com
"Have beer with your breakfast boxty" as you hang with friends and "football" fans amid the "nooks and crannies" of this "dependable" Center City Celtic pub; it's "cookie-cutter" to some ("Irish bars should never become chains"), but chances are you'll be happy if you're looking for "a full belly and to satisfy a thirst for a few dollars."

Famous 4th Street Delicatessen   22   13   17 $18
700 S. Fourth St. (Bainbridge St.), 215-922-3274
"Clean at last, clean at last, thank God almighty, it's clean at last" kvell fans who "close their eyes" and find themselves on the "Lower East Side" at this "landmark" in Queen Village; legions leave any thoughts of cholesterol "at the door" and set upon "amazing", "cartoonishly large" sandwiches and "hearty" matzo ball soups; P.S. "don't plotz when you see the bill."

Farmicia   17   19   17 $35
15 S. Third St. (bet. Chestnut & Market Sts.), 215-627-6274; www.farmiciarestaurant.com
A "commitment to locally grown, organic foods" helps sustain interest in this "comfortable", "vegetarian"-friendly Old City Continental also known for "fabulous" breads (courtesy of the on-site Metropolitan Bakery); still, some "intrigued by its environmental mission" seek a prescription for "inconsistent" fare that can fall "flat."

Fatou & Fama   ▽ 14   8   13 $17
4002 Chestnut St. (40th St.), 215-386-0700; www.fatouandfama.com
"Want a cab? you can always find a driver" eating or picking up "interesting" food at this University City Senegalese/soul fooder; it's best to "come with an open mind", and expect "no decor to speak of" along with fare that's deemed "cheap" and "average."

Fayette Street Grille   23   14   21 $34
308 Fayette St. (bet. 3rd & 4th Sts.), Conshohocken, 610-567-0366; www.streetgrille.info
Devotees of this "popular" New American BYO in a Conshy storefront suggest making a reservation on account of

food that's a "bargain" considering the "excellent" quality (especially the $31 prix fixe dinner) and "amiable" staff; the "bare-bones" quarters may be "tight", but it doesn't matter since many loyalists just lovette.

Fellini Cafe   19 | 13 | 17 | $24 |
2216 Walnut St. (bet. 22nd & 23rd Sts.), 215-972-0860
31 E. Lancaster Ave. (bet. Cricket Ave. & Rittenhouse Pl.), Ardmore, 610-642-9009
St. Albans Shopping Ctr., 3541 West Chester Pike (Rte. 252), Newtown Square, 610-353-6131; www.fellinicafe.net
It's downright Fellini-esque trying to figure out the ownership of this "always packed" collection of BYO Italians that grew out of the Ardmore original, but fans can list at least 8½ attributes including "good", "solid" food "piled high on your plate" ("you get the whole box of pasta") and a "friendly" staff that seems "right off the boat"; notwithstanding "gaudy" settings complete with fake grapes and stucco, the whole package comes "cheap."

Fergie's Pub ●   17 | 16 | 19 | $18 |
1214 Sansom St. (bet. 12th & 13th Sts.), 215-928-8118; www.fergies.com
You "leave America behind when you walk through the doors" of this "dark", "authentic" Irish taproom, a "must for your next Center City pub crawl"; the combination of "standard" even "unfailingly good" bar food, quizzo and live music make it the perfect pit stop for pubbers.

Fez Moroccan Cuisine   ▽ 21 | 25 | 23 | $34 |
620 S. Second St. (bet. Bainbridge & South Sts.), 215-925-5367; www.fezrestaurant.com
"Prepare for a wild ride" to Morocco complete with "belly dancers" at this mainstay off South Street, where you "sit on couches or pillows" and indulge in multicourse "feasts" with, ideally, a "group" of friends or, for the full-on "sensual" experience, a "date"; "friendly" service and hookahs mean you'll likely b'steeya-in' awhile.

Figs ⊘   22 | 17 | 19 | $30 |
2501 Meredith St. (25th St.), 215-978-8440; www.figsrestaurant.com
As "cute" and compact as a "crib", this Fairmount Mediterranean BYO purveys a "delicious" mix of flavors, from the "exotic" (Moroccan) to the "down-home" (American); the "fabulous" weekend brunches and "attentive" service are more reasons to celebrate – just bring cash to do so, since they only take green.

Fioravanti ☒   ▽ 23 | 14 | 22 | $34 |
105 E. Lancaster Ave. (bet. Beach St. & Brandywine Ave.), Downingtown, 610-518-9170
"Minimal" decor belies "first-rate" Continental cooking from an open kitchen at this "small" Downingtown BYO

also prized for its affordable weekday prix fixe along with a tasting menu for kids; "no reservations" for parties under six can add up to "waits."

Fish Tank on Main – – – M
4247 Main St. (Rector St.), 215-508-0202
Now swimming in Manayunk's Main Street scene is this Northern Italian–seafood BYO, whose moderate prices may help bait fans to its digs – those being, as the name suggests, nautically themed and dominated by a large salt-water fish tank.

Flavor ▽ 22 18 17 $26
(fka Thai Pepper)
372 W. Lancaster Ave. (Conestoga Rd.), Wayne, 610-688-5853
Both "patrons and staff are clearly devoted" to this retooled Wayne Thai (the former home of Thai Pepper); the remodel has "enhanced" the look, and as for the "consistently good" menu, the addition of more items is a "welcome change"

FORK 24 22 22 $44
306 Market St. (bet. 3rd & 4th Sts.), 215-625-9425; www.forkrestaurant.com
Officially a Philly "institution", this "NYC-ish" Old City New American bistro eschews "flash" and has legions who "never hesitate to return" for "sophisticated", "consistently high-quality" food dispensed by an open kitchen in a "handsome" art-filled setting; owner Ellen Yin "runs a tight ship", so "attentive", "knowledgeable" service is no mystery; in sum, it's good tines all around; P.S. for an "excellent", "quick" nosh for less cash, visit next-door Fork: etc., the prepared foods adjunct.

FOUNTAIN RESTAURANT 28 28 29 $82
Four Seasons Hotel, 1 Logan Sq. (Benjamin Franklin Pkwy.), 215-963-1500; www.fourseasons.com
"As good as it gets" sizes up this *Survey*'s winner of the triple crown (No. 1 for Food, Decor and Service) in the Four Seasons Hotel; Philly's "elite" "live it up" and find "a treat for all the senses" in an "opulent" setting that showcases Martin Hamann's "divine" New French–Continental cuisine and "formal", yet "low-key" service that gives you the "royal treatment" ("they could serve me Cheerios and I'd think it was the best meal I ever had"); yes, the "shockingly high" tabs may be hard to absorb, but they're easily justified, especially for "expense-account" or "special-occasion" visits; N.B. jacket required.

Fountain Side 18 14 18 $30
537 Easton Rd. (Meetinghouse Rd.), Horsham, 215-957-5122
"Regular Joes feel at home" at this "large" and "bustling" Horsham Italian-American BYO in a strip mall near Willow

Grove Naval Air Station; notwithstanding the "dreaded" statues in the parking lot and a setting inside with all the ambiance of a "banquet hall", many enjoy "good" pastas plus prime ribs and steaks that "aren't bad for the price."

Four Dogs Tavern   14 | 15 | 15 | $31 |
1300 W. Strasburg Rd. (Telegraph Rd.), West Chester, 610-692-4367; www.fourdogstavern.com
Loyalists lap up the "lovely" ambiance of the patio and live music at this New American in West Chester; meanwhile, inside the converted-barn space, "glorified" pub grub and a "lively" bar scene keep tails wagging; the place "doesn't take itself too seriously", so you can expect "simple" delights from the food, even while some say "this old dog needs new tricks."

Four Rivers   ∇ 24 | 12 | 17 | $23 |
936 Race St. (bet. 9th & 10th Sts.), 215-629-8385
"Spicy", "delicious" dishes overflowing with "flavor" make you feel confident" that this Chinatown BYO provides a "true" Szechaun experience; considering that low tabs mean you can order "freely", many maintain "barebones" decor is just water under the bridge.

Fox & Hound ◑   11 | 12 | 13 | $21 |
1501 Spruce St. (15th St.), 215-732-8610
King of Prussia Mall, 160 N. Gulph Rd. (Mall Blvd.), King of Prussia, 610-962-0922
www.totent.com
"They're just sports bars, man" sums up this "jock-infested" duo that has more televisions and kinds of beer than China has people; though they might be "awesome" for hanging out and downing a few cold ones, expect few victory laps for "passable" American food some would hunt down only if their big-screen "died during a game."

Franco's Pastaria Restaurant   22 | 18 | 21 | $31 |
1549 S. 13th St. (Tasker St.), 215-755-8900; www.francoandluigis.com
You "can't beat the entertainment factor" at this "romantic" South Philly BYO Italian where "waiters serenade you" with opera and show tunes between "large-portioned" courses of "tasty", "homestyle" food; all told, "you don't even need a pulse to enjoy this place."

Frederick's   20 | 19 | 19 | $50 |
757 S. Front St. (Fitzwater St.), 215-271-3733
It's "Sinatra" time at Fred Vidi's "upscale" South Philly Italian catering to "longtime regulars" who sup on "generous" servings of "great" fare and chat over the piano player tickling the ivories in an "over-the-top" setting that's "worth" the trip alone; P.S. note that "you may feel out of place if you're under 50."

Freight House, The ◗ | 19 | 21 | 18 | $41 |

Doylestown SEPTA Station, 194 W. Ashland St. (Clinton Ave.), Doylestown, 215-340-1003; www.thefreighthouse.net

This "happening", "big city"–style Doylestown New American in a "cavernous" space next to the SEPTA train station draws a host of "hot chicks" and "yuppie lawyers" who gather for "happy hour" and "dancing" amid "intense" noise; while a few find the food "hit-or-miss", many think things are right on track here.

FRIDAY SATURDAY SUNDAY | 22 | 18 | 21 | $40 |

261 S. 21st St. (bet. Locust & Spruce Sts.), 215-546-4232; www.frisatsun.com

Exemplifying "staying power" after all these years is Weaver Lilley's "quirky" Center City "classic" that's still well worth "revisiting" for its patented, "decadent" cream of mushroom soup and other Traditional American food, "very fair" wine prices and "super-romantic" brownstone setting; it "hasn't changed in years", and that "ain't a bad thing at all"; P.S. the upstairs Tank Bar is "rendezvous" central.

Fuji Mountain | 20 | 15 | 18 | $30 |

2030 Chestnut St. (20th St.), 215-751-0939; www.fujimt.com

"Inventive" rolls of "surprising quality" can be had at this tri-level Japanese sushi specialist in Center City, but it's the sake bar and lounge that folks are floating to; you'll "feel like you traveled halfway around the world" for "rockin'" karaoke that supplies a "*Lost-in-Translation*" vibe.

Funky Lil' Kitchen ⊠ | – | – | – | E |

232 King St. (Penn St.), Pottstown, 610-326-7400; www.funkylilkitchen.com

Center Citizens make the hour-long drive to blue-collar Pottstown for Michael Falcone's little, urbane BYO surprise, whose open kitchen spins clever riffs on New American cooking; though the newcomer is a 'burb dweller, prices in this kitchen are on the citified side.

FuziOn | 24 | 17 | 22 | $35 |

Center Point Shopping Ctr., 2960 Skippack Pike (Valley Forge Rd.), Worcester, 610-584-6958; www.fuzionrestaurant.com

"Great karma" is at work at this "low-key" French-Asian "standout" in central Montco known for "creative" "Center City"–quality cooking; the "BYO factor", "nice" outdoor seating and "personal" service keep patrons "going back."

Gables at Chadds Ford, The | 21 | 21 | 19 | $46 |

423 Baltimore Pike (Brintons Bridge Rd.), Chadds Ford, 610-388-7700; www.thegablesatchaddsford.com

Brandywine Valley day-trippers and locals alike endorse this "civilized" New American seafooder in a former 1897 barn; aside from the "chic" "rusticity" of its setting, there's "good" fare, and many know to "ask for a table outside" on the "beautiful" patio and "listen to the sounds from the nearby waterfall."

GAYLE ⌧
26 | 19 | 24 | $58

617 S. Third St. (bet. Bainbridge & South Sts.), 215-922-3850;
www.gaylephiladelphia.com

"Go and be adventurous" at former Le Bec-Fin executive chef Daniel Stern's "little" New American off South Street, a "casual" though still upscale newcomer blowing away fans with "knowledgeable" service and "well-executed", "complex" fare that deftly combines the "experimental" and "classic"; N.B. it's à la carte Mondays–Wednesdays, but prix fixe only Thursdays–Saturdays.

Geechee Girl Rice Café ⇪
▽ 25 | 18 | 18 | $22

5946 Germantown Ave. (bet. Haines & Harvey Sts.),
215-843-8113; www.geecheegirlricecafe.com

There's "down-home" Southern soul "with a dose of sophistication" on the menu of this BYO storefront in Germantown that has adherents praising its "fabulous" "low-country" cooking (particularly the "best" greens "north of the Mason-Dixon"); service is appropriately "hospitable" and "slow."

General Lafayette Inn & Brewery, The
18 | 18 | 18 | $29

The General Lafayette Inn, 646 Germantown Pike (Church Rd.),
Lafayette Hill, 610-941-0600; www.generallafayetteinn.com

"Phenomenal" beers, "solid" pub grub and "relaxed" vibe come together in a historical "General-Lafayette-slept-here"setting at this Lafayette Hill Traditional American reportedly inhabited by the spirits of Revolutionary War soldiers; nowadays, "young professionals" haunt the bar, while an "older crowd" favors the dining room – generally.

General Warren Inne
24 | 23 | 23 | $47

General Warren Inne, Old Lancaster Hwy. (Warren Ave.),
Malvern, 610-296-3637; www.generalwarren.com

"Bring the parents" for beef Wellington and bananas Foster at this newly renovated, "elegant" Colonial "hide-away" in Malvern; "high-quality" Traditional American cookery complements the "wonderful" service with a "flourish" (i.e. tableside preparations), and those under the spell of the place's "romance" may want to "book one of the rooms upstairs."

Genji
22 | 15 | 17 | $35

1720 Sansom St. (bet. 17th & 18th Sts.), 215-564-1720;
www.genjionline.com

"People come from all over" to "roll up to the sushi bar", "chat with the chefs and chow down" at this "upscale" Center City Japanese proffering fish "so fresh you'd think it had a pulse"; it's perhaps a bit "pricier than others", so if someone else is paying, take advantage and "go omakase."

Geno's Steaks ●⋈　　　　19 | 7 | 13 | $10

Italian Mkt., 1219 S. Ninth St. (Passyunk Ave.), 215-389-0659;
www.genossteaks.com
"There's nothing better at 3 AM" than to "wait in line" to tear
into "sloppy goodness in every bite" at Whizard Joe Vento's
"classic", "neon"-accented 24/7 cheese steak stand; it's a
"true piece of Americana" and what keeps South Philly "on
the map" – just be prepared for debates about "that other
place" across the street and do your best to quickly "figuring
out what and how to order" – preferably in English.

Georges'　　　　　　　21 | 24 | 21 | $49

503 W. Lancaster Ave. (Gallagher Rd.), Wayne, 610-964-2588;
www.georgesonthemainline.com
Georges Perrier's "down-home" Eclectic alternative to his
Center City showcases "fills a need", offering Main Liners
"action" at the "popular" bar and "solidly good" fare in the
farmhouse-style main dining room; those who aren't that
impressed ("inconsistent" dishes) are in the minority;
N.B. Sunday is BYO, with a $5 corkage fee.

GILMORE'S ⊠　　　　　27 | 23 | 27 | $55

133 E. Gay St. (bet. Matlack & Walnut Sts.), West Chester,
610-431-2800; www.gilmoresrestaurant.com
Peter Gilmore (an alum of Georges Perrier) "amazes" with
his Classic French West Chester BYO widely regarded as
the "Le-Bec the of 'burbs" for its "fantastic" "special-
occasion" cuisine served by an "attitude-free" staff; at 35
seats, scoring a reservation in the the snug, "intimate"
quarters means either many redials or divine intervention.

Gioia Mia　　　　　　　19 | 14 | 18 | $40

2025 Sansom St. (bet. 20th & 21st Sts.), 215-231-9895;
www.gioiamiaphl.com
Fabrizio Pace's "talent" is evident at this white-tablecloth
Center City newcomer, a "delightful" find serving
"delicious" Central Italian dishes complemented by a
select list of varietals; reports of a "cheerful" staff help
bring joy to early enthusiasts.

Gnocchi ⋈　　　　　　22 | 15 | 19 | $26

613 E. Passyunk Ave. (bet. Bainbridge & South Sts.), 215-592-8300
"Go for the namesake" dish and come away happy at this
affordable, no-reserve Italian BYO operating in "tight",
exposed-brick quarters off South Street; the "attentive"
staff "screaming" over the "noise" is "part of the fun", even
if the cash-only policy isn't.

Goji Tokyo Cuisine　　　– | – | – | M

2001 Hamilton St. (20th St.), 215-569-1667;
www.gojirestaurant.com
Samurai armor enshrined in a glass case is the focal
point of this stylish Cityview Condos newcomer, the first

U.S. offshoot of a Japanese chain; there's much more than sushi and tempura on a diverse menu that features delicate cuisine from the Edo period (reflecting the history of the family who owns this spot) along with more contemporary offerings.

Golden Pheasant Inn ▽ 25 | 23 | 22 | $48 |

Golden Pheasant Inn, 763 River Rd. (13 mi. north of New Hope), Erwinna, 610-294-9595; www.goldenpheasant.com

"French country dining at its best" is the specialty of this "special-occasion" destination north of New Hope in Upper Bucks "worth the ride" for its "simply excellent" cuisine and "charm"; regulars regale with tales of "romance" given both its inn setting and location near the Delaware Canal.

Gourmet ⊠ ▽ 25 | 14 | 21 | $34 |

3520 Cottman Ave. (Frankford Ave.), 215-331-7174

The Youjongdee family was among the pioneers of French-Thai cooking when they opened this "perennial favorite" in an "out-of-the-way" Northeast Philly storefront a quarter century ago; though calls have gone out to "change the menu", most insist they've "never had a bad meal" and say it's still "worth" finding a meter on Cottman Avenue for.

Grace Tavern ◑ 19 | 14 | 18 | $18 |

2229 Grays Ferry Ave. (bet. South & 23rd Sts.), 215-893-9580

"Love this place" sizes up the appeal of this "bohemian" neighborhood tavern in emerging Grays Ferry slinging up "cheap" and "tasty" bar chow such as blackened green beans on its N'Awlins-accented New American slate; beerwise, qualified quaffers confess the on-tap selection is "very good."

Grey Lodge Pub ◑⊄ – | – | – | ⌐ |

6235 Frankford Ave. (bet. Harbison Ave. & Robbins St.), 215-624-2969; www.greylodge.com

A bona fide destination for brewhounds is this dimly lit Northeast Philly bar, whose downstairs attracts with the requisite dartboards and TVs but also with the place's claim to fame – the craft beers backed by a well-schooled staff; the low-priced gastropub vittles are reserved for the upstairs dining area.

Grill, The 23 | 25 | 25 | $57 |

Ritz-Carlton Philadelphia, 10 S. Broad St. (Chestnut St.), 215-523-8000; www.ritzcarlton.com

Fantasists feel "a king could come strolling in" at any moment to the Ritz-Carlton's "clubby" New American, a destination for Philly's "elite"; "escape" Center City's "madness" via one of the city's most "beautifully appointed" settings enhanced by "top-notch" food and "pampering worthy of the price tag."

Grill Restaurant   ▽ 15 | 22 | 20 | $46

Westin Philadelphia, 99 S. 17th St. (bet. Chestnut & Market Sts.),
215-575-6930; www.westin.com

You "get lots of attention" at the Westin's "rarely crowded" New American, so if your meal "involves a serious business conversation" and you need a "quiet retreat", it may be a good bet; though "dependable" to its backers, some surveyors sear the offerings as "unimaginative" "hotel food."

Gullifty's   13 | 11 | 13 | $23

1149 W. Lancaster Ave. (bet. Franklin & Montrose Aves.),
Rosemont, 610-525-1851; www.gulliftys.com

Abetted by its "remarkable" number of beers, along with burgers and 'zas, this "hopping" Main Line sports bar lives up to its rep as a "late-night" haunt of "'Nova students" and "those trying to relive their college days"; so "bring your earplugs" and get set for "merely mediocre" vittles, "dingy" digs and servers "who have little clue how to wait tables."

Half Moon Saloon ⌧   ▽ 17 | 16 | 15 | $28

108 W. State St. (Union St.), Kennett Square, 610-444-7232;
www.halfmoonrestaurant.com

The "loud and smoky" downstairs of this Kennett Square New American features a long bar dispensing "exceptional" brews, while the "airy" deck upstairs is a sure bet "for sure" in the summer; they call it a "saloon", but who knew a place like this could have "good", "interesting" food?

Hamlet Bistro ⌧   ▽ 21 | 18 | 20 | $32

7105 Emlen St. (bet. Durham St. & Mt. Pleasant Ave.),
215-247-5800; www.hamletbistro.com

It seems all the village wants to turn out for this "adorable" (i.e. it has only 28 seats) Mount Airy BYO yearling that charms with "tasty", affordable American-Eclectic dishes and a "welcoming" vibe; to its supporters, there's no question that it "impresses."

Hank's Place ⌐   22 | 10 | 18 | $15

1410 Baltimore Pike (Creek Rd.), Chadds Ford,
610-388-7061

They crank out "awesome" breakfasts for some of the "best prices in the state" at this "friendly", "down-home" Traditional American diner in Chadds Ford; you'll have to "tolerate the lines" on weekends, but whether you're fighting a "hangover" or preparing to visit Brandywine Valley, it's a tough act to beat.

Happy Rooster   19 | 13 | 17 | $38

118 S. 16th St. (Sansom St.), 215-963-9311;
www.thehappyrooster.com

Beyond a "dive-bar" facade is this small and "offbeat" Center City spot still pulling off "surprisingly good" French-American pub food amid a "dark" "supper-club" setting that's pure "vintage '60s"; in all, it's a testament to its success that many have come to roost here for nearly 40 years.

Hard Rock Cafe ◗ | 11 | 18 | 13 | $26 |
1113-31 Market St. (12th St.), 215-238-1000; www.hardrock.com
They're a "rockin'" and their eardrums are a "burstin'" at Philly's outpost of the American chain near the Pennsylvania Convention Center in Center City; it's "great if you have teens in tow" and is still serving up a burger-centric American menu, memorabilia and "more tourists than the Statue of Liberty"; P.S. "don't go there to get your taste buds rocked", which is why wags dub it "the Hard Luck Cafe."

Harmony Vegetarian | ▽ 20 | 11 | 19 | $17 |
135 N. Ninth St. (bet. Cherry & Race Sts.), 215-627-4520
This Chinese veggie specialist in Chinatown "works magic" ("you'll never know it's not the real thing") with its all-you-can-eat dim sum ($20 for two) that's a "dream come true"; even meat eaters are in sync about "not missing the beef" when there's this much "flavor" going around.

Haru | 19 | 23 | 18 | $39 |
241-243 Chestnut St. (3rd St.), 215-861-8990; www.harusushi.com
"Wear your good threads" for a night out in Old City at this "chic" Manhattan transplant tagging "NYC prices" to Japanese fare served in a "soothing" renovated bank building space; though the sushi is a source of debate ("very good" vs. "mediocre") and service isn't ("disappointing"), for some the place "oozes potential"; N.B. there's an upstairs lounge for sake sipping.

Havana | 16 | 14 | 15 | $30 |
105 S. Main St. (bet. Mechanic & New Sts.), New Hope, 215-862-9897; www.havananewhope.com
"Young things on the prowl" keep Havana "hot night" on the patio of this New Hope "institution"; certainly "the place to be" for "nightlife", drinks and "people-watching", most deem the New American food "ok" and add that despite the name, those looking for Cuban comestibles won't find it here.

Hibachi | 18 | 16 | 19 | $28 |
Pier 19 N., 325 N. Columbus Blvd. (Callowhill St.), 215-592-7100
240 W. Swedesford Rd. (west of Valley Forge Rd.), Berwyn, 610-296-4028
985 E. Lancaster Ave. (off Rte. 30 bypass), Downingtown, 610-518-2910
Benjamin Fox Pavillion, 261 Old York Rd. (Township Line Rd.), Jenkintown, 215-881-6814
145-147 S. State Rd. (bet. Bobbin Mill Rd. & Dora Dr.), Springfield, 610-690-4911
"Kids", "groups" and "first dates" seem entranced by this "bargain" Japanese steakhouse chain renowned for chefs offering "frenetic", "dazzling" performances on

grills ("who needs a movie after dinner?"); while gourmets find the food just "ok", most focus on "keeping their eyes" fixed on the show for any wayward shrimp "doing a double axel, triple toe loop combo or quadruple Lutz."

HIGH STREET CAFFÉ   25 | 17 | 22 | $35

322 S. High St. (Dean St.), West Chester, 610-696-7435; www.highstreetcaffe.com

"Loud" and "funky" is this West Chester BYO storefront, where expats "close their eyes" and swear they're "back in New Orleans"; Cajun-Creole lovers lap up "superb" vittles aided by "helpful" service in a room so "tight" you quickly "get to know your neighbor."

Hikaru   21 | 17 | 19 | $32

4348 Main St. (Grape St.), 215-487-3500
607 S. Second St. (bet. Bainbridge & South Sts.), 215-627-7110

Even "sushi snobs" salute the "good" raw fare at these twins in Queen Village and near the canal in Manayunk (the latter sporting a "nice" river view); while adults admit the food's a bit "pricey", kids are "entertained" by the "overlooked" cooked dishes dispensed from the grills.

H.K. Golden Phoenix ◐   20 | 10 | 14 | $21

911 Race St. (bet. 9th & 10th Sts.), 215-629-4988

The dim sum's "yum" and the prices "low" at this huge Chinese eatery in Chinatown specializing in family-style offerings fit for "banquets" and offering a "varied" selection of fare ("I can't remember how many dishes I tried"); on some nights the "waits can be long", and on most nights the service "isn't exactly classy."

HONEY'S SIT 'N EAT ⇗   24 | 19 | 17 | $14

800 N. Fourth St. (Brown St.), 215-925-1150

"If your Jewish bubbe" ruled the stove at an "old roadside" joint down South, you'd grasp the concept of this "funky" Jewish-Southern breakfast/luncher; it seems all of Northern Liberties "lines up" for its "extensive menu" of "tasty" comfort dishes served by "seemingly idle" servers who may keep you waiting "an eternity for your food to arrive"; P.S. and honey, it's best to "get there early."

Horizons ⌺   ▽ 24 | 18 | 21 | $35

611 S. Seventh St. (South St.), 215-923-6117; www.horizonsphiladelphia.com

Habitués have happily followed Rich Landau (who turns out the "best" vegan fare around) and Kate Jacoby's "amazing" standby from its Willow Grove roots to South Street; the relaxing split-level space is decorated in natural woods, with a dining room upstairs and a lounge downstairs dispensing various drinks; P.S. a selection of the wines is produced from organic grapes, so "getting a buzz can come with a clear conscience."

Hosteria Da Elio
21 | 13 | 19 | $33

615 S. Third St. (bet. Bainbridge & South Sts.), 215-925-0930
"Don't judge a small Italian eatery by its decor", since the pastas are "delicious" and the other dishes "skillfully prepared" at Elio Sgambati's "intimate" BYO trattoria off South Street; P.S. if "cramped" isn't your style, skip the dining room for the "quaint" patio.

Hotel du Village ⌧
▽ 22 | 24 | 24 | $50

Hotel du Village, 2535 River Rd. (Phillips Mill Rd.), New Hope, 215-862-9911; www.hotelduvillage.com
"Solid", "classic" country French food lures city slickers to this eatery in a 20-room lodgelike inn outside of New Hope; the "elegant", "Tudor-style" dining room, "old-world" airs and "helpful" service make "perfect romantic evenings" a sure thing; N.B. dinner only, and closed Mondays and Tuesdays.

Hunan
▽ 20 | 15 | 19 | $26

47 E. Lancaster Ave. (Rittenhouse Pl.), Ardmore, 610-642-3050
"Flashier competitors" have little on this "quiet" Ardmore Chinese BYO where adherents gather for "interesting", "reasonably" priced food including some of "the best hot-and-sour soup anywhere"; the staff aims to "please", and they "never rush you" either.

Hymie's Merion Deli
17 | 8 | 14 | $18

342 Montgomery Ave. (Levering Mill Rd.), Merion Station, 610-668-3354
Servers in "bad moods" "yell" and dole out "pounds" of pastrami and other "reliable" deli gut busters at this Merion mainstay frequented by Main Line "seniors" and "families"; "long lines at all hours" are to be expected, so "don't dillydally" when ordering; P.S. many are "so in love" with the pickle bar.

Il Cantuccio ⌧⇄
23 | 15 | 19 | $29

701 N. Third St. (Fairmount Ave.), 215-627-6573
"Bring a bottle of wine" to this "tiny", "bustling" and "friendly" neighborhood BYO fave in Northern Liberties, and they'll pair it with "superior" Italian food that's a "bargain"; "reservation times can be pure fiction" (you'll likely "wait" even if you made one), and "don't ask for coffee" because "someone is always waiting for your seat."

Illuminare
18 | 23 | 17 | $31

2321 Fairmount Ave. (bet. 23rd & 24th Sts.), 215-765-0202; www.illuminare2321.com
Whether you're up for a "casual" meal or a "romantic" rendezvous, this Italian near the Art Museum is a bright option; while things dim a bit with "spotty" service, the "excellent" brick-oven pizzas shine, as does the "gorgeous" wood-and-glass decor and "beautiful" courtyard.

Il Portico
21 | 20 | 19 | $52

1519 Walnut St. (bet. 15th & 16th Sts.), 215-587-7000;
www.il-portico.com
"Old-style elegance" sets the scene at this chandeliered,
"special-place-for-special-people" Walnut Street Italian
where denizens bask in "serene" environs and take in
"good" dishes; still, detractors diss "overpricing" and want
to show "hit-or-miss" service the door.

Il Sol Tuscan Grill
17 | 15 | 16 | $38

255 N. Sycamore St. (Durham Rd.), Newtown, 215-968-5880;
www.ilsoltuscangrill.com
It "rocks on the weekend" at this Bucks venue serving
Tuscan specialties in "noisy" quarters; but even fans of the
food ask for a "major update" of the "worn-out" decor
that's "trapped in the '80s" and "iffy" service.

Il Tartufo ⊄
22 | 18 | 20 | $38

4341 Main St. (Grape St.), 215-482-1999
The "food's for savoring" at this "charming" cash-only
Manayunk Tuscan (part of the Il Portico and Tira Misu family)
that proves "you don't need to drive into the city" for "wonderful" Italian dining; come summer, some say sidewalk
seating allows for prime "people-watching" on Main Street.

Imperial Inn ●
20 | 12 | 18 | $22

146 N. 10th St. (bet. Cherry & Race Sts.), 215-627-5588
Heaven is a bowl of dim sum is the word on this imperially
resilient, "banquet"-size Chinatown landmark, whose
"consistent", "quality" Chinese fare gives the place
"street cred" even if decor that "hasn't changed in three
decades" doesn't; the staff generally "takes good care of
you", even if service is sometimes "slower" if you can't
speak the language.

Independence Brew Pub ●
14 | 15 | 15 | $23

1150 Filbert St. (bet. 11th & 12th Sts.), 215-922-4292;
www.independencebrewpub.com
For brew food, TVs or happy hour, this "fun" American pub
beneath the Pennsylvania Convention Center may do the
trick; though it's a tepid tea party to some who seek independence from the place ("why did I go here with the
Reading Terminal Market across the street?"), others find
it useful for "great" beers and a burger.

Indonesia
∇ 18 | 13 | 19 | $22

1029 Race St. (bet. 10th & 11th Sts.), 215-829-1400;
www.indonesiarestaurant.com
If you're interested in "authentic" Indonesian, try the "outstanding" value of a tasting menu plead partisans of this
"tasty departure from the rest of the Chinatown" offerings;
veterans point out, however, that the food "brings back
fond memories, but without the taste."

Inn at Phillips Mill ⊘   23 24 23 $49

Inn at Phillips Mill, 2590 N. River Rd. (Phillips Mill Rd.), New Hope, 215-862-9919

"Get a room and make it a night" at this BYO French "getaway" housed in a "quaint" 18th-century farmhouse in the "woods" outside of New Hope; sure, the food's "solid", but it's the setting that gives it "charm in spades", thanks to a "cozy" setting complete with fireplaces and "beautiful" garden for alfresco dining; N.B. cash only.

Io E Tu Ristorante   21 14 21 $38

1514-20 S. Ninth St. (bet. Dickinson & Tasker Sts.), 215-271-3906

"Bring an appetite" to Ristorante Pesto's South Philly cousin, where you'll see "families" enjoying "well-prepared" Italian "home cooking" and a "down-to-earth" vibe ("I was kissed on both cheeks!"); bring a good memory since you can expect a "long recitation" of specials.

Iron Hill Brewery & Restaurant 17 17 18 $26

30 E. State St. (bet. Church & Monroe Sts.), Media, 610-627-9000 ☽

Shoppes at English Village, 1460 Bethlehem Pike (Welsh Rd.), North Wales, 267-708-2000

3 W. Gay St. (High St.), West Chester, 610-738-9600 ☽
www.ironhillbrewery.com

"So glad there's more than one" of this "upmarket" suburban New American brewpub chain exclaim enthusiasts who endorse "interesting" comfort food that rarely "disappoints" while it "hits every price range"; naturally, the beer selections are "outstanding", and the "helpful" staffers are "so friendly, I thought I was home."

Isaac Newton's   15 13 16 $23

18 S. State St. (Washington Ave.), Newtown, 215-860-5100; www.isaacnewtons.com

"Mommies", "kids" and young adults gravitate to this New American pub in the middle of Newtown to chow down on "better-than-average" fare from a "huge", reasonably priced menu; all the "meeting and greeting" generates lots of "noise" that's further abetted by a "lively" late-night bar scene and beer from a list so large it "boggles the mind."

Isaac's Restaurant & Deli   17 12 16 $13

Crossroads Sq., 630 W. Uwchlan Ave. (off Pottstown Pike/ Rte. 100), Exton, 484-875-5825

Shops at Thornberry, 66 E. Street Rd. (Wilmington Pike), West Chester, 610-399-4438
www.isaacsdeli.com

For a sit down or on the fly bite, this "more-San-Fran-than-NYC" deli chain has Pennsylvanians singing about "fresh" and "healthy" pretzel-bun sandwiches (named after birds) that are expedited by a "speedy" staff in "tropical" digs; the prices please, but bigbirds squawk over "skimpy" portions.

Italian Bistro
15 14 16 $26

211 S. Broad St. (bet. Locust & Walnut Sts.), 215-731-0700
2500 Welsh Rd. (Roosevelt Blvd.), 215-934-7700
www.italianbistro.com

"It ain't South Philly", but this "easy-on-the-pocket" Italian chain puts out "big" helpings of "decent" fare and an atmosphere that brings to mind "Olive Garden" (your "aunt from the Midwest" may be happy); big plus: "they know how to get you in and out" if you have a show to catch.

Izzy & Zoe's
20 13 13 $13

Hamilton Village Shops, 224 S. 40th St. (bet. Locust & Walnut Sts.), 215-382-2328

"Free" pickles, "great" sandwiches and "waits" in line are the norm at this "crowded" deli/bagelry on Penn's campus; you can also bank on the staff "taking a long time" to put together an order, then "messing it up", so make sure to attend anger management class or read Gandhi before going.

Jack's Firehouse
18 19 18 $35

2130 Fairmount Ave. (bet. 21st & 22nd Sts.), 215-232-9000;
www.jacksfirehouse.com

Elk – emu – "dare to eat bear?" – "is this heaven or what?" ask amazed acolytes of this Fairmount Southerner captained by Jack McDavid (he creates "country cooking at its best") in a "unique" old firehouse setting that befits the "adventurous" menu; those who think the place's "fire is going out" can at least take comfort in the "great" bar area.

Jake's
25 21 23 $51

4365 Main St. (bet. Grape & Levering Sts.), 215-483-0444;
www.jakesrestaurant.com

"Main Line yuppies" are still happily "slumming it" at Bruce Cooper's "sophisticated" Manayunk New American; it maintains its rep as "the grande dame" of Main Street with "skillfully prepared", "splurge"-worthy food and "impeccable" service; the seating's "tight", especially at peak times, so expect to almost "sit in your neighbor's lap."

Jamaican Jerk Hut ⊉
20 12 14 $18

1436 South St. (15th St.), 215-545-8644

Yes, Nicola Shirley's cash-only BYO Center City Jamaican may look "low budget", and "slow" service "isn't always on the ball", but if you bring your own rum and sit out back for "good", "authentic" goat curry, oxtail and jerk chicken, you'll think you're in paradise; P.S. it's no longer a "best-kept secret" since its appearance in the movie *In Her Shoes*.

J.B. Dawson's
17 17 18 $27

Pilgrim Garden Shopping Ctr., 5035 Township Line Rd./Rte. 1 (Fairway Rd.), Drexel Hill, 610-853-0700
Shoppes at Flowers Mill, 92 N. Flowers Mill Rd. (Rte. 213), Langhorne, 215-702-8119

(continued)
J.B. Dawson's
440 Plymouth Rd. (W. Germantown Pike), Plymouth Meeting,
610-260-0550
www.jbdawsons.com
Settle into a "comfy" booth for "reasonably" priced steaks
and babybacks at this "manly" American that's "not bad
for a chain"; the "team approach to service takes some
getting used to", and bring a "miner's helmet" to find your
way around a setting as "dark" as a "tomb."

Jim's Steaks ◑   22 | 9 | 14 | $10
431 N. 62nd St. (bet. Callowhill St. & Girard Ave.),
215-747-6615 ⊅
Roosevelt Mall, 2311 Cottman Ave. (Bustleton Ave.),
215-333-5467
400 South St. (4th St.), 215-928-1911 ⊅
Stony Creek Shopping Ctr., 469 Baltimore Pike (Sproul Rd.),
Springfield, 610-544-8400
www.jimssteaks.com
"Ask fast" ("'Whiz with' is all you need to say") and you
shall receive what many regard as the "best" sandwiches
around at this "sine qua non", "no-frills" Philly cheese
steak quartet; for just about everyone, it's "worth the long
lines at all hours of the day" – and the "emergency angio-
plasty" you may need.

John Harvard's Brew House   14 | 14 | 15 | $24
Springfield Square Shopping Ctr., 1001 Baltimore Pike
(Lincoln Ave.), Springfield, 610-544-4440
629 W. Lancaster Ave. (Old Eagle School Rd.), Wayne,
610-687-6565
www.johnharvards.com
"Stick to the basics" – "great" beers and the bar – at
these "cavernous" American chain brewhouses, and most
maintain you'll make out fine; some even profess that although the chow won't make it into the "Ivy Leagues" of
food, it's "reliable" nonetheless.

Johnny Brenda's ◑   ▽ 21 | 13 | 16 | $18
1201 Frankford Ave. (Girard Ave.), 215-739-9684;
www.johnnybrendas.com
"Standard Tap's even cooler cousin" is this "funky" Fishtown
"winner", a bi-level bar whose "divey" demeanor belies the
"fab" sandwiches and other American-Eclectic vittles that
are "way beyond bar fare"; a jukebox and pool table make
it more "hipster" hang than" "grandfather's social club."

Johnny Mañana's   15 | 16 | 16 | $23
4201 Ridge Ave. (Midvale Ave.), 215-843-0499;
www.johnnymananas.com
"Great" margaritas and "big" burritos help enliven this
East Falls Mexican sporting a "good" bar that suits the

"fun" "college" ambiance; while the weekend mariachi guitarists lends an air of "authenticity", "flavorless" fare doesn't sit well with purists.

Jonathan's American Grille　　16 21 17 $31
Jenkintown Train Station, Greenwood Ave. & Township Line Rd., Jenkintown, 215-885-9000; www.jonathansamericangrille.com
This new Traditional American inside the Jenkintown train station shows promise: while the modern space has been "beautifully" designed and the menu is "varied", "uneven" service and food derails things somewhat; still, with some "fine tuning", this whistle stop should be a "keeper."

Jones ⬤　　　　　　　20 21 19 $29
700 Chestnut St. (7th St.), 215-223-5663; www.jones-restaurant.com
Cross "*The Brady Bunch*" with a little "Frank Lloyd Wright", then throw in some mac 'n' cheese and meatloaf, and you've got Stephen Starr's "campy" Washington Square American, a "retro" den complete with shag rugs and a "Chevy" vibe; the comfort food's "done right" and the servers "genuinely peppy" – ain't that swell?

Jong Ka Jib　　　　　▽ 25 17 21 $16
6600 N. Fifth St. (66th Ave.), 215-924-0100
"Keep it a secret" plead backers of this "bargain" BYO Korean in the Olney section of Koreatown, lest others find out about "wonderfully" "satisfying" tofu and barbecue plus the "little dishes they serve with them"; a meal may go more smoothly "if you can communicate with the staff", but the majority gets by deliciously.

Joseph Ambler Inn　　　　21 23 21 $44
Joseph Ambler Inn, 1005 Horsham Rd. (bet. Stump & Upper State Rds.), North Wales, 215-362-7500; www.josephamblerinn.com
"Peace and tranquility" reign at this New American, a favorite in Central Montco for "expense-account meetings", "celebrations" or "romance"; the fare may "not challenge", but it's "well made" (and complemented by a "good" wine list), while the "beautiful" patio works wonders.

Joy Tsin Lau ⬤　　　　19 12 14 $19
1026 Race St. (bet. 10th & 11th Sts.), 215-592-7226
Boosters bum rush this big Chinatown "fave" for reasonably priced dim sum that's "worth the chaos" of weekend "crowds"; "trust the locals" they say, since the fare's, "hands down, the best", though "sticky tables" and "mechanial", "harried" service are tsins.

Kabobeesh　　　　　　▽ 21 6 14 $12
4201 Chestnut St. (42nd St.), 215-386-8081
"Rub shoulders with half the cabbies in the city" at this "no-frills" University City Pakistani kebab-ery, where you

step up to the "counter" for the "real deal" at "unbeatable" prices; there's "nothing more filling", and the service is "friendly" to boot.

Kabul   21 15 18 $23
106 Chestnut St. (bet. Front & 2nd Sts.), 215-922-3676;
www.kabulafghancuisine.com
This "understated" long-running BYO "sleeper" takes you out of "loud and sceney" Old City via "delectable" Afghan dishes and a setting that "charms"; there's nothing more you can ask for besides an "excellent value" and a staff that is "as attentive as possible."

KARMA   24 16 18 $29
114 Chestnut St. (bet. Front & 2nd Sts.), 215-925-1444;
www.thekarmarestaurant.com
"Philadelphia must have done something good in a previous life" to deserve this "exceptional" Old City Indian (that also spun off a South Jersey satellite); while the colorful setting sparks some debate ("unremarkable" or "attractively sexy"), the "consistently excellent" fare and "eager" staff create good vibes.

K.C.'s Alley ◑   ▽ 14 13 17 $18
10 W. Butler Pike (Main St.), Ambler, 215-628-3300
Say "*Cheers!*" and you'll know the deal at this "nothing-fancy" Ambler American bar prized for its "cold" beers and "good" burgers; the service is "friendly" and the music "fun", so in other words, it's a "perfect neighborhood" joint.

Khajuraho   22 15 15 $27
Ardmore Plaza, 12 Greenfield Ave. (W. Lancaster Ave.),
Ardmore, 610-896-7200; www.khajurahoindia.com
Supplying "manna" in Ardmore is this Indian BYO serving "superb" (if "slightly pricey") fare that's perfect for vets and "neophytes" (i.e. "spicy" or not); those put off by "patchy" service and sometimes "tiny" portions head to the "highly recommended" "bargain" of a buffet; P.S. "distracting" images of characters striking "sensual poses" are naught for the weak.

Kibitz in the City   22 8 13 $15
703 Chestnut St. (7th St.), 215-928-1447
"What deli food should look, smell and taste like" is the consensus on this "cafeteria-style" standard near Washington Square cranking out "fabulous", "ridiculously overstuffed" sandwiches ("my jaw hurts just thinking about them") and chopped liver to make "your bubbe cry"; N.B. unaffiliated with the Cherry Hill spot of the same name.

Kildare's ◑   15 20 17 $24
4417 Main St. (1½ blocks southeast of Green Ln.), 215-482-7242
509-511 S. Second St. (bet. Lombard & South Sts.), 215-574-2995
(continued)

(continued)
Kildare's
826 W. DeKalb Pike (N. Gulph Mills Rd.), King of Prussia, 610-337-4772
1145 W. Baltimore Pike/Rte. 1 (Hwy. 476), Media, 610-565-8886
18-22 W. Gay St. (High St.), West Chester, 610-431-0770
www.kildarespub.com
Fresh-faced fans "mix it up" over comfort food and Guinness at these "college-y" Irish pubs; they're surely cheaper than taking a trip "across the Pond", and the fare's "decent" and "filling, but note that when the live bands start playing, remember this: "noise, yes; conversation, no."

KIMBERTON INN   25   24   25 $45
2105 Kimberton Rd. (Hares Hill Rd.), Kimberton, 610-933-8148; www.kimbertoninn.com
This Traditional American "tucked away" in the wilds of Chester County has "been around for years and years" (as in since 1796), and adherents talk up "very good" cookery and a "refined yet unstuffy" setting perfect for "Sunday brunch" and "romantic" dinners around "multiple" fireplaces; "attentive" service caps an overall "consistently excellent" experience.

Kingdom of Vegetarians   ∇ 21   9   18 $17
129 N. 11th St. (bet. Arch & Race Sts.), 215-413-2290
Just say "all-you-can-eat dim sum" and savor the flavors to come at this humble Chinatown BYO, a "palace" for vegans and vegerians that "even pleases carnivores"; not only is the menu big, but with prices this low, you'll think you're in paradise.

King George II Inn   21   20   21 $41
102 Radcliffe St. (Mill St.), Bristol, 215-788-5536; www.kginn.com
Bristol colonists seem smitten by this circa-1681 Traditional American "landmark" near the Riverside Theater offering a "beautiful" view of the Delaware; while commoners find the fare "reliable", Tories tout it as "fit for a king" and add "good" service isn't too far behind.

Kisso Sushi Bar   21   16   19 $30
205 N. Fourth St. (Race St.), 215-922-1770
"All sushi, all the time" could be the catchphrase of this "calming", orange-walled Japanese BYO on the fringe of Old City, a "mecca" for fanatics endeared by "expert", "lovingly prepared" fish; while some complain about "minuscule" portions and "limited" options (there's no cooked fare here), many swim away happy.

Knight House   25   20   23 $46
96 W. State St. (Clinton St.), Doylestown, 215-489-9900
A "Knight to remember" sums up sentiment on Tom Frank's Doylestown New American that's enlivened by both chef Will Lewis' "delicious" preparations and "excellent" ser-

vice; if prices and "cramped" seating detract for some, "try the pub menu" and secure a spot on the "lovely" patio.

Koi ☒ ▽ 18 14 17 $26
604 N. Second St. (bet. Fairmount Ave. & Green St.), 215-413-1606
Kisso's similarly orange-hued, "space-agey" Japanese-Korean twin in Northern Liberties makes a "good effort" at supplying "fresh" sushi, cooked fare and "fast", "attentive" service; if the "unremarkable" experience leaves some feeling "empty", others want to fish again in these waters ("give it another shot").

Konak 20 20 19 $31
228 Vine St. (bet. 2nd & 3rd Sts.), 215-592-1212;
www.konakturkishrestaurant.com
"A sultan" would be happy enough to swing in this "cavernous" Turkish "bringing the Bosphorus" to Old City with "authentic" food and decor; "pleasant" service and "reasonable" prices delight all, and there's live music and belly dancing (Fridays) for "something different."

Kristian's Ristorante 24 20 22 $47
1100 Federal St. (11th St.), 215-468-0104;
www.kristiansrestaurant.com
"Not your typical South Philly pasta and gravy joint" is this "elegant" yet "homey" Italian showcase for chef-owner Kristian Leuzzi's "beautiful" food supported by service as "gracious" as can be; suburban partisans pine "if only it were closer" so it could become their neighborhood haunt.

La Belle Epoque Café ▽ 18 16 18 $31
38 W. State St. (Olive St.), Media, 610-566-6808;
www.labelleepoquecafe.com
"When they get it right, it's a beautiful thing" at this Media enterprise featuring crêpes and other assorted hits from the French bistro repertoire; all in all, it's a "good" value and a "welcome bit of France" for the neighborhood; N.B. you can choose a wine from their list, or bring your own for a $10 corkage fee.

La Boheme 22 16 19 $36
246 S. 11th St. (bet. Locust & Spruce Sts.), 215-351-9901
Athmane Kabir's "high-energy" French BYO storefront near Center City's Jefferson Hospital attracts with "friendly" airs and "solid" food (and a "bargain" $30 prix fixe), making it a "great date spot – even with your spouse"; some liken it to "eating in a sardine can" (read: "tiny"), but "when it comes down to it", it's still a crowd-pleaser.

LA BONNE AUBERGE 26 27 26 $75
Village 2 Apartment Complex, 1 Rittenhouse Circle (River Rd.),
New Hope, 215-862-2462; www.bonneauberge.com
An auberge to remember is Gerard Caronello's "formal", "precious" French serving up a "romantic" ambiance,

"super" food and "super" service to "special-occasion" seekers; the 18th-century farmhouse setting (within a New Hope apartment complex) evokes the French "country-side", though "stratospheric" prices bring everyone back to reality; N.B. dinner only, Thursdays–Sundays.

La Cava   23 | 14 | 20 | $35
60 E. Butler Ave. (bet. Cavalier Dr. & Ridge Ave.), Ambler, 215-540-0237
There's nary a taco or fajita in sight marvel gringos who dine at this "upscale" Mexican BYO in "understated" Ambler digs, where chef-owner Carlos Melendez is "on a crusade" to change the "American definition" of south-of-the-border fare by delivering "true", "mouthwatering" creations to "gourmets"; "personable" service is part of the secret to its success.

La Collina 🗷   20 | 18 | 21 | $46
37-41 Ashland Ave. (Jefferson St.), Bala Cynwyd, 610-668-1780
The "best" Dover sole is just one reason fans are drawn to this "old-school" Bala Cynwyd Italian landmark over-looking the Schuylkill Expressway and catering to a clientele "on the senior side" of life (but also to those looking for a "terrific first-date place"); sure the staff's a tad "rough around the edges", but for "very good" food, few in its class beat it.

La Colombe ⬦   22 | 17 | 17 | $7
4360 Main St. (bet. Grape & Levering Sts.), 215-483-4580
Rittenhouse Sq., 130 S. 19th St. (bet. Sansom & Walnut Sts.), 215-563-0860
www.lacolombe.com
Philly fauxhemians flock to these "Euro" coffeehouses (this *Survey*'s Top Bang for the Buck) where caffeine cognoscenti and "hipsters" wait in line to sit and linger over what's widely considered the "best coffee in town – make that the country" – while sampling some "excellent" pastries; "people-watching" is "fun", "eavesdropping" on an "amazing diversity of conversations" is de rigueur and the "cold", "cooler-than-you" 'tude from the staff seems to fit the scene well.

LACROIX AT THE RITTENHOUSE   27 | 27 | 27 | $79
Rittenhouse Hotel, 210 W. Rittenhouse Sq. (bet. Locust & Walnut Sts.), 215-790-2533; www.lacroixrestaurant.com
For a taste of what "the gods on Olympus eat", there's no better example than Jean-Marie Lacroix's "dreamy" French extravaganza in the Rittenhouse Hotel; count on "culinary mastery", with a menu devised of three-, four- and five-course "artfully presented" small plates, a "modern", "tranquil" room overlooking the Square and "sublime" service; true, you'll have to dip heavily into your piggy bank, but it's undeniably sure to impress; N.B. post-*Survey*,

Lacroix has yielded the reins to new executive chef Matt Levin; jacket required at dinner.

La Famiglia ⊠ 23 21 21 $61
8 S. Front St. (bet. Chestnut & Market Sts.), 215-922-2803; www.lafamiglia.com
This "top-of-the-line" Italian in Old City combines an "old-school fancy" ambiance (jackets are required), "excellent", "old-fashioned" food and an "extensive" wine list; while service is "gracious" for many, some feel it doesn't necessarily make you feel like *famiglia* (they're "haughty"), and everyone agrees that it's best enjoyed when out on "expense-account or big-deal nights."

La Fontana Della Citta ▽ 18 16 18 $37
1701 Spruce St. (17th St.), 215-875-9990
"Pre-theater" crowds think this new "warm and welcoming" Center City BYO is a "great" addition to the mix, offering "classic" Italian food and a staff that "tries hard" to please; others, though, want to wait for them to shake out "the kinks" before passing final judgment.

Lai Lai Garden 21 21 21 $32
1144 DeKalb Pike (Skippack Pike), Blue Bell, 610-277-5988; www.lailaigarden.com
Blue Bell's "high-end" Pan-Asian has its devotees who dig the "varied" and "fresh" Chinese, Thai and Japanese selections (and some of the "best sushi in the 'burbs'"); though dinner is slightly "pricey" ("stick to lunch!"), a "caring" staff and "pretty" decor make the package ever more "yum yum."

Lakeside Chinese Deli ⊅ 24 5 20 $16
207 N. Ninth St. (Race St.), 215-925-3288
"Best dim sum in Philly – ugliest restaurant in town" is the 411 on this "cheap" Chinatown BYO that's "not a deli, and not near a lake"; it's also prized for its "fantastic" soups and beloved for takeout, and you'll be "well looked after" by the "friendliest people" around.

La Locanda del Ghiottone ⊅ 22 16 19 $32
130 N. Third St. (Cherry St.), 215-829-1465
This "cramped" Old City locanda of all things Italian is where lovers come for "intimacy" and foodies arrive to partake of "awesome" fare in portions "hearty" enough to make a glutton blush; the "entertaining", "friendly" waiters are "real pros" and are also adept at keeping tables turning (i.e. they'll "rush you" on weekends if necessary).

La Lupe ● 23 8 12 $14
1201 S. Ninth St. (Federal St.), 215-551-9920
"Ahh, the fresh tortillas", "tasty" tacos and other "cheap", "terrific" eats are why "homesick" Mexicans seek out this "no-frills" South Philly BYO cantina in what was once a

garage; don't expect fast service (how do you say "slow as molasses" *en español*?), but do expect it to be "friendly."

La Na Thai-French Cuisine   20   15   19 $28
33 W. State St. (bet. Jackson & Olive Sts.), Media, 610-892-7787
This "tiny" Thai-French BYO in a Media storefront gets "a thumbs-up" for cuisine that displays an "amazing array" of "flavors, colors and textures"; if the menu's a "bit stale", many more focus on the quality of the fare and are also sold on "good" service and "reasonable" prices.

Landing, The   19   21   18 $40
22 N. Main St. (Bridge St.), New Hope, 215-862-5711;
www.landingrestaurant.com
As the name suggests, the "lovely" outdoor deck may be what this New Hope New American is all about, since, for many, it doesn't get any better than "whiling away a summer night" alfresco style and taking in the Delaware River and "pretty good", if "pricey" fare; regulars also report that you'll get a "cozy" feeling dining before the fireplace in winter.

L'ANGOLO   26   15   22 $35
1415 W. Porter St. (Broad St.), 215-389-4252
It's "well worth" braving South Philly's "double-parking traps" and bringing your "best Barolo" to pair with Davide Faenza's "outstanding" Southern Italian cooking at this "upbeat" BYO trattoria, where the chef's wife, Kathryn, oversees a "charming" floor crew who "aim to please"; keep in mind, "you may need a shoehorn to get in", but after all the "amazing" food, "you'll need a wheelbarrow to get out."

La Pergola   17   10   17 $22
42 Shewell Ave. (Main St.), Doylestown, 215-230-9936
726 West Ave. (Old York Rd.), Jenkintown, 215-884-7204
The clientele at these "drab", "low-cost" suburban twins appreciate "ample" platters from a "great" array of "tasty" Middle Eastern and Eastern European "soul food"; service can be "slow", which is what you'd expect when it seems there's "one waiter for the whole place"; N.B. Doylestown has a small wine list, while Jenkintown is BYO.

Las Cazuelas   23   18   21 $25
426 W. Girard Ave. (bet. 4th & 5th Sts.), 215-351-9144;
www.lascazuelas.net
A "roaming" mariachi serenades faithful fans and helps bring the house down at this "cozy" and "colorful" Northern Liberties Mexican BYO, though the "authentic", affordable fare that'll "knock your socks off" probably takes center stage; in all, it's got charm and then some.

La Terrasse ⊠   –   –   –   M
3432 Sansom St. (bet. 34th & 36th Sts.), 215-386-5000
Though it's hard to tell the impact of a mid-*Survey* chef turnover at this French-American University City cafe in-

stitution, the early line is that the menu's been "revital-
ized"; what hasn't changed is the "collegial" atmosphere,
which makes it ideal for "professors" and Pennsters.

Latest Dish, The   20   16   18 $29
613 S. Fourth St. (bet. Bainbridge & South Sts.), 215-629-0565;
www.latestdish.com
This New American tavern off South Street serves up an
"original" menu that surprises, along with a "casual" vibe
enforced by a modern setting complete with copper-
covered tables; the beer selection is "great", and for extra
"hip", hit Fluid, the nightclub upstairs.

La Veranda   22   19   20 $55
Penn's Landing Pier 3, 5 N. Columbus Blvd. (bet. Arch &
Market Sts.), 215-351-1898; www.laverandapier3.com
The "waterfront" view and "large" quantities of "excellent" (albeit "pricey") Italian dishes are the hallmarks of
this "*Sopranos*"-esque favorite near Penn's Landing; beyond the quality of the cooking, however, look for "especially nice" treatment for regulars, and watch newbies get
a dose of "indifference."

La Vigna   ▽ 19   17   20 $40
1100 S. Front St. (Federal St.), 215-336-1100;
www.lavignarestaurant.com
"*Molto bene!*" exclaim enthusiasts of this "affordable" but
still "dressy" South Philly Italian in Pennsport featuring
"delicious" vittles, "gracious" service and a wine cellar
that accommodates larger groups; while "you'll never
have to worry about meeting Dracula" or a date after dinner (i.e. lots of "garlic"), this one's more than "worth it."

LE BAR LYONNAIS ⌀   28   23   25 $58
1523 Walnut St. (bet. 15th & 16th Sts.), 215-567-1000;
www.lebecfin.com
"Philly" Georges Perrier's "hidden" Center City "gem" beneath Le Bec-Fin continues to impress gourmets who
crave an "intimate" meal with "spectacular" French bistro
food and "fantastic" service but can't fork over a "whole
paycheck" at the mother ship upstairs; it's even better
when you can visit the bar at peak times and gaze at the
"impressive examples of plastic surgery."

LE BEC-FIN ⌀   28   27   27 $120
1523 Walnut St. (bet. 15th & 16th Sts.), 215-567-1000;
www.lebecfin.com
Still "the pinnacle" of Philly restaurants is Georges
Perrier's "big-bucks" haute Center City French institution
that "bows to no other" in its class and is a "must-see"
"must-experience" "masterpiece" that's de rigueur "before dying"; indeed, the "magnificent" food (including the
"unbelievable" dessert cart), ornate, "beautiful Parisian"
setting and "perfect" service from a "fleet" of waiters all

leave you as "breathless" as the "sticker-shock"-inducing bill, but it's all worth the admission to "one of the best ever"; N.B. jacket required at dinner.

Le Castagne ⊠ 22 | 22 | 20 | $49
1920 Chestnut St. (20th St.), 215-751-9913;
www.lecastagne.com
The Sena family's "upscale", "contemporary" Northern Italian in Center City has regulars talking up the "delicious" food on par with crosstown relative La Famiglia and chalking up its "charming" ambiance to a "knowledgeable" staff that oozes "tons of class without pretension" – even if a few point out the pace can run a little "slow" (i.e. "they don't rush you").

Lee How Fook 23 | 12 | 18 | $21
219 N. 11th St. (bet. Race & Vine Sts.), 215-925-7266
"Eat where the locals do" confide fans of this BYO, a "friendly" "mom-and-pop" Cantonese shop in Chinatown where you may "feel like a sardine" but you'll sate yourself with "superior" examples of Chinese cookery; some are too busy eating the "heavenly" fare to notice a "revamped" decor, though most still marvel about "low" prices.

Le Jardin 17 | 22 | 18 | $46
Art Alliance Bldg., 251 S. 18th St. (Rittenhouse Sq.),
215-545-0821; www.lejardinsquare.com
The name gives away the appeal of this "romantic" French-Mediterranean "oasis" in the Art Alliance Building near Rittenhouse Square; beyond a "beautiful" garden area for dining, "inconsistent" food gets in the way of the ambiance, though some say "when the place is solid, it's capable of great meals."

Lemon Grass Thai 21 | 16 | 18 | $24
3626-30 Lancaster Ave. (36th St.), 215-222-8042
Henderson Sq., 314 S. Henderson Rd. (Pennsylvania Tpke.),
King of Prussia, 610-337-5986
"Evil Jungle Princess", "Young Girl on Fire" and other "exotically" named dishes are "real conversation pieces" and help "break the ice" at these "bargain" Thais; the "reliably good" fare can come "fast" – or "rushed" – especially when it's "busy"; N.B. both Lancaster (separately owned) and King of Prussia are BYO.

Liberties ▽ 16 | 16 | 16 | $24
705 N. Second St. (Fairmount Ave.), 215-238-0660;
www.libertiesrestaurant.com
You'll have a "blast" as long as you stick with the "great" fries and burgers and expect nothing more at this saloon-like American, one of the "original" pubs in Northern Liberties; loyalists laud its longevity, adding that it helps when both the tabs are this "reasonable" and the beer keeps flowing.

Little Fish　　24 | 12 | 19 | $35
600 Catharine St. (6th St.), 215-413-3464
"Little only describes the size" of John Tiplitz's "quirky", "guppy-sized" BYO seafooder in Queen Village, and afishionados dispense with "elbow-room" issues and pack in like "sardines" to sit "almost in the kitchen" for "astonishingly" fresh fare served by a "sweet" staff; P.S. though you'd better "beware of flying pans", this one's a catch if you can get a seat.

Little Marakesh　　▽ 19 | 22 | 21 | $33
1825 S. Limekiln Pike (Twining Rd.), Dresher, 215-643-3003; www.littlemarakesh.com
"If you have all night for a feast" and have the urge to "get up and dance with the belly dancer", this "cozy" Moroccan "den" in a Dresher strip mall is sure to make for an "amazing" experience; bring "friends" and be prepared to eat "authentic" food "with your hands" and take in a touch of North African "culture."

Little Pete's　　15 | 7 | 17 | $15
219 S. 17th St. (Chancellor St.), 215-545-5508 ◗⊄
The Philadelphian, 2401 Pennsylvania Ave. (bet. 24th & 25th Sts.), 215-232-5001
"Partiers" in search of "after-hours" face-stuffing or "hangover" curatives look no farther than this Center City "classic" Greek "dive" known for "dirt-cheap" diner grub and "lovable" waitresses who "call you hon"; "you'll be full for weeks" – of food, "geriatrics" and "characters at the counter"; N.B. 17th and Chancellor is open 24/7.

Loie　　17 | 15 | 15 | $32
128 S. 19th St. (bet. Sansom & Walnut Sts.), 215-568-0808; www.loie215.com
Lounge lizards keep crawling to this regularly "packed" French-American club-cum-eatery off Rittenhouse Square selling "reliable" if not "very good" bistro cooking and a "hot", "trendy" vibe; enter after 9 PM "at your own risk", as the music is pumped "beyond disco level" and the place morphs into a Penn romper room; N.B. the Decor score may not reflect a post-*Survey* renovation.

LOLITA ⊄　　25 | 18 | 21 | $34
106 S. 13th St. (bet. Chestnut & Sansom Sts.), 215-546-7100; www.lolitabyob.com
"The hype is true": "taste buds" are "twirling" over this "convivial", "sleek" temptress, a Center City nuevo Mexican BYO where a "good-looking crowd" gathers for Marcie Turney's "imaginative" takes on traditional *comida* that carries prices so "reasonable" they put "flashier places to shame"; bring cash, "your own tequila" (they'll make "fresh" "*fantastico*" margaritas for you) and patience, since "waits" are not unheard of.

London Grill   18   16   16 $33
2301 Fairmount Ave. (23rd St.), 215-978-4545;
www.londongrill.com
"Is it a bar or is it a restaurant?" is the question, but it
doesn't matter since the "soul of Fairmount", Michael and
Terry McNally's "long-running" New American hangout,
still produces "reliable" "pub" fare suited for "imbibers
and noshers", and more "gourmet" items for Art Museum
denizens; despite "haphazard" service, nearly all agree
this place offers "just what you need sometimes."

Long's Gourmet Chinese   17   12   16 $23
2018 Hamilton St. (bet. 20th & 21st Sts.), 215-496-9928
Opinions are mixed over this Chinese eatery a few blocks
from the Art Museum: one camp considers the fare "tasty",
"healthy" and "creative" and the staff "friendly", while
naysayers scoff at the name (the eats are "not gourmet")
and would just as soon contemplate driving to Chinatown.

LOS CATRINES/TEQUILA'S   24   23   23 $38
1602 Locust St. (16th St.), 215-546-0181;
www.tequilasphilly.com
With "beautiful" decor complete with murals including
"dancing skeletons", "phenomenal" Mexican cuisine and
an "incredible" selection of tequilas, this "engaging", "upscale" Center Cityite keeps south-of-the-border fans
streaming in; if you can deal with "waits" (thanks in part to
"no reservations"), once you're seated, expect servers so
"attentive" you'd think they were "reading your mind."

Lourdas Greek Taverna ⊄   19   13   17 $31
50 N. Bryn Mawr Ave. (Lancaster Ave.), Bryn Mawr, 610-520-0288
"Bring earplugs and cash" to this Greek BYO, a "family"-
run feedery offering a taste of the "Mediterranean" right
near the Bryn Mawr train station; the "small" room is
"spare" but it still "charms", and the food is "homey" and
"good", but lourd knows, this taverna can cost more "than
a flight to Athens."

L2   20   17   20 $33
2201 South St. (22nd St.), 215-732-7878; www.l2restaurant.com
Boosters "cuddle up on velvet sofas" and soak up a setting
that's half "Russian Orthodox Church" and half "Turkish
bordello" at this "date"-perfect Center City West
Traditional American; "consistently good" eats are the
standard here, as is the "enjoyable" bar and "slow" but
genuinely "warm" service.

Ludwig's Garten   16   17   17 $26
1315 Sansom St. (bet. Broad & 13th Sts.), 215-985-1525;
www.ludwigsgarten.com
Teutonic tattlers do jigs over this Bavarian biergarten in
Center City, a slice of Deutschland in Philly complete with

an "extensive" suds selection enhanced by potato pan-cakes, schnitzel and other dishes "full of hearty German wonderfulness"; even nein-ilists chuckle and admit the "tchotchke", "kitsch" and fräuleins in full "St. Pauli Girl" getups are "worth seeing."

Ly Michael's
21 | 16 | 22 | $36

101 N. 11th St. (bet. Arch & Cherry Sts.), 215-922-2688;
www.lymichaels.com
FuziOn's "upscale" though still affordable relative opposite the Convention Center features "wonderful" Asian cooking that "beats the moo goo gai pan out of the usual Chinatown places"; the "owners care" about their customers, and it shows in the "accommodating" service.

Maccabeam
▽ 21 | 6 | 12 | $15

128 S. 12th St. (bet. Sansom & Walnut Sts.),
215-922-5922
Ok, it's "not the classiest" place, and there's "no decor " whatsoever (and "no service with a smile"), but this "inex-pensive" Center City kosher Israeli beams in other ways, namely by serving "yummy" falafel, hummus and other hits; it's one of the "best Middle Eastern greasy spoons" around – just don't go there on a Friday night or any time Saturday (it's closed for Sabbath).

Madame Butterfly
▽ 21 | 16 | 19 | $36

34 W. State St. (Main St.), Doylestown, 215-345-4488
While some think the food just "ok" and the service "slow", many fans beg to differ and are aflutter over this Doylestown Japanese, calling it "Zen-like" and insisting it excels at sushi ("very good") and service ("attentive"); P.S. either way, come "prepared to spend."

Maggiano's Little Italy
19 | 18 | 18 | $31

1201 Filbert St. (12th St.), 215-567-2020
King of Prussia Mall, 205 Mall Blvd. (Gulph Rd.), King of Prussia,
610-992-3333
www.maggianos.com
Big appetites, "Tums" and patience are necessary to deal with "endless waits" and "endless amounts" of "tasty" Italian food served "family-style" at these "convivial" chain outlets; "kitschy" "old-world" decor impresses, as do "bags of leftovers" for "next-day feasts", even if these joints are "about as Italian as Nebraska."

MAINLAND INN
26 | 23 | 25 | $48

17 Main St. (Sumneytown Pike), Mainland, 215-256-8500;
www.mainlandinn.org
"Understated" is another name for this central Montco "secret" decorated in "18th-century Americana" that "lives up to its rep" as "one of the best" in the 'burbs with "sub-lime" New American food and service that makes you "forget about traveling to Center City"; insiders advise if

you want to make an impression on someone, check out the $21.95 Sunday brunch.

MAJOLICA 🏶   25 20 24 $44

258 Bridge St. (bet. Gay & Main Sts.), Phoenixville, 610-917-0962

Hardscrabble "Phoenixville is rising from the ashes", and the proof is in the quick popularity of Andrew Deery and Sarah Johnson's New American BYO, a "find" operating in an old tavern; devotees make the jaunt for "exciting" food that tempts you to "eat off of everyone else's plate", and after you factor in "friendly" service, "does wow cover it?"

Mama Palma's ⊄   23 13 18 $21

2229 Spruce St. (23rd St.), 215-735-7357

This "family-friendly" "mom-and-pop" BYO Italian on Fitler Square is "still rockin' the brick-oven scene" with "awesome" "thin"-crust pizzas dished out in a "chaotic" setting that's "a step up from no-frills"; a "true Philly staff" (that is, sometimes "brusque", sometimes "pleasant") "takes care of your kids", and are known to dole out "freebies" sometimes.

Mamma Maria   ▽ 19 14 18 $48

1637 E. Passyunk Ave. (bet. 11th & 12th Sts.), 215-463-6884; www.mammamaria.info

"You go, Mamma": "you can't leave hungry" or thirsty after one of Maria Chiavatti's "*molto bene*" seemingly "nonstop" multicourse dinners at her "homey" Italian BYO in the "heart of South Philly", and with wine and cordials comped, you'd be wise to "get a taxi" home; P.S. even the "unimpressed" concede "everyone needs to try Mamma at least once."

Manayunk
Brewery & Restaurant   17 17 17 $25

4120 Main St. (Shurs Ln.), 215-482-8220; www.manayunkbrewery.com

"Pour me another one" cry "yuppie" loyalists of this "lively" Manayunk brewhouse and "staple" in a refurbished textile mill; the "diverse" burgers-to-sushi slate is "straightforward", "good" and "reasonably priced" plus the "bumping" scene is abetted by scores of "beautiful people" and, best of all, a "wonderful" outdoor dining area overlooking the canal.

Mandarin   23 16 16 $30

190 Lancaster Ave. (Malin Rd.), Frazer, 610-647-5488; www.margaretkuos.com

Margaret Kuo's BYO mainstay in Frazer receives raves as the "best" of its kind on the "far western Main Line" for "delicious" Chinese food (along with sushi and tempura); indeed, the fare "hits a gong", especially the Peking duck, and the staff is "friendly", but some hammer home you should learn "Chinese if you want your order to be correct."

Mandarin Garden   22 | 14 | 20 | $23 |
91 York Rd. (Davisville Rd.), Willow Grove, 215-657-3993
This "reliable" 20-year-old Chinese opposite the Willow Grove train station is "still at the top" of its game with "friendly" service and "terrific" fare that consistently delivers; while "drab" digs are no Garden of Eden, the majority concludes this one surpasses other "typical" joints in its genre.

Mandoline Ⓢ   22 | 12 | 18 | $38 |
213 Chestnut St. (bet. 2nd & 3rd Sts.), 215-238-9403
Todd Lean's "excellent" New American cooking at his Old City BYO is an "example of the success of Philadelphia's BYOs" and a reason why devotees keep coming back "more than once" to this "postage stamp"–size space; overall, from the looks and taste of things, it's clear folks are "trying hard" here.

Mantra ◐   – | – | – | M |
122 S. 18th St. (Sansom St.), 215-988-1211
Zanzibar Blue's Albert Paris has carved himself a spot (literally) by designing the decor and building the black walnut and butterwood bar of his modestly priced Pan-Asian near Rittenhouse Square; an array of sakes and shochus are added attractions for lounge lizards.

Marathon Grill   18 | 13 | 15 | $20 |
1339 Chestnut St. (Juniper St.), 215-561-4460
Commerce Sq., 2001 Market St. (bet. 20th & 21st Sts.), 215-568-7766 Ⓢ
1818 Market St. (19th St.), 215-561-1818 Ⓢ
121 S. 16th St. (Sansom St.), 215-569-3278
200 S. 40th St. (Walnut St.), 215-222-0100
www.marathongrill.com
"Quick, "wholesome" bites are the specialty of these "über-urban", "upscale" New American chain spots that go the distance to satisfy the "insane" number of fans who sup there breakfast, lunch and dinner; think smoothies, sandwiches and such, "low" prices and "hit-or-miss" service (though it can be "fast at lunch"); N.B. Commerce Square and South 40th serve alcohol.

Marathon on the Square   18 | 14 | 16 | $25 |
1839 Spruce St. (19th St.), 215-731-0800;
www.marathongrill.com
Marathon Grill's "bustling", "furniture"-filled Rittenhouse Square outpost (and brunch "staple") has "something for everyone" on its menu, namely "uniformly good" gourmet diner staples (even at "11 PM") at "fair" prices; "congenial" staffers help make it a "home away from home" for the Square's hip "twentysomethings."

Marco Polo
20 14 18 $33

Elkins Park Sq., 8080 Old York Rd. (Church Rd.), Elkins Park, 215-782-1950; www.mymarcopolo.com

Even though chef Lo is no longer there, diners point their compasses to this "dependable", "workmanlike" Elkins Park Italian seafooder serving "delectable" pasta and "excelling" at fish; adventurers who've journeyed here compliment its "relaxed" vibe and "sports-bar-ish" atmosphere.

Margaret Kuo's
23 23 20 $39

175 E. Lancaster Ave. (Louella Ave.), Wayne, 610-688-7200; www.margaretkuos.com

At Margaret Kuo's "sophisticated" and "tranquil" Chinese-Japanese in Wayne, "Mother Hen (Mrs. Kuo) watches over" her "amazing" Peking ducks and other "superb" (and "pricey") fare; meanwhile, in the dining room, the "dramatic", "eye-popping" tri-level setting features original Sung Dynasty pieces and an indoor waterfall.

Margaret Kuo's Media
24 21 18 $31

6 W. State St. (Jackson St.), Media, 610-892-0115; www.margaretkuos.com

The folks "live to please" at Margaret Kuo's "unpretentious" outpost in Downtown Media, and many talk up how the kitchen pulls off both "wondrous" Japanese ("fab" sushi) and Chinese cuisine rivaling the "more ballyhooed emporiums in Philly"; even those who think the "pretty" renovations pumped up prices slightly are still keen on eating here.

Margaret Kuo's Peking
24 20 20 $32

Granite Run Mall, 1067 E. Baltimore Pike (Middletown Rd.), Media, 610-566-4110; www.margaretkuos.com

Though in the "uncharming" environs of the Granite Run Mall, Margaret Kuo's "classy" original is a "little slice of Asian heaven" specializing in "world-class" Chinese-Japanese fare that "arrives with a smile"; no surprise then that for 30-plus years, it's been "worth the schlep."

Maria's Ristorante on Summit
▽ 23 17 21 $29

8100 Ridge Ave. (Summit Ave.), 215-508-5600

Amid pizzeria-heavy Roxborough dwells the D'Alicandra family's affordable Italian "treasure", a quintessential "neighborhood" spot that charms with its "excellent" slate of classic dishes along with "welcoming" service that echoes the sunny, golden decor; P.S. it's a "solid" choice when "taking the parents to dinner."

Marigold Kitchen 🗷
25 18 22 $45

501 S. 45th St. (Larchwood Ave.), 215-222-3699

Acolytes of "culinary artistry" are all over this "hidden" New American BYO in a touched-up West Philly Victorian, the showcase for chef Michael Solomonov who twirls his "magic wand" over "eccentric", yet "excellent" dishes; many also endorse the service, which is "well-informed" considering what's on the plate "ain't mama's cooking."

Marrakesh ⊅ | 22 | 24 | 22 | $33 |

517 S. Leithgow St. (South St.), 215-925-5929
The Kouchacji mother-daughter team still offers "memorable" dining events – not just meals – at their "dark" Moroccan in Queen Village; "sit back" against "soft pillows" with a "crowd" and "eat with your hands" ("who needs utensils" since the place is this "sexy"?), but first wear "loose-fitting clothes" since everyone leaves "full."

Marra's | 21 | 11 | 16 | $22 |

1734 E. Passyunk Ave. (bet. Moore & Morris Sts.), 215-463-9249
"Incredible" thin-crust pies and classic "red-gravy" chow draw "visitors" and regulars to this "homey" pizza/pastaria that's so "quintessentially" South Philly "it's almost a caricature of itself"; "bring a thick skin" for "gruff" (yet "lovable") service and a "big appetite", and you'll see why this "tradition" has been around for four generations.

MARSHA BROWN | 21 | 26 | 19 | $56 |

15 S. Main St. (Bridge St.), New Hope, 215-862-7044;
www.marshabrownrestaurant.com
"Well-heeled" crowds settle in amid the pews, murals and stained glass of this "chic" Creole-Southerner in a "beautifully" refurbished New Hope church; devotees don't lie, the "large" helpings of food may "fall short of wonderful" but can still "feed a family of four" , while others are quick to ordain it "expense-account" central.

MATYSON ☒ | 24 | 18 | 22 | $41 |

37 S. 19th St. (bet. Chestnut & Market Sts.), 215-564-2925;
www.matyson.com
"Come to be dazzled" and "splurge" a bit at Matt and Sonjia Spector's (hence, Mat-y-son) "little gem" of a BYO in Center City that has legions admiring "attentive, but not overbearing" service, "ever-changing" New American savory preparations that "deserve all the raves they get" and "sublime" desserts; alas, it's no shock then, for "gone are the days one could just walk in" and get a seat.

Max & Erma's | 13 | 13 | 14 | $21 |

1205 E. Lancaster Ave. (Exton Bypass), Downingtown,
610-873-0473
180B Mill Rd. (Egypt Rd.), Oaks, 610-650-8014
www.maxandermas.com
Crayons and "great" burgers mean you can expect to "dine with a zillion kids" at these suburban chainsters, an American duo that is "a step up from TGI Friday's, but not much of a step up"; still, with the "scoop-your-own-sundae bar" and "warm", "delicious" chocolate chip cookies, some say the places are even "safe for your fourth date."

Maya Bella   17 | 14 | 17 | $38

*119 Fayette St. (bet. 1st & 2nd Aves.), Conshohocken,
610-832-2114*

This "earnest", "romantic" BYO in Conshy has some touting
Le Bec-Fin alum Ken Shapiro's Eclectic fare, pointing out
"pleasant surprises" along the way (the "goat cheese ravioli
is one of the best dishes I've ever eaten"); yet critics who
tire of "flashlight fun" (it's "too dark") also aver the place
suffers from "unrefined" service and "mediocre" fare.

Mayfair Diner ●   16 | 14 | 18 | $15

7373 Frankford Ave. (Bleigh Ave.), 215-624-4455

Feeding hungry hordes, 24 hours a day, seven days a week
is this "landmark" "stainless-steel"–decorated Northeast
diner, a "pillar of the community" "holding its own" by
serving "classic" Americana for nearly 75 years; some
even enjoy going here just to get a picture of "what diner
life used to be like" way back when.

McCormick & Schmick's   20 | 20 | 20 | $45

*1 S. Broad St. (Penn Sq.), 215-568-6888;
www.mccormickandschmicks.com*

Yes, it's a "chain" and the fare "isn't imaginative", but for
the sheer "assortment" of "fresh" fish, this "large" venue
on the Avenue of the Arts is a "keeper" and "one of the
most reliable seafood houses around"; while it's a "favorite" for "professional types" and theatergoers for lunch
and dinner, insiders also recommend it for its "great"
happy-hour scene.

McFadden's ●   11 | 15 | 13 | $22

*Citizens Bank Park, 1 Citizens Bank Way (Pattison Ave.),
215-952-0300*
*461 N. Third St. (bet. Spring Garden & Willow Sts.),
215-928-0630; www.mcfaddensphilly.com*

"Watch the youth of America party" at these big-screen-
heavy restaurants/bars, one in Northern Liberties, the other
attached to Citizens Bank Park; sanguine sorts say they're
"a nice way to finish off a Flyers or Phillies game" and that
you'll be happy if you "don't expect anything more" than
the typical burgers and brew lineup, while a few crabby
kinds find "wave after wave of Coors Light swillers" and
"barely passable food" as part of their McFailings.

McGillin's Olde Ale House ●✉   15 | 17 | 18 | $18

*1310 Drury St. (bet. Chestnut & Sansom Sts.), 215-735-5562;
www.mcgillins.com*

Kickin' it "olde"-school is this circa-1860 Irish alehouse
tucked away in a Center City back alley; everyone "feels
right at home" over beers, wings and other "standard, but
good" pub grub in the "friendliest joint this side of the
Atlantic" – no wonder it's the "favorite bar in all of Philly"
for so many.

MELOGRANO
25　16　20　$37

2201 Spruce St. (22nd St.), 215-875-8116

"Pure joy" sums up this "minimally" decorated yet "inviting" (and "tiny") Tuscan BYO corner bistro, a Fitler Square "treasure" where you must "arrive as soon as it opens" to avoid the crowds who await Gianluca Demontis' "simple" and "beautifully prepared" fare that's "not to be missed" and "warm", "professional" staff that works the "deafening" room; now, if only they "took reservations."

Melrose Diner ◐
17　12　18　$15

1501 Snyder Ave. (15th St.), 215-467-6644;
www.melrose-diner.com

Look up" 'diner' in Webster's" and you'll see a picture of dis South Philly 24"/7 "institution" cranking out "solid" grub that fulfills everyone from "tattooed guys in undershirts" to "club-goers" to "whoever performed that day at the Wachovia Center"; service comes courtesy of "welcoming", "puffy-haired" waitresses who "could shuttle food around in their sleep", and while "sharing a booth with strangers is for the birds", everyone knows it's a "requirement to stop in this place, like running up the steps of the Museum of Art."

Melting Pot, The
20　17　20　$41

1219 Filbert St. (bet. 12th & 13th Sts.), 215-922-7002
8229 Germantown Ave. (Southampton Ave.), 215-242-3003
www.meltingpot.com

"Playing with your food" is just one of the "guilty pleasures" you'll indulge in at this chain fondue duo near the Pennsylvania Convention Center and in Chestnut Hill – the other concerns "cheese, chocolate and hot oil" ("what more can you ask for?"); meals here make for "great" dates or "nights out with friends", even though the penny-wise ask, now, "I paid how much to cook my own food?"

Mendenhall Inn
18　19　19　$48

Clarion Inn at Mendenhall, 323 Kennett Pike (1 mi. south of Rte. 1),
Mendenhall, 610-388-1181; www.mendenhallinn.com

"History abounds" at this "romantic", "genteel" New American inn place and Brandywine Valley "standard" known for "wonderful" Sunday brunches, "solicitous" service and "reliable" cuisine; in short, it's a "safe choice" for your "aunt" or to "celebrate."

Mercato ⊄
24　18　21　$36

1216 Spruce St. (Camac St.), 215-985-2962;
www.mercatobyob.com

Find yourself "elbow-to-elbow" with your neighbor at this "hip", cash-only BYO, a "great addition" to Center City dining that's earning accolades with R. Evan Turney's "fresh, creative" spins on Italian-American cuisine; overall, this "new kid on the block" is a keeper; N.B. they take reservations Sundays–Thursdays from 5–6:30 PM.

Meridith's
21 | 18 | 20 | $32

10 Leopard Rd. (Lancaster Ave.), Berwyn, 610-251-0265;
www.merudiths.com

"Find a place to park" then join the crowds who flock to this "lively" Berwyn Med-Eclectic BYO warmed by "friendly" service and "charming" Tuscan-influenced decor; look for "delicious" breakfasts and lunches (and dinners Tuesdays–Sundays) from a place just "perfect for the neighborhood."

Meritage Philadelphia ✍
24 | 22 | 22 | $58

500 S. 20th St. (Lombard St.), 215-985-1922;
www.meritagephiladelphia.com

Now under new ownership is this "elegant", 40-seat Center City Euro-Eclectic, where chef Grant Brown blends culinary influences from the Mediterranean into "unusual", albeit "delectable" dishes; "enthusiastic" service and, as the name suggests, an "amazing" wine list helps most overlook the somewhat "pricey" tabs.

Mexican Post
18 | 13 | 16 | $22

104 Chestnut St. (Front St.), 215-923-5233 ◐
Franklin Mills, 4501 Woodhaven Rd. (southeast of Knights Rd.),
215-632-6959 ✍
www.mexicanpost.com

"Pitchers of margaritas" and "generous" helpings of "cheap" and "good" "Amerimex" cooking "hit the spot" for "college students", "singles" and "bachelorettes" at this "Lone-Star quality" Mexican mini-chain that grew out of an Old City "dive bar"; while protestors post complaints of "so-so" fare, amigos love that these "party" parlors are "too crowded – which is a good sign."

Mezza Luna
22 | 18 | 21 | $39

763 S. Eighth St. (Catharine St.), 215-627-4705

"Old-world charm" is at work at this "classic" Roman-style South Philly Italian hailed for its "warmth" "from the minute you walk in" and "gratifying" Italian cooking, especially "gnocchi that'll change the way you look at gnocchi"; aside from "parking" woes, just about everyone who goes here ends up "moonstruck."

Mikado
19 | 17 | 18 | $34

66 E. Lancaster Ave. (Churchwood Rd.), Ardmore, 610-645-5592

Main Liners "quell their craving" for sushi and tempura with this "pleasant" Japanese BYO from the owners of Thai Pepper; the "lunch bento box" is a hit, and the "volcano roll a taste explosion", even though some find that "sunken seating" makes it "hard to get up."

Mimosa
▽ 20 | 8 | 13 | $35

901 South St. (9th St.), 215-238-0144

Franco Iovino's Italian BYO off South Street is praised for its "carefully prepared" Italian favorites and touches such as a comp "glass of wine" if you forget to bring your own; despite "reasonable" prices, some can't dismiss "erratic" performances from the staff and a "stark" setting.

Mimosa Restaurant　　　∇ 22 | 18 | 20 | $40
2 Waterview Rd. (West Chester Pike), West Chester, 610-918-9715; www.mimosa-restaurant.com
"Extraordinary care in the kitchen" shows in Gilles Moret's "wonderful" dishes at this "hard to find, easy to love" West Chester Eclectic BYO offering "interesting pairings of ingredients" and "efficient" service; its Tuscan-inspired decor and "easygoing" air help blot out the strip-center locale.

Mio Sogno　　　　　　∇ 22 | 18 | 19 | $44
2650 S. 15th St. (Oregon Ave.), 215-467-3317
Don't say "gravy house" when describing this "refeshing change from typical South Philly Italians", a "quality" place "worth the effort" of visiting on account of "good" cooking and a "feel-good" atmosphere; though a "tad pricey", chances are you'll come away "impressed."

Mirna's Café　　　　　　22 | 16 | 19 | $33
Center Sq., 758 DeKalb Pike (Skippack Pike), Blue Bell, 610-279-0500
417 Old York Rd. (West Ave.), Jenkintown, 215-885-2046 ✍
www.mirnas.com
You "get your money's worth" of "fab", "zesty" Med fare at these suburban BYO twins; ok, the tables are "close together" and the noise can be "unbearable", but the service is "attentive", and overall, fans think things here make for a "winning" formula; N.B. Jenkintown reopened post-*Survey* after a recent renovation.

Mixto　　　　　　　　　21 | 21 | 18 | $31
1141 Pine St. (bet. Quince & 12th Sts.), 215-592-0363; www.mixtophilly.com
The comida at this "sexy", brick-walled Center City Latin is so "yummy" and the vibe so "lively" you'll feel "like doing the salsa mid-meal"; the scene's enhanced by "fabulous" sangrias and a bar on the second floor ("bring earplugs"), and it's probably safe to expect service that ranges from "good" to "where's my waiter?"

MONK'S CAFE ◑　　　　　22 | 15 | 17 | $25
264 S. 16th St. (Spruce St.), 215-545-7005; www.monkscafe.com
Hops-happy habitués think this "incredibly crowded", "dark" Center Cityite just might be the "best beer hall west of Antwerp"; staffers who "love what they pour" ("don't you dare ask for a Miller Lite") from the "largest" selection of Belgian brews in the U.S. also dish out "awesome" hits (i.e. mussels and frites), and since most are willing to ignore "long, long waits", most think it all adds up to "perfection."

Monte Carlo Living Room ⊠

18 | 19 | 19 | $60

150 South St. (2nd St.), 215-925-2220
A "formal" affair in the midst of "Mardi Gras"-esque South Street, this "old standby" still churns out "special-occasion" Italian fare that suits "business dinners"; neither the "dated" decor nor "costly" tabs appeal, but there's always "dancing" in the club upstairs to take the sting out of things.

Moonstruck

21 | 22 | 21 | $40

7955 Oxford Ave. (Rhawn St.), 215-725-6000;
www.moonstruckrestaurant.com
Claire Di Lullo and Toto Schiavone's "old-world" Italian in Fox Chase has long been beloved as an "oasis in a desert of concrete and traffic" (in other words, Northeast Philly); aside from "tasty" food, both a layout that provides "intimacy" and "knowledgeable" service imbue the place with "class", and even those struck by somewhat "high prices" call this one their "home away from home."

More Than Just Ice Cream

20 | 12 | 17 | $17

1119 Locust St. (12th St.), 215-574-0586
"Bring your sweet tooth but leave your pancreas at home" before digging into the "delightfully obscene" ice creams and "heavenly" deep-dish apple pies at this "chill", "diner-type" American joint in Wash West; since "yummy" burgers and sandwiches round out the rest of a "comfort-food-central" menu that's "much better than you'd expect", don't be surprised if you catch yourself noshing the night away.

Moriarty's ◗

17 | 14 | 17 | $21

1116 Walnut St. (11th St.), 215-627-7676;
www.moriartysrestaurant.com
"Beer, burgers, wings – that's all you need to know" about this "reliable", "no-fuss" Center City pub "favorite" popular with "Forrest Theatre"–goers and the "Jefferson Hospital crowd" who like to "chase it all down" with a shot of "Saturday night karaoke"; realists realize it's best to "just pass the pitcher."

MORIMOTO

27 | 27 | 25 | $72

723 Chestnut St. (bet. 7th & 8th Sts.), 215-413-9070;
www.morimotorestaurant.com
Even with '*Iron Chef*' Masaharu Morimoto spending time in the new namesake NYC offshoot, Stephen Starr's "trendy" "neo"-Japanese "masterpiece" in Center City is still a "must visit" for "sublime", "Tokyo-quality" sushi and "exciting" fusion fare in a "surreal" and "seriously sexy" setting complete with "changing mood lights"; "flawless" service is part of an overall experience that feels like "winning the lottery", so it's advised to "splurge" to take advantage of what will be a "memorable" meal ("you won't be sorry, even when you get the bill").

Morning Glory Diner ⌷   22 | 11 | 16 | $16
735 S. 10th St. (Fitzwater St.), 215-413-3999;
www.morningglorydiner.com
"This is why the sun rises every morning" crow devotees of
Sam Mickey's "steadfast", cash-only Bella Vista breakfast-
luncher where lines are "wrapped around the block" for
"to-die-for" "biscuits" and other coffee-shop "comfort
food galore" served by "friendly" staffers; those seeking
"instant gratification" go on weekdays.

MORTON'S, THE STEAKHOUSE   24 | 20 | 23 | $62
1411 Walnut St. (bet. Broad & 15th Sts.), 215-557-0724
Pavilion at King of Prussia Mall, 500 Mall Blvd. (DeKalb Pike),
King of Prussia, 610-491-1900
www.mortons.com
Beef eaters' "mouths water" even before they enter one of
these "well-run" Center City and KoP carnivoriums, where
"hefty" prices accompany dishes so "big" that "one baked
potato could feed all the *Desperate Housewives*", and
where the "outstanding" steaks are served with "enthusiasm and polish" in an "old-men's club" setting; P.S. the
same people who sniff at "show-and-tell" spiels from the
staff are willing to tag along if "someone else is buying."

MOSHULU   20 | 25 | 20 | $51
Penn's Landing, 401 S. Columbus Blvd. (Delaware River),
215-923-2500; www.moshulu.com
"Bring your sea legs" and an open mind to this "romantic"
albeit "pricey" New American on a 100-year-old four-
masted ship anchored at Penn's Landing; despite somewhat "erratic" service, those expecting a "tourist trap"
are pleasantly "shocked" with cap'n Ralph Fernandez's
"tasty" Polynesian-influenced New American menu, and
since "nothing beats" the views of the Delaware from the
deck, it's clear this one floats many a boat.

Mother's Rest. & Wine Bar   17 | 15 | 16 | $31
34 N. Main St. (bet. Bridge & Randolph Sts.), New Hope,
215-862-5857
Although this New Hope stalwart has a "new life" (it's also
a wine bar now), the vibe still is a mix of "quirky"/"hippie"
and "upwardly mobile"; along with "good" Traditional
American savories are desserts "to die for" and "no pretense", even if some swear the staff "takes early retire-
ment after serving your entree."

Mr. Martino's Trattoria ⌷   20 | 20 | 22 | $28
1646 E. Passyunk Ave. (bet. Morris & Tasker Sts.),
215-755-0663
"Just the sweetest ambiance ever" inhabits this "cute"
Italian BYO residing in an old hardware store in South
Philly; after what seems like "entering another world",
patrons sit down to "good" "home"-cooked meals (albeit

from a "limited" menu) brought to table by "pleasant" servers – but only at dinner on Fridays–Sundays (they're closed the rest of the week).

Ms. Tootsie's ⊘   ▽ 24 | 17 | 19 | $26 |
1314 South St. (S. 13th St.), 215-731-9045
There's "real" soul food (e.g. "mac 'n' cheese that lives up to its name") plus some items with a "twist" to satisfy all comers to this South Street BYO; N.B. in the works at press time is a major renovation that will more than double the space and add a lounge area and a private room.

Murray's Deli ⊘   18 | 7 | 13 | $17 |
285 Montgomery Ave. (Levering Mill Rd.), Bala Cynwyd, 610-664-6995; www.murraysdeli.com
"Unhinge your jaw" for "great" "overstuffed" sandwiches and other chow at this Bala "staple" locked in a "battle" for Main Line deli supremacy with Hymie's across the street; adherents simultaneously love the "grungy charm" that "never disappoints" yet blast both "tight quarters" and "service without a smile" from an "uncaring" staff.

Museum Restaurant   19 | 20 | 19 | $37 |
Philadelphia Museum of Art, 2601 Benjamin Franklin Pkwy. (26th St.), 215-684-7990
After being "cultured", stop in for "tasty" fare at the Philadelphia Museum of Art's "understated" eatery, a New American providing both "lovely interludes" for art fans and a "good", "creative" menu that mimics the exhibit (e.g. Cézanne-wich); overall, most find it a "treat", even if they think it costs a little too much Monet.

Mustard Greens   23 | 16 | 22 | $28 |
622 S. Second St. (bet. Bainbridge & South Sts.), 215-627-0833
"Fresh, light" and "clean" is the word on the "nouvelle" cuisine at Bon Siu's "serene" Chinese in "charmingly spare" Queen Village quarters; forget about "gloppy sauces" – this is a "healthy" alternative to "greasy" joints, and it's all enhanced by "pleasant" servers who hand out "steamed towels at the end."

My Thai   20 | 14 | 17 | $24 |
2200 South St. (22nd St.), 215-985-1878
"A Thai grandmother must have decorated" this "quiet", "affordable" South Street "gem" near Graduate Hospital; most know to "pop in" for $15.95 weekend prix fixes and "reliably good" cooking that "never fails" and comes with "warm" service.

Nam Phuong   24 | 9 | 15 | $18 |
1100-1120 Washington Ave. (11th St.), 215-468-0410
This "always crowded", "warehouse-size" Vietnamese near the Italian Market turns out "delightful" pho and other "authentic" dishes at "bargain basement" prices;

while it adheres to the "restaurant school" dictum "get 'em in, get 'em out", and meals here are "like eating in a mess hall", all told, it offers up some of the best food "this side of Saigon."

NAN ⊠　　　　　　　　　　26 16 21 $38
4000 Chestnut St. (40th St.), 215-382-0818;
www.nanrestaurant.com
Word is "from the outside, you'd never guess that you're in for one of the best meals" around at "talented" chef-owner Kamol Phutlek's French-Thai BYO, a "jewel" in University City's "lower rent district"; they "get all the courses right" say the amazed when describing the "exceptional" fare, though it also helps when service is this "good."

Nan Zhou　　　　　　▽ 23 7 16 $10
Hand Drawn Noodles ⇄
927 Race St. (bet. 9th & 10th Sts.), 215-923-1550
"If you want decor and service, don't come here", but "if you want the best bowl of noodle soup in Chinatown" then head to this cash-only BYO vending "miraculously" good noodles at "criminally" "cheap" prices ("I would have paid double"); P.S. watching the "experienced" staff at work provides a "good show."

NECTAR　　　　　　　　24 26 22 $51
1091 Lancaster Ave. (Manchester Ct.), Berwyn, 610-725-9000;
www.tastenectar.com
"Porsche"- and "Beemer"-driving Main Liners love the "party" scene at the "Buddakan of the 'burbs", Michael Wei and Scott Morrison's "beautiful" multilevel Berwyn Pan-Asian, where the scene is buoyed by both Patrick Feury's "fantastic" fare and an "active" bar when the nectar flows; P.S. "septuagenarians who can't read the menu in the darkness" can "ask for a table upstairs."

New Delhi　　　　　　　　19 10 15 $15
4004 Chestnut St. (bet. 40th & 41st Sts.), 215-386-1941;
www.newdelhiweb.com
It's all about the "cheap" and "awesome" buffets ($5.95 at lunch, $8.95 at dinner) at this "college dining hall in disguise" near Penn that have helped make Indian "food lovers" out of countless students; ok, the service may not be four-star, but it's "attentive", and the modest decor ("hey, they painted") doesn't bother anyone.

New Tavern, The ⊠　　　　　16 16 17 $35
261 Montgomery Ave. (Old Lancaster Rd.), Bala Cynwyd,
610-667-9100; www.thetavernrestaurant.com
Bala-ites weigh in on Nick Zarvalas' "friendly" Greek-influenced Traditional American: one camp insists the fare off the "diverse" slate is "good" and "wholesome", while others describe "inconsistent" food and wonder if they take "Medicare" given the number of "blue hairs" in attendance.

New Wave Café ◐ | 19 | 10 | 17 | $26 |

784 S. Third St. (Catharine St.), 215-922-8484;
www.newwavecafe.com

Chef "Ben [McNamara] is back, and so am I" proclaim supporters of this "funky", "smoky" Queen Village watering hole serving "all the old favorites" – "reasonably" priced "upscale" New American food – that "surpass expectations"; in short, it "feels like home again."

Next ⊅ | 21 | 17 | 19 | $40 |

223 South St. (bet. 2nd & 3rd Sts.), 215-629-8688;
www.nextbyob.com

To escape South-Street "bustle", step down into this "subterranean" cash-only New American BYO, a "best-kept secret" serving "imaginative" "well-prepared" dishes from a "constantly changing" menu; decorwise, the "crisp", "modern" design pleases as much as it "relaxes."

Nido | ▽ 21 | 17 | 22 | $28 |

1514 W. Ritner St. (Hicks St.), 215-755-0860

"If you can find a place to park", you're good to go at this shoebox-size South Philly Italian BYO where Michelle Iovino cooks "delicious" food; that it mixes a "neighborhood" and "upscale" vibe makes it even more "worth the trip."

Nifty Fifty's ⊅ | 19 | 19 | 18 | $13 |

2491 Grant Ave. (Roosevelt Blvd.), 215-676-1950
2555 Street Rd. (Knights Rd.), Bensalem, 215-638-1950
1900 MacDade Blvd. (Kedron Ave.), Folsom, 610-583-1950
www.niftyfiftys.com

Doo right by yourself and swing into one of these "neon"-lit joints that "turn back the clock"; in fact, definitely "bring the whole family" too for "the best" shakes, burgers and fries, and be "as loud as you want" to compete with the "screaming kids"; it all proves once again that the "'50s" and "Dick Clark" "will never get old."

Nineteen (XIX) | – | – | – | E |

Park Hyatt at the Bellevue, 200 S. Broad St. (Walnut St.),
215-893-1234; www.parkhyatt.com

Replacing Founders is this 19th-floor overlook, a New American seafooder in the Park Hyatt; the striking decor boasts soaring ceilings and an enormous pearl chandelier hovering above the circular, mosaic-tiled bar, the showcase for a sparkling selection of raw bounty from the sea; N.B. the cafe side is open for breakfast, lunch and dinner.

Nodding Head | 17 | 13 | 17 | $22 |
Brewery & Restaurant ◐

1516 Sansom St., 2nd fl. (bet. 15th & 16th Sts.), 215-569-9525;
www.noddinghead.com

There's appeal beyond the "bobblehead collection" at this "relaxed" pub on Sansom Street, namely "good" and somewhat "fancified" bar food that's inevitably washed down or preceded by "kick-butt" brews (and "thank God they're cheap"); what with "comfy" booths and "rock" on the sound system, "dude, it's a hip place."

North by Northwest
15 | 16 | 15 | $28

7165 Germantown Ave. (bet. Mt. Airy & Mt. Pleasant Aves.), 215-248-1000; www.nxnwphl.com
This "casual" Mount Airy Traditional American nightspot sports exposed brick and tin ceilings, but the main attractions just may be the "fantastic" nightly music lineup; though "good", the food can be "notoriously average", causing some to point their compasses elsewhere.

N. 3rd ●
22 | 18 | 18 | $25

801 N. Third St. (Brown St.), 215-413-3666; www.norththird.com
The term 'pub grub' "doesn't do justice" to Peter Dunmire's New American dishes (from foie gras to quesadillas) at this "trendy" Northern Liberties corner spot that "sets the standard for great bar food"; you'll likely "never have a bad meal" here, and the "eclectic" decor (featuring "Christmas-tree" lights and "interesting" artwork for sale) works.

Ocean Harbor
19 | 12 | 14 | $21

1023 Race St. (bet. 10th & 11th Sts.), 215-574-1398
"Rolling carts" bearing "outstanding" dim sum wind up at your table at this "noisy", "non-touristy" and modestly decorated Chinese outlet in Chinatown; the food is some of the "best" of its kind, but know that meals here require assertive countermeasures to deal with a staff that "rushes you in and rushes you out" amid a scene of "mass confusion."

Ogontz Grill & Sidewalk Café
– | – | – | I

7152 Ogontz Ave. (bet. Homer St. & Walnut Ln.), 215-424-7100
Burgeoning West Oak Lane locals sit and relax at this casual Southern-style American (and Chestnut Grill relative) for ribs and such, and more contemporary dishes in a setting brightened by art from African-American artists; live jazz on weekends keeps things hopping, while the large patio area's perfect for alfresco noshing.

Oishi
– | – | – | I

2817 S. Eagle Rd. (Durham Rd.), Newtown, 215-860-5511
Purveying a range of Japanese, Thai and Korean comestibles is this minimalist Newtown Pan-Asian BYO, where the counter-service seating allows acolytes to survey the action; aside from the allure of the fare, inexpensive tabs make waits (especially on weekends) inevitable.

Old Guard House Inn ⊠
23 | 21 | 22 | $52

953 Youngsford Rd. (Righters Mill Rd.), Gladwyne, 610-649-9708; www.guardhouseinn.com
This "steady" 70-year-old Main Line eatery housed in a "rustic" 200-year-old log cabin–like building "still rocks"

its "old-guard" clientele with "consistently excellent" German-influenced American fare ("think warm food on a cold night") and "great" service; P.S. if you want to dine with the "fresh-from-the-golf-course" crowd, be prepared to "drop big bucks" before entering this house.

Old Original Bookbinder's   18 | 20 | 19 | $52 |

125 Walnut St. (2nd St.), 215-925-7027; www.bookbinders.biz
Back after a "beautiful success" of a renovation is this restored seafood landmark in Old City that has fans "walking down memory lane" and reveling in a setting that blends "old Philly charm" and "modern" sensibilities and still includes "celebrities, dignitaries, politicos" and "tourists" on any given night; the service team is "friendly", and as for the "pricey" fare, expect "good" if "uninspiring" eats – but then again "tradition, not food, is the lure" here.

Olive Tree Mediterranean Grill ⊠ ▽ 23 | 14 | 20 | $26 |

379 W. Uwclan Ave. (Peck Rd.), Downingtown, 610-873-7911; www.olivetreegrill.com
Surveyors have recently "discovered" this casual Downingtown Greek BYO operating in strip-mall digs and serving "wonderful" homespun food (think Greek salads, souvlaki and calamari); reports indicate that the "welcoming" service is as pleasing as the "authentic" eats.

Ooka Japanese   23 | 18 | 20 | $32 |

110 Veterans Ln. (Main St.), Doylestown, 215-348-8185
1109 Easton Rd. (Fitzwatertown Rd.), Willow Grove, 215-659-7688
For Japanese "outside the city limits", "it doesn't get any better" than at these "friendly" and "sleek" venues that delight with "exciting" choices of "wonderfully fresh" sushi and entertain "young and old" in the "fun" hibachi areas; overall, it's apparent the "delicious" food is worth the "waits"; N.B. Doylestown has a license, and Willow Grove is BYO.

Orchard, The   ▽ 24 | 22 | 23 | $56 |

503 Orchard Ave. (Rte. 1), Kennett Square, 610-388-1100
In the "shadow" of Longwood Gardens is this "warm" Kennett Square BYO whose "minimalist", "contemporary" setting shows off James Howard's "fantastic looking", daily changing New American fare (it "can hold its own with that of any big-city place") abetted by "skilled" service; N.B. there's a $5 corkage fee.

Ortlieb's Jazzhaus ☽   ▽ 16 | 17 | 17 | $27 |

847 N. Third St. (Poplar St.), 215-922-1035
Get a taste of the "past" at this "old-time" candlelit Northern Liberties jazz house that's been serving up "great" live acts for nearly 20 years; true, folks "go for the music" and not necessarily the "hit-or-miss" Cajun food, but for an "enjoyable" evening, it's a Philly "must."

Osaka
23　19　19　$36

8605 Germantown Ave. (Evergreen St.), 215-242-5900
372 W. Lancaster Ave. (Strafford Ave.), Wayne, 610-902-6135
"High-quality", "beautifully" presented Japanese cuisine – particularly the "amazing" sushi – is the hallmark of this piscine-centric duo; they further appeal with "fabulous" sakes for adults, a fish tank (Lancaster Avenue) that "entertains" the kids and "wonderfully accommodating" (though sometimes "slow") service.

Ota-Ya
23　14　19　$31

10 Cambridge Ln. (Sycamore St.), Newtown, 215-860-6814;
www.ota-ya.com
"Fresh", "unique" raw fare comes from sushi "masters" while the "delicious" cooked items delight just about everyone else at these "cozy" albeit "pedestrian"-looking Japanese BYOs in Bucks and Lambertville warmed by a "friendly" staff that "knows all their customers"; N.B. the Jersey branch is dinner only.

Otto's Brauhaus
17　14　17　$24

233 Easton Rd. (Pine Ave.), Horsham, 215-675-1864;
www.ottosbrauhaus.com
"More than ample" are the portions and plenty are the Hummel figurines at this "dark" authentically Teutonic taphaus in Horsham where "dad" and local "Rotary clubbers" convene for "artery-clogging" brats, schnitzel and other German goodies and "excellent" brews; in sum, it's all *gut* for what it is, and the Sunday night buffet is "a hit."

Overtures
24　23　23　$50

609 E. Passyunk Ave. (bet. Bainbridge & South Sts.), 215-627-3455
Peter LamLein continues to create "lovely" music in the kitchen of his "romantic" French-Med BYO off South Street, arguably "Philly's best-kept secret" for "terrific" midweek prix fixes "worthy of your finest wines; it's all complemented by "excellent" service in a "jewel box" of a setting featuring trompe l'oeil paintings and "beautiful" flower arrangements; in other words, "bravo!"

Pace One
∇ 19　19　18　$42

Pace One Country Inn, 341 Thornton Rd. (Glen Mills Rd.), Thornton, 610-459-3702
City slickers gladly "take a ride to the country" for this "elegant" American in Thornton offering "lots of nooks and crannies" that allow for "quiet conversations"; if a few find the fare "doesn't stand out too much", fans think the "romantic" charm here "makes the good food taste better."

Paganini Pizza & Cafe
∇ 18　18　20　$27

72 W. State St. (Clinton St.), Doylestown, 215-348-9600
The pastas are the "high point" at Paganini Trattoria's more "casual" offspring across the street in Doylestown that's

"good" for "quick", "inexpensive" Italian meals chased with wine; warm weather provides an excuse for some to sit on the "great" patio, and the related wine bar next door allows oenophiles to browse.

Paganini Trattoria ▽ 18 | 16 | 16 | $33

81 W. State St. (Clinton St.), Doylestown, 215-348-5922
"Well worth the price" to its backers is this "date"-worthy Doylestown Italian offering "straightforward" fare that tends to "hit the spot"; protestors play the whole thing down, lamenting "nothing-special" fare served by a staff whose "attitude" makes them seem like they were "recruited from a reform school."

Palace of Asia 20 | 17 | 18 | $29

Best Western Inn, 285 Commerce Dr. (bet. Bethlehem Pike & Pennsylvania Ave.), Fort Washington, 215-646-2133
"Cravings for curry" are duly satisfied at this "out-of-the-way" Indian in an "unlikely" location in Fort Washington's Best Western; those who size up the environs that "leave something to be desired" "shouldn't be discouraged" – most recommend the food here, saying it's "tasty" and the service "attentive."

Palm 22 | 19 | 21 | $59

Park Hyatt at the Bellevue, 200 S. Broad St. (Walnut St.), 215-546-7256; www.thepalm.com
"Boys with all the marbles" come to play at this "paradise for power brokers", a "clubby" steakhouse "institution" in the Park Hyatt that gets so "crowded" you'll feel like you're dining "in the middle of a busy highway"; sure, the "high-priced" steaks and lobsters are "consistently good", but some note it's the "show" of "characters on the walls – and at the tables" that intrigues the most; P.S. "lunch offers the best viewings."

PALOMA ⊠ 26 | 18 | 25 | $49

6516 Castor Ave. (bet. Hellerman St. & Magee Ave.), 215-533-0356
In a "food-starved", "down-at-the-heels" Northeast Philly area resides this "haute" French-Mexican "standout" wowing those who've been to its "relaxing" space for Adan Saavedra's "artistic" presentations backed by "reasonably" priced wines and "excellent" service; for some who're thinking twice about making the trip, consider that food "doesn't get any better than this."

Paradigm ⊠ 17 | 19 | 17 | $38

239 Chestnut St. (bet. 2nd & 3rd Sts.), 215-238-6900; www.paradigmrestaurant.com
"Young" 'uns check in to this "dark", "modern" American in Old City for "chocolate martinis" and a "too-cool-for-school" setting populated by fellow "beautiful people" throughout; those who stay for dinner speak of "standard" fare that "needs updating", and everyone's still amazed at

the "cool" bathrooms and the "doors that fog up when you lock them."

Paradiso   21 | 20 | 19 | $48 |
1627-29 E. Passyunk Ave. (Tasker St.), 215-271-2066;
www.paradisophilly.com
"Upscale comfort food at its best" is the line on Lynn Rinaldi's "modern" Italian bistro exuding "sophistication" on the Passyunk Avenue strip; there's a "wonderful" wine list and a "friendly" crew that "tries hard" to boot, but note that such a "classy" package comes with "pricey" tabs.

¡PASIÓN!   25 | 23 | 23 | $55 |
211 S. 15th St. (bet. Locust & Walnut Sts.), 215-875-9895;
www.pasionrestaurant.com
"Seviche worth its weight in gold" and other "spectacular" Nuevo Latino fare "make believers out of skeptics" at Guillermo Pernot's "romantic" Center City "stunner" whose "tropical" vibe makes it feel like "Miami" even when it's "January" in Philly; for "extra entertainment" or at least to take your mind off the bill (it's "not cheap"), sit at the "kitchen bar" and watch the crew at work.

Passage to India   18 | 13 | 14 | $21 |
1320 Walnut St. (Juniper St.), 215-732-7300
Find buffets ($7.99 lunch, $9.99 dinner) that "never disappoint" at this "nothing-fancy" Center City Indian convenient to the theaters; if it looks a "little frayed" around the edges to some, it hooks most on its "nice vegetarian options" and overall appeal as a "passage to good, inexpensive" food for the 'hood.

Patou   19 | 17 | 17 | $43 |
312 Market St. (bet. 3rd & 4th Sts.), 215-928-2987;
www.patourestaurant.com
The "Côte d'Azur" comes to Old City via Patrice Rames' "hip", "high-ceilinged" nautically themed French-Med; but surveyors seem adrift on its attributes, with some praising the "thought and care" put into the fare and point out it "won't break the bank", while others are "disappointed" with "inconsistent" eats and service and think the interior more "waiting area than restaurant."

Pat's King of Steaks ◑⇥   20 | 7 | 12 | $10 |
1237 E. Passyunk Ave. (9th St.), 215-468-1546;
www.patskingofsteaks.com
"People continue to argue" if this 24/7 cheese steak stand at Ninth and Passyunk is the "best in town" (or at least better than Geno's across the street); those who vote for the "king" join a crowd of "celebrities, millionaires and your neighbor" who can't get enough "artery-clogging" sandwiches on rolls as "crusty" as the staff, who both "capture the essence of South Philly" and want you to "have the lingo down when you order" ('wit' means "with onions", pal).

Pattaya Grill　　　　　　18 | 14 | 17 | $22
4006 Chestnut St. (40th St.), 215-387-8533
Pennsters swear by this "quaint" University City Thai for
"reliably tasty" cooking from an "extensive" menu, albeit
one "without surprises"; "you can bring anyone" to this
place, and they'll probably come away pleased on account
of "budget"-friendly tabs and a glass-enclosed sunroom
that gives a "wonderful sense of the outdoors."

Peacock on the Parkway ⊠　16 | 14 | 16 | $32
1700 Benjamin Franklin Pkwy. (17th St.), 215-569-8888;
www.peacockontheparkway.com
For a "reasonable" expense, this "family-run" Center City
Med BYO on the parkway is a "good standby", especially
when you snag a spot on the sidewalk patio; despite having
the "friendliest" staff around, "ok" fare and "tired" decor
have some surmising it's "time for a new concept."

Penang ◑⊄　　　　　　21 | 17 | 17 | $23
117 N. 10th St. (bet. Arch & Cherry Sts.), 215-413-2531
"Adventurous" foodies look to this "bustling", "contemporary" Malaysian chain link in the middle of Chinatown for
"big", "bold" dishes that "please all the senses"; "eat
quickly and talk elsewhere", since servers who try to keep
up work at the "speed of light" amid a "continuous din;
P.S. if the cash-only policy annoys, at least this place
"won't put a hole in your pocketbook."

Penne　　　　　　　　18 | 18 | 17 | $37
Inn at Penn, 3611 Walnut St. (36th St.), 215-222-0200;
www.pennerestaurant.com
Watching the "heavenly" pastas being made before your
eyes gives this "fancified" Italian in the Inn at Penn the
nickname "penne campus"; though some insist the "hit-
or-miss" service is "out of its (Ivy) League" and suggest
"South Philly" for the "real" deal when it comes to food,
many maintain this spot is a "surprisingly good" option to
"typical campus fare."

Pepper's Cafe ⊠⊄　　　∇ 22 | 6 | 20 | $17
2528 Haverford Rd. (Eagle Rd.), Ardmore, 610-896-0476
Main Liners seek out Kate Rapine's "tiny hut" for "yummy"
pastas and other "superb" Italian food dished out by "caring", "friendly" folks; with just a few seats and not much
decor inside, most head for the patio or opt for takeout, the
latter a "working mom's dream" come true.

Persian Grill　　　　　　21 | 11 | 20 | $27
637 Germantown Pike (Crescent Ave.), Lafayette Hill,
610-825-2705
Instantly recognized by its "turquoise" pond out front and
easily mistaken for a "small diner" from its exterior is this
"low-key" Montco mainstay that has fans "purring" over

"very good" Persian cooking; what's more, the prices are "good" (the lunch specials are a "great" deal) and the service "gracious."

P.F. Chang's China Bistro   21 | 20 | 19 | $29

Shoppes at Brinton Lake, 983 Baltimore Pike (Brinton Lake Rd.), Glen Mills, 610-545-3030; www.pfchangs.com

"Nutty" waits measured in "hours" and "overcrowded" conditions are what Chang-ees come to expect at these chain spots, where "eager-to-please" staffers work "cavernous" rooms loaded with seemingly "faux artifacts" and serve "all sorts" of Chinese "fusion" fare (though "everyone comes for the lettuce wraps"); so, who knew something so "inauthentic" could be this "fun"?

Philadelphia Fish & Co.   21 | 18 | 19 | $39

207 Chestnut St. (2nd St.), 215-625-8605

"The name may sound boring", but the fare at Kevin and Janet Meeker's Old City seafooder provides a useful example of how "excellent" "simple preparations from quality products" can be; "pleasant" service and a bar menu that's "the best bargain in town" mean this longtimer's still a "keeper"; P.S. their burgers are a "favorite."

Philly Crab & Steak House   19 | 14 | 17 | $30

Grant & Academy Shopping Ctr., 3334 Grant Ave. (Academy Rd.), 215-856-9510
355 York Rd. (Street Rd.), Warminster, 215-444-9208

"Basic" is the byword for these surf-'n'-turf twins operating in the Northeast and Warminster, with aficionados talking up "good" comestibles and "warm" service; some just want them to "turn on a few lights" and address "drab" digs ("wish they would redecorate").

Pho 75 ⌐   20 | 5 | 12 | $10

823 Adams Ave. (Roosevelt Blvd.), 215-743-8845
1122 Washington Ave. (12th St.), 215-271-5866

"Soups made with love" are the draw at these "welcoming" Vietnamese "fast"-fooders in the Lower Northeast and Italian Market where you get "heaping", "filling" bowls of pho for "less than 10 bucks"; fans seem willing to put up with "bare-bones", "dismal" digs for some of the "best" food of its kind around.

Pho Xe Lua   ▽ 25 | 6 | 16 | $15

907 Race St. (9th St.), 215-627-8883

"Order whatever the guy at the next table is eating" and you'll be happy at this "crowded" Chinatown spot where Philly's Vietnamese clientele "meet" and greet behind a "neon train engine in the window" to slurp up "glorious" pho (i.e. "Vietnamese penicillin"); would-be designers note they "must be passing what they've saved in decorating costs to the customer", because phogeddaboudit – prices here are a "steal."

Picasso
▽ 19 | 18 | 18 | $37

36 W. State St. (Olive St.), Media, 610-891-9600;
www.picasso-bar.com
Small plates of "good" Italian-Spanish food provide a "nice complement" to the fare at the next-door (and related) La Belle Epoque at this wine-focused Media bar with a "bistro-like" vibe; the "people-watching" possibilities are "great", and the overall scene is enhanced by live music some nights.

Piccolo Trattoria
21 | 13 | 19 | $26

32 West Rd. (Eagle Rd.), Newtown, 215-860-4247
"Good", "homemade" Italian cookery trumps the "strip-mall" locale of this "small" Bucks BYO where "waits" and "friendly", "brisk" service are the norm; the "exceptionally varied" menu including "extensive" daily specials help generate popularity.

Pietro's Coal Oven Pizzeria
19 | 14 | 16 | $23

121 South St. (bet. Front & 2nd Sts.), 215-733-0675
1714 Walnut St. (bet. 17th & 18th Sts.), 215-735-8090
www.pietrospizza.com
"Mouthwatering" "thin-crust" pies and "humongous" salads sate "the entire family" at this "rustic" Italian trio considered "heaven" by pizza pros; ok, the service ranges from "passable" to "slow", and so what if they're "too loud" (go ahead and "bring your baby") to carry on a conversation?

PIF ⊅
26 | 15 | 23 | $44

Italian Mkt., 1009 S. Eighth St. (Kimball St.), 215-625-2923
"Oenophiles" "break out their best" bottles for the "superb" food at David Ansill's cash-only, "true" *petit* French bistro BYO near the Italian Market; the strains of Edith Piaf" in the background complete the "Parisian" vibe and "warm" service "makes you want to move in", but just bring more than a few euros to cover somewhat "pricey" tabs.

Pink Rose Pastry Shop
21 | 15 | 16 | $12

630 S. Fourth St. (Bainbridge St.), 215-592-0565;
www.pinkrosepastry.com
With "too many delicious desserts" to choose from, it's "hard not to have your sweet-tooth life changed" after walking out of this "local blessing" of a Queen Village bakery purveying "rich, enticing" pastries to fans who tend to "indulge"; some even like the "froufrou" "Victoriana" of the decor, which seems to suit the mood and "homey" goods.

Pizzicato
20 | 16 | 18 | $31

248 Market St. (3rd St.), 215-629-5527
The "reasonably" priced "quality" food shows a "surprising consistency" and encourages "repeat visits" to these "understated", "laid-back" Italians good for "quick bites" at lunch or dinner before or after the theater (Old City) or shopping (Marlton, which is BYO).

Places! Bistro   ▽ 17 16 16 $41

People's Light & Theatre Co., 39 Conestoga Rd. (Lancaster Pike), Malvern, 610-647-8060

Don't worry about getting to the theater "on time" since this "quaint" Malvern New French in an old farmhouse sits right next to the People's Light & Theatre Company; but reviews nonetheless are mixed, with admirers applauding "solid" fare while critics pull the curtain down on a "limited menu" of "ordinary" stuff.

Plate   16 18 16 $34

Suburban Sq., 105 Coulter Ave. (Anderson Ave.), Ardmore, 610-642-5900
8460 Limekiln Pike (Ogontz Ave.), Wyncote, 215-885-3636
www.platerestaurant.com

You'll say "Center City" to yourself after paying a visit to one of these "contemporary" Traditional American comfort-fooders in Suburban Square and Montco; though some cite "uneven" fare and service "snafus", for others, they "don't disappoint" as they cater to everyone from "families with finicky kids" to "trendy" types.

Plough & the Stars   18 19 18 $31

123 Chestnut St. (2nd St.), 215-733-0300; www.ploughstars.com

"When the city's snowed in", it's comforting that the fireplace "burns bright", the "Guinness" flows and bands play "wonderful" music at this "authentic" Irish pub inside a high-ceilinged converted bank in Old City; fans also favor the "good" (and "inventive") fare and "friendly", "gabby" staffers, while insiders advise the "saving grace" of an upstairs for "oldsters" who want to escape the youngsters at the "smoky" bar.

Plumsteadville Inn   ▽ 20 21 21 $38

Plumsteadville Inn, Rte. 611 & Stump Rd. (4 mi. north of Doylestown), Plumsteadville, 215-766-7500

Partisans are plumb pleased with this "charming" eatery located in a 1751 Bucks County inn with "lots of character"; while there's a fair share of backers enjoying the "good old-fashioned" Traditional American cookery amid a "cozy" "Colonial" ambiance, some lament "banquet-hall" fare and choose to opt out instead.

Pod   22 24 20 $44

Inn at Penn, 3636 Sansom St. (bet. 36th & 37th Sts.), 215-387-1803

"Crazy lights and funky nights" translate into "out-of-this-world" experiences at Stephen Starr's "futuristic" Pan-Asian on the Penn campus, where college kids and "hip" "tweens" spend "mommy and daddy's money" and opt to sit in the "cool" private pods for "high-quality" eats (enhanced by "pretty" staffers) or grab "tempting" sushi delivered via conveyor belts; P.S. "I don't think we're in Kansas anymore" since this place seems like it's on "LSD."

Pompeii Cucina D'Italia
20 | 19 | 18 | $42

1113 Walnut St. (bet. 11th & 12th Sts.), 215-829-4400;
www.pompeiirestaurant.com

Although in Center City, this "upscale" Italian opposite the
Forrest Theater feels like "South Philly", what with its
"romantic" ambiance and "red-sauce" specialties; despite "variable" service, many enjoy this spot for "hearty"
pre-theater repasts; N.B. the Food score may not reflect a
post-*Survey* chef change.

Pond Restaurant ⊠
– | – | – | E

175 King of Prussia Rd. (E. Lancaster Ave.), Radnor, 610-293-9411

Bistro Cassis ⊠
175 King of Prussia Rd. (E. Lancaster Ave.), Radnor, 610-293-9521

For his solo debut, chef Abde Dahrouch, an alum of
Restaurant Taquet, has set up a posh (and pricey) Radnor
French-Med in the former home of Passerelle; one of the
Main Line's more notable outdoor settings feature a ter-
race for alfresco dining, a small bridge leading to the restaurant and a pond filled with swans; N.B. the adjacent
bistro is suited for quicker, more casual meals.

Porcini ⊠
23 | 12 | 20 | $31

2048 Sansom St. (bet. 20th & 21st Sts.), 215-751-1175;
www.porcinirestaurant.com

A "friendly" welcome and "delicious" pastas are the forte
at the Sansone brothers' Rittenhouse Square–area Italian
BYO where loyalists "endure cheek-to-jowl" seating at one
of the few "coveted tables"; so bring "earplugs and
football pads", and keep in mind no reservations make it
"harder to get into than Yale Law."

Porky & Porkie
▽ 18 | 12 | 18 | $20

1111 S. 11th St. (bet. Ellsworth St. & Washington Ave.),
215-468-8389

"Friendly" staffers "go out of their way" to teach "neophytes" a little technique at this grill-it-yourself BYO, a
Korean BBQ buffet near the Italian Market; "all you can
eat" means "happy, happy meat comas" are easily in-
duced, though just remember to "leave the shirt with the
dangling sleeves at home" and that "you'll smell like
charred beef for days."

Portofino
20 | 18 | 21 | $38

1227 Walnut St. (bet. 12th & 13th Sts.), 215-923-8208;
www.portofino1227walnut.com

Get a "very good" meal in before seeing a show at this
"nicely refurbed", longstanding Center City Italian whose
"delightful" servers are skilled at the art of "getting you to
the theater on time"; even though it's a moderately "upscale" kind of place (i.e. expect somewhat "high" prices),
fans applaud the 20 percent discount on your meal when
you show the staff your ticket.

Positano Coast 20 | 21 | 19 | $38
212 Walnut St., 2nd Fl. (bet. 2nd & 3rd Sts.), 215-238-0499;
www.lambertis.com
Lamberti's "trendy", "bright and sunny" Italian small-plater
next to the Ritz Five offers a "crowd-pleasing" scene complete with "airy" mural-filled environs that take you to the
"Amalfi Coast" and patrons nibbling on fare that makes
their "taste buds sing"; while "filling yourself up can turn
into an expensive proposition", just about everyone seems
happy to coast right in here.

Primavera Pizza Kitchen 18 | 20 | 16 | $28
7 E. Lancaster Ave. (Cricket Ave.), Ardmore,
610-642-8000
Ashbridge Shopping Ctr., 853 E. Lancaster Ave. (Uwchlan Ave.),
Downingtown, 610-873-6333; www.primaverapk.com
These "affordable" Italians (one in a "hangar"-size space
in Downingtown and the other occupying a former
Ardmore bank building) attract "kids", "adults" and those
on "dates" with "well-prepared" pastas and pizzas and
bar scenes; N.B. now separately owned.

PRIME RIB 25 | 25 | 24 | $63
Radisson Plaza Warwick Hotel, 1701 Locust St. (17th St.),
215-772-1701; www.theprimerib.com
Tame the "carnivore in you" at this "old-school" Warwick
steakhouse supplying "top-of-the-line" steaks to a well-
heeled crowd who dig the "quiet" "Rat Pack"-esque setting and "amazing" piano music (the "crowning touch");
you'll feel like a "royal" sitting in the "cushy", "thronelike
chairs" while "attentive" servers pamper you, and though
your "budget will be eaten up quickly" here, it still "doesn't
get any better than this"; N.B. jackets required in the main
dining room, but upstairs is more casual.

Public House at Logan Square 14 | 15 | 15 | $25
1801 Arch St. (18th St.), 215-587-9040;
www.publichousephilly.com
"What a meat market" marvel followers of the action at
this "upscale" Center City American bar "loaded" with
"after-work attorneys" and other "young professionals"
who congregate for the "hot" happy hour in the "cool",
"warehouselike" space; "passable" fare suggests more
"social scene" than cuisine here, and some note "shaky"
service in this house.

Pub of Penn Valley ◗ 19 | 12 | 20 | $27
863 Montgomery Ave. (bet. Brookhurst & Narbeth Aves.),
Narberth, 610-664-1901; www.pubofpv.com
"Bump into someone you know" at this "low-key",
"*Cheers*"-like Main Line Tudor-style taphouse, whose staff
"greets customers with a smile"; it's "popular", so "expect
to wait" for "satisfying" Eclectic pub fare ("who knew?")

that's "a cut above" the norm; P.S. "bless their hearts" for the no-smoking policy at dinner.

Pumpkin ⊽
22 15 19 $38
1713 South St. (17th St.), 215-545-4448
On an "up-and-coming" patch of South Street is this "cute" New American storefront BYO, the brainchild of Hilary Bor and chef Ian Moroney that's carving out a reputation for using "fresh", local ingredients for its "excellent" food (hence, the "limited" menu changes daily); N.B. with only 28 seats, reservations are recommended.

Qdoba Mexican Grill
16 8 11 $11
230 S. 40th St. (Locust St.), 215-222-2887
1528 Walnut St. (16th St.), 215-546-8007
www.qdoba.com
Think "cheap", "pretty good" burritos with all the "fixin's you can point to" and you'll understand why folks "are out the door" ready to order at one of these "dependable" Mexican "cafeteria"–style chainsters, whose "assembly-line" service is heralded for its "Germanlike efficiency"; most find the three "dependable" even if some insist "Americanized" fare means they hear the sound of "millions of Mexicans crying."

Radicchio
23 15 21 $36
402 Wood St. (4th St.), 215-627-6850; www.radicchio-cafe.com
"Be prepared to wait in line" with a "who's who" of Philly's chefs who spend their off nights savoring "fantastic" cooking at this "rustic", "noisy as hell" Old City Italian BYO specializing in "exceptionally" prepared fish; "caring" servers make you think you're "in Italy", but "no reservations" mean you have to "come early" for the trip (and don't go on weekends "unless you like hanging out at street corners").

Ralph's ⊽
20 14 18 $31
Italian Mkt., 760 S. Ninth St. (bet. Catharine & Fitzwater Sts.),
215-627-6011; www.ralphsrestaurant.com
Philly's "red-gravy" "treasure" has "history" (over 90 years of it) to spare and still "never lets you down" with its "belly-filling" favorites that seem tailor-made for the "Sinatra"-esque setting; boosters bring cash (though there's an ATM on the premises) and "ask for an upstairs table" because there's "little elbow room" and lots of "tourists" downstairs.

Rangoon
23 11 20 $21
112 N. Ninth St. (bet. Arch & Cherry Sts.), 215-829-8939
It might be as stylin' as a "Holiday Inn", but regulars urge you to round up everyone you know and head to this "affordable" Center City Burmese (on the edge of Chinatown) whose "gracious" servers deliver simply "amazing" fare including a thousand-layer bread that'll take you "a step closer to Nirvana"; overall, it offers a "wonderful break" from the same old, same old.

Ravenna
21 | 17 | 19 | $38

2960 Skippack Pike (Valley Forge Rd.), Lansdale, 610-584-5650
"Every bite" of the "inspired" Northern Italian cooking is
"memorable" at Rachel and Shawn Sollberger's "lovely",
rustic Lansdale BYO decorated like a "Tuscan" trattoria;
"high weekend noise levels" is perhaps the most precise in-
dicator of its appeal.

Raw Sushi & Sake Lounge
– | – | – | M

1225 Sansom St. (bet. 12th & 13th Sts.), 215-238-1903
Behind the velvet rope at this exciting new Center City
Japanese restaurant/lounge is a creative mix of sushi and
cooked dishes supported by an enviable list of 40 sakes;
those who like their setting sleek will likely dig the arched
bamboo ceiling, glass-tiled walls, granite bar and lanterns
dangling from the ceiling.

Ray's Cafe & Tea House ☒
▽ 21 | 11 | 19 | $19

141 N. Ninth St. (bet. Cherry & Race Sts.), 215-922-5122
There's "skillfully prepared", "healthy" Taiwanese cuisine
at Grace Chen's "charming" Chinatown tearoom, but the
star of the show is the "amazing" coffee that's brewed
with a glass siphon (it's "alchemy"), making for the "finest"
cup around, though one that'll "take a bite out of your
pocketbook"; P.S. the staff is "so nice" that it's a "pleasure
to eat here."

READING TERMINAL MARKET ☒
24 | 14 | 15 | $13

51 N. 12th St. (Arch St.), 215-922-2317;
www.readingterminalmarket.org
"A must-see destination for tourists and residents" is
this "foodies' paradise", a Philadelphia "landmark" and
"bazaar" on one-square block next to the Pennsylvania
Convention Center; some 30-odd "stands" feature "every
cuisine" and comestible imaginable amid a "living, breath-
ing, working" farmer's market with folks from the Amish and
Mennonite communities (Wednesdays–Saturdays); in all,
it's "a jewel in Philly's gastronomic" and cultural crown.

Red Sky
17 | 17 | 17 | $40

224 Market St. (bet. 2nd & 3rd Sts.), 215-925-8080;
www.redskylounge.com
Get past the "clublike facade" of this "swank" Old City
Eclectic and discover "better-than-expected" fare
(though the dishes try "a bit too hard to be creative" for a
few); some say the "menu is hard to read in the dim, red
mood lighting" – a possible sign that this place is more
"popular for the trendy bar" scene.

Rembrandt's ◗
19 | 17 | 18 | $33

741 N. 23rd St. (Aspen St.), 215-763-2228; www.rembrandts.com
Fans of this "long-running" Fairmount American hangout
paint a picture of "hearty", "interesting" American fare

and "friendly" service, even when the occasional "kid" pops in; aside from the "down-to-earth" atmosphere, the "great" bar and entertainment (quizzo and live jazz) make it "worthwhile", "even if you're not from the neighborhood."

RESTAURANT ALBA 🖾   26 | 20 | 23 | $44

7 W. King St. (Warren Ave.), Malvern, 610-644-4009; www.restaurantalba.com

"Excellent" sums up this "cozy" Malvern BYO bistro that "books up early" with grateful western-suburbanites who enjoy peeking into Rose Tattoo alum Sean Weinberg's open kitchen, where the chef turns out "wonderful" New Americana from a wood-burning grill.

Restaurant Taquet 🖾   23 | 22 | 21 | $54

Wayne Hotel, 139 E. Lancaster Ave. (Wayne Ave.), Wayne, 610-687-5005; www.taquet.com

Things are about as "solid" as can be at Jean-Francois Taquet's "civilized", "fine-dining" New French–Med in the Wayne Hotel; the kitchen (entrusted to chef Clark Gilbert) offers Main Line "gastronomes" and "movers and shakers" some "deliciously" "modern" presentations of "very good" food, while the "more informal" bar area pleases as much as the "delightful" patio.

Rib Crib ●🖾🗗   23 | 5 | 15 | $18

6333 Germantown Ave. (bet. Duval St. & Washington Ln.), 215-438-6793

You'll know the ribs got "soul" once you start feasting on the "great" slow-cooked specialties at this "legendary" Germantown BBQ; it's true, expect to "stand in line" for a long time, but it's all worth the effort when you consider how "good" the stuff is; N.B. remember: no seating means all the gnawing is done somewhere else.

Ristorante Il Melograno   ∇ 23 | 18 | 23 | $44

Mercer Square Shopping Ctr., 73 Old Dublin Pike (N. Main St.), Doylestown, 215-348-7707; www.ilmelogranodoylestown.com

Bucks Countians enjoy "classic" Italian cookery in "plentiful" portions at this "small", white-tablecloth strip-mall "surprise" outside Doylestown; claims of "dependable" from "start to finish" extend to the "congenial" service, and it almost goes without saying reservations are highly suggested.

Ristorante La Buca 🖾   22 | 17 | 22 | $49

711 Locust St. (bet. 7th & 8th Sts.), 215-928-0556; www.ristlabuca.com

Guiseppe Giuliani, the proprietor of this Italian in a "basement" on Washington Square, still "loves" his clients, and after more than a quarter-century, his "high-class", "old-world" standard "still has what it takes", proving itself with "fabulous" seafood from a rolling cart, a "great" wine list and a staff that "knows how to take care of its patrons";

if a few think it "needs a breath of fresh air", the longevity
of this "standard" mutes the criticism.

Ristorante Mediterraneo   22   20   19 $43

*Pine Run Corners, 303 Horsham Rd. (Easton Rd.), Horsham,
215-672-5595; www.ristorantemediterraneo.net*

Many a Horshamite has something to say about this "romantic" Italian prized for its "delicious" fish and pastas;
most are impressed with "reliable", "personalized" service
from a staff with "deep" "accents", while others "feel like
intruders" and warn "don't order the specials unless you
ask the price"; N.B. plans are underway for a late 2006 move.

Ristorante Panorama   22   20   21 $49

*Penn's View Hotel, 14 N. Front St. (Market St.), 215-922-7800;
www.pennsviewhotel.com*

Pleasing patrons comes easy at this "refined" yet "happening" Penn's View Hotel trattoria with a solid rep for its
"amazing" wine flights from an "unmatched" by-the-glass
selection backed by "delicious" pastas; it's a "high-
priced" proposition, though one "you enjoy returning to."

Ristorante Pesto ☒   21   19   19 $34

*1915 S. Broad St. (bet. McKean & Mifflin Sts.), 215-336-8380;
www.ristorantepesto.com*

"Bring some Chianti" and "come hungry" to Io E Tu's "upbeat" BYO bro' across from St. Agnes; "wonderful" Italian
food (and specials "longer than the regular menu") awaits
you, as does a "friendly" vibe and rustic setting filled with
antiques and terra-cotta – all factoring in to its success.

Ristorante Positano   18   19   18 $41

*21 W. Lancaster Ave. (bet. Ardmore & Cricket Aves.),
Ardmore, 610-896-8298*

As "comfy" as a "robe and slippers" is this Ardmore Italian
"standby", whose defenders call it an "underappreciated"
"taste of Italy" on account of its reliably "good" meals; a few
foes, however, taste "variable" food that "lacks pizzazz."

Ristorante Primavera   19   15   19 $36

148 South St. (2nd St.), 215-925-7832
*184 W. Lancaster Ave. (Conestoga Rd.), Wayne,
610-254-0200*

"favorite" for "good, basic" Italiana are these "neigh-
rhoody" twins on South Street and the Main Line whose
easant" service makes you "feel right at home"; criti-
ns of a "menu that could use an update" are muted
n "generous" helpings and a reasonable bill arrive.

torante San Marco ☒   24   21   20 $47

*V. Bethlehem Pike (Dager Rd.), Spring House, 215-654-5000;
v.sanmarcopa.com*

beyond your normal budget" for the "excellent", "old-
ol" Italian food and atmosphere to match at this

polished Central Montco "special-occasion" destination; the piano bar is a "nice touch", though service is a subject of much debate ("wonderful" vs. "arrogant").

Ristorante Verona ⊠   ▽ 23 19 22 $37
288 Lancaster Ave. (bet. Green St. & Wallace Ave.), Frazer, 610-644-7464; www.ristoranteverona.com
An "attentive" staff and owners bring Frazer fans who "look forward" to visiting this Italian BYO yearling serving "very good" dishes; there's much to "love" here, and the consensus is it's "nice to have a South Philly–style restaurant in this area."

Rock Bottom   15 15 15 $23
Restaurant & Brewery ◐
Plaza at King of Prussia Mall, 1001 Mall Blvd. (DeKalb Pike), King of Prussia, 610-337-7737; www.rockbottom.com
Women shoppers send their "husbands or boyfriends" to this Southwestern pub chain link in the Plaza at King of Prussia Mall; the boys ring up "great" brews and chow down on "standard" bar vittles, and while the place is "too busy for its own good" (i.e. the "service needs work"), at least there are "fewer whiny kids here than at TGI Friday's."

Roller's at Flying Fish ⊅   21 15 18 $34
8142 Germantown Ave. (bet. Abington Ave. & Hartwell Ln.), 215-247-0707; www.rollersrestaurants.com
"Quirky" chef-owner Paul Roller "hasn't lost his touch", still whipping up food that's "as good as ever" in his newly relocated (just down the street) Chestnut Hill Eclectic; it's as "reliable" as it was in the old spot (and perhaps, "less noisy"), but you still need to bring cash since plastic won't get you anywhere.

Roselena's Coffee Bar   19 21 18 $32
1623-1625 E. Passyunk Ave. (bet. Morris & Tasker Sts.), 215-755-9697
Although this "feminine" BYO in the Italian Market serves "good" Italian fare at lunch and dinner, many reserve it for its "delicious" desserts "with the girls"; the "adorably" "froufrou" Victorian setting provides a perfect venue for "catty conversations."

Rose Tattoo Cafe ⊠   22 22 20 $37
1847 Callowhill St. (19th St.), 215-569-8939; www.rosetattoocafe.com
It's a regular "urban jungle" in there admire Tennessee Williams-ites of this "wrought-iron" adorned New American near the Free Library that "enchants" with an "A+-for-romance" setting teeming with "lush plant life" and "reliably good" fare and service; P.S. the "pretty" balcony offers perfect perch for people-watching.

Rose Tree Inn
24 | 18 | 20 | $43

1243 N. Providence Rd. (Rte. 1), Media, 610-891-1205
"Class" abounds at this "old-fashioned" Media Traditional American serving an "old-guard" crew "superbly executed" dishes; while an "update" of the "outdated" decor is called for, this mainstay is still "one of the nicest places" to "impress business associates", "parents or grandparents" over a leisurely paced meal.

Rouge
21 | 21 | 17 | $43

205 S. 18th St. (bet. Locust & Walnut Sts.), 215-732-6622
Neil Stein's "chichi", New American pad on Rittenhouse Square has a lock on burgers (the "best"), "people-watching" (even "better") and "attitude"; show off your "most recent blonde" to the rest of the "hot clientele" who suck up "prime" window and sidewalk seats, and while there's little doubt food is "secondary" to the "scene", "no matter what other place comes along, this is still going to be the hippest joint in town."

Roux 3
23 | 21 | 19 | $45

4755 West Chester Pike (Crum Creek Rd.), Newtown Square, 610-356-9500; www.roux3.com
Main Liners seeking something "Center City" turn to this "modern" Newtown Square New American featuring "creative", if at times "terrific" fare and a "hip" vibe (and a "bargain" of a $20 prix fixe dinner); but for the "slow" service, overall, this place is doing a "commendable" job.

Royal Tavern ◑
– | – | – | I

937 E. Passyunk Ave. (bet. Carpenter & Montrose Sts.), 215-389-6694
"Thank the Lord" say those whose prayers have been answered with this "inviting" Bella Vista tavern; the gastropub roster comprises vegan and vegetarian dishes, along with meaty options, all served in typically dark, woody quarters.

ROY'S
22 | 22 | 22 | $49

124-34 S. 15th St. (Sansom St.), 215-988-1814; www.roysrestaurant.com
"Your taste buds will thank you" while dining at Roy Yamaguchi's "mini-vacation" to Hawaii, a Center City link in the chain serving Big Island fare in "airy" environs showcasing an open kitchen that "enlivens" the experience; if a few critics call it "inconsistent", far more maintain it's as solid as a "well-oiled machine."

Ruby's
16 | 15 | 15 | $16

Suburban Sq., 5 Coulter Ave. (Anderson Ave.), Ardmore, 610-896-7829
Brinton Lake, 919 Baltimore Pike (Brinton Lake Rd.), Glen Mills, 610-358-1983

(continued)

(continued)

Ruby's
*Plaza at King of Prussia Mall, 160 N. Gulph Rd. (DeKalb Pike),
King of Prussia, 610-337-7829
www.rubys.com*

Model trains run "round the track" above the "roomy" booths at this "classic" "'50s-style" diner chain where "students", "stay-at-home moms" and their tots feast on "good" burgers, fries and shakes while ignoring attendant "calories and cholesterol"; a few fuddy-duddies frown and say it's a "kidfest" and advise to get ready to fight the brigades of "strollers."

RUTH'S CHRIS STEAK HOUSE | 22 | 21 | 22 | $57 |
*260 S. Broad St. (Spruce St.), 215-790-1515 ◑
220 N. Gulph Rd. (DeKalb Pike), King of Prussia, 610-992-1818
www.ruthschris.com*

Your "cholesterol number may explode", but that's the price many eagerly pay for "wonderful" beef sheathed "in butter" at these satellites in the "old-school" steakhouse chain; while "worth the loot" for most who find the pair's protein "consistently good", some scoff "standard" eats mean you can "do better" somewhere else.

Rx | 23 | 18 | 21 | $31 |
4443 Spruce St. (45th St.), 215-222-9590; www.caferx.com

Set up in a former pharmacy is this "cute" Eclectic where "arty" acolytes swear by Ross Essner's "natural-organic" approach to food, one that knits the "high-end" to the "homey"; the servers are as "warm" as the "laid-back" atmosphere, and the "amazing" Sunday brunch is prescribed to boost everyone's attitude.

Sabrina's Café | 25 | 15 | 20 | $21 |
910 Christian St. (bet. 9th & 10th Sts.), 215-574-1599

"If your stomach can handle the long waits", this "hopping" Eclectic BYO "hideout" in the Italian Market is "not to be missed" for "hands down" the "best" breakfast and brunch vittles served by "friendly hipsters" in a "comfortable", "shabby-chic" space; insider's tip: it's somewhat of a "secret", but the dinners are "real good" too.

Saloon | 23 | 22 | 21 | $62 |
*750 S. Seventh St. (bet. Catharine & Fitzwater Sts.),
215-627-1811; www.saloonrestaurant.net*

You "gotta love the steak and vino, baby" (and "waitresses") at this upmarket, Amex or cash-only Italian steakhouse, a "rite of passage" for followers who know to become a "regular" or at least go with one; "you get what you pay for" (and "you pay a lot"), but this "experience" may just be worth it alone for its "clubby" scene complemented by the South Philly holy trinity of "meat, gold chains and high hair."

Salt & Pepper ⊄   ▽ 21 | 16 | 23 | $32
746 S. Sixth St. (Fitzwater St.), 215-767-0202
Under new owners is this "cute" and "so-small" New American Bella Vista BYO that's "serving the neighborhood well" thanks to John DeSantis' "short" but "tasty" menu of seasonal dishes turned out from an open kitchen.

Sang Kee Asian Bistro   22 | 17 | 18 | $26
339 E. Lancaster Ave. (Remington Rd.), Wynnewood,
610-658-0618; www.sangkeeasianbistro.com
"We needed this", exclaim Main Liners who "wait in the crowded foyer" of this Wynnewood BYO "star" offering "succulent" Peking duck and other "delicious" Chinese dishes enjoyed without the "parking headaches" associated with the original; "fast-talking" waiters and "noise" may not pass the Zen test, but "moderate" prices compensate.

Sang Kee Peking Duck House ⊄   23 | 9 | 17 | $20
238 N. Ninth St. (Vine St.), 215-925-7532
Reading Terminal Mkt., 51 N. 12th St. (bet. Cuthbert &
Filbert Sts.), 215-922-3930 ⊠
The food – not the decor – "does the talking" at Michael Chow's Chinatown Chinese (with a Reading Terminal Market relative), where's it's wise to "fast before going" since you "can't stop eating" the "phenomenal" duck and noodle soups that are the "best on the East Coast"; N.B. cash only.

Sansom Street Oyster House   19 | 14 | 18 | $34
1516 Sansom St. (bet. 15th & 16th Sts.), 215-567-7683;
www.sansomoysters.com
A last "bastion of Philly's oyster houses" is this "venerable" Center City seafooder that remains "popular" for its "timeless", "basic" bivalves (they bring back "memories") and for its "excellent" raw bar; though a few deep-six it as "tired" and say the "senior crowd" keeps it afloat, most are still willing to drop anchor at this "page from the past."

SAVONA   27 | 26 | 25 | $69
100 Old Gulph Rd. (Rte. 320), Gulph Mills, 610-520-1200;
www.savonarestaurant.com
For a "special occasion" (like "winning the lottery") Main Liners "heartily recommend" this "formal" yet "convivial" "winner" in Gulph Mills for Andrew Masciangelo's "glorious" French-Italian menu, an "incredible" 1,000-label wine list and "romantic" Riviera-style setting; "mind-reading" servers tend to a well-heeled crowd so enthralled they thought they "owned the place."

Sazon   ▽ 19 | 8 | 20 | $19
941 Spring Garden St. (10th St.), 215-763-2500;
www.sazonrestaurant.com
"Good", traditional Venezuelan cooking is the special seasoning of this Northern Liberties BYO on Spring Garden; fans

savor "affordable" prices and a "personable" staff in "no-frills" "dinerlike" digs brightened by "interesting" artwork.

Scannicchio's   22 18 22 $32
2500 S. Broad St. (Porter St.), 215-468-3900;
www.scannicchio.com
The key is to "come hungry" and don't worry about "spelling the name" of this "fab" BYO (and outpost of the Atlantic City original) "red gravy"-ite "convenient to the stadiums" in South Philly; by the way, "yummy" Italian fare and "darling" service are standard operating procedure at this place.

Seafood Unlimited   22 12 18 $28
270 S. 20th St. (Spruce St.), 215-732-3663;
www.seafoodunlimited.com
Even "sophisticated" types marvel at "delicious" fish dishes and "fair" prices at this "unassuming" seafooder off Rittenhouse Square; service is "friendly", and while "not-so-terrific" decor means it's best to take the "longtime sweetie and not a new date", overall, things are shipshape here.

Serrano   21 19 21 $34
20 S. Second St. (bet. Chestnut & Market Sts.), 215-928-0770;
www.tinangel.com
"Carnivores" and "vegetarians" agree the food "doesn't disappoint" at this Old City Eclectic whose "narrow", "cozy" environs are "romance"-friendly and servers treat you like "you're being waited on by a close friend"; if you crave "great" live music, head upstairs to the Tin Angel.

Seven Stars Inn   20 17 20 $49
Hoffecker Rd. & Rte. 23, Phoenixville, 610-495-5205;
www.sevenstarsinn.com
"Manly" chophouse fare – "lots of it" ("1 meal = 3 days of leftovers") – is the main show at this circa-1736 Chester County "staple"; but while some insist the surf 'n' turf lineup is "excellent", others judge the "quantity-trumps-quality" food ideal only for "eating contests" and dis a look that could "use some dressing up."

Shanachie   16 18 18 $27
111 E. Butler Ave. (Ridge Ave.), Ambler, 215-283-4887;
www.shanachiepub.com
A "pub in the truest sense of the word" is this "modern", "convivial" Ambler Irish venue favored for its "interesting" "more-than-just-potatoes" menu and "wonderful" live music; for a "change of pace", this hangout impresses.

Shangrila   24 21 22 $36
(fka Shangrila 120)
120 W. Swedesford Rd. (Valley Forge Rd.), Devon, 610-687-8838;
www.shangrila120.com
Praised for its "extensive" and "excellent" Asian fusion menu is this "upscale" Devon "sleeper", where the "elo-

quence" to the dish presentations matches the "contemporary" quarters; savvy Main Liners are also quick to applaud "excellent" service and a "good deal" of a Sunday brunch.

SHANK'S & EVELYN'S LUNCHEONETTE 🖂🖵
26 | 6 | 17 | $13

932 S. 10th St. (Carpenter St.), 215-629-1093
"Don't ever $%#@* change!" is the war cry of "characters" who frequent this "hole-in-the-wall" South Philly luncheonette for the "great" Italian home cooking, especially the "best sandwiches in the world"; the seats are "few and far between" and the setting brims with "attitude" (be prepared to be "yelled at" by the folks behind the counter).

Shiao Lan Kung ☽
25 | 9 | 18 | $22

930 Race St. (bet. 9th & 10th Sts.), 215-928-0282
The salt-baked shrimp is the stuff of "dreams" at this "small" Chinese Chinatown BYO whose looks may be "lacking" but where the "excellent" quality of the food "speaks for itself"; you may have to "wait or share a table with strangers", but it's worth it since "this is the only place" you need to go when in the neighborhood.

Shiroi Hana
23 | 17 | 21 | $32

222 S. 15th St. (bet. Locust & Walnut Sts.), 215-735-4444;
www.shiroihana.com
If you're looking for "simple, fresh" sushi that "won't bust your budget", this "serene", "low-key" Japanese near the Kimmel Center "can't be beat"; "don't expect fireworks" from the food – just pleased patrons who know "great" service when they see it.

Shula's Steak House
20 | 17 | 19 | $52

Sheraton Philadelphia City Ctr., 17th St. (Race St.),
215-448-2700; www.donshula.com
The "NFL crowd" and "business travelers" think Don Shula "should get another Super Bowl ring" for backing this "sports-enthusiasts'" steakhouse chain in the Sheraton Philadelphia City Center; though some blow the whistle on "overpricing", "linebacker-sized" portions of beef fill many a belly, and what fan in their right mind would pass up chowing down "next to a photo of Larry Csonka?"

Siam Cuisine
21 | 14 | 17 | $26

925 Arch St. (bet. 9th & 10th Sts.), 215-922-7135
Buckingham Green Shopping Ctr., 4950 York Rd. (Rte. 202),
Buckingham, 215-794-7209
Village at Newtown, 2124 S. Eagle Rd. (bet. Durham &
Swamp Rds.), Newtown, 215-579-9399
www.siamcuisinepa.com
These "reliable" Thai triplets are standbys for their "good, basic" fare accompanied by "hospitality"; some, however, are fit to be thai'd when they think of "hit-or-miss" service and portions that "should be larger"; N.B. Newtown is BYO.

Siam Cuisine at The Black Walnut
▽ 22 | 19 | 21 | $38

80 W. State St. (bet. Clinton & Hamilton Sts.), Doylestown, 215-348-0708; www.siamcuisinepa.com

"Lovely" servers deliver "imaginative" French-Thai offerings that range from "good to superb" at this "upscale" eatery (the posh link in the Siam Cuisine chain) on Doylestown's Restaurant Row; P.S. the patio and garden "charm" in the warmer months.

Siam Lotus ⓩ
▽ 22 | 19 | 18 | $26

931 Spring Garden St. (bet. 9th & 10th Sts.), 215-769-2031; www.siamlotuscuisine.com

Despite the "sketchy location" "next to a gun shop", this Center City spot may be the "sexiest place to get great Thai food" around, and the "sweet" servers working the "stylish" room fit right in; it's "worth a try", and even the late-night bar scene doesn't disappoint.

Silk Cuisine
▽ 22 | 15 | 20 | $23

656 W. Lancaster Ave. (bet. Lee Ave. & Penn St.), Bryn Mawr, 610-527-0590

En-thai-cing the Main Line is this "dependable" Bryn Mawr BYO cooking up "yummy" Thai dishes (including an "ample" array of vegetarian options) at "best-buy" prices; it's "more than worth the parking hassle" when you have that "curry craving."

Simon Pearce on the Brandywine
19 | 24 | 20 | $44

1333 Lenape Rd. (Pocopson Rd.), West Chester, 610-793-0948; www.simonpearce.com

"Dramatic" views of the Brandywine River" and "beautiful" glass works blown at the on-site factory and sold at the attached store are the hallmarks of this "country" New American near West Chester; some take pains to point out the "quasi-gourmet comfort food" and "special" service, even while others feel shattered by "high" prices.

Singapore Kosher Vegetarian
▽ 19 | 13 | 18 | $18

1006 Race St. (bet. 10th & 11th Sts.), 215-922-3288

Give "praise" unto "seitan" say supporters of this "quiet" Chinatown mainstay churning out "interesting" stuff that makes even carnivores "forget they're not eating meat"; if the goods "don't rise above average" for critics, no one wants to beef about low tabs.

Sitar India
▽ 19 | 9 | 16 | $17

60 S. 38th St. (bet. Chestnut & Market Sts.), 215-662-0818

For a "deal" of a meal, hit this BYO University City Indian buffet specialist, where Pennsters "come to feed" on "tasty" dishes for a few rupees ($6.95 at lunch, $9.95 at dinner); fans want to keep it a "secret" lest this spot starts raising the rates.

Slate Bleu   ▽ 21 18 19 $52

100 S. Main St. (Green St.), Doylestown, 215-348-0222;
www.slatebleu.com
Mark Matyas (of NYC's La Grenouille fame) heads this new, "sophisticated" French bistro that's a "wonderful" addition to Doylestown; the chef's "very good" dishes help offset early reports about kinks in service (it "needs help").

Sly Fox Brewery   11 11 15 $22

519 Kimberton Rd. (bet. Prizer & Steven Stars Rds.),
Phoenixville, 610-935-4540
312 N. Lewis Rd. (Royersford Rd.), Royersford, 610-948-8088
www.slyfoxbeer.com
When you're in the mood to "chill" over "drinks with friends", these "boisterous" twin suburban brewpubs can make for a "decent" stop; low ratings, however, support the view that many are "seduced" by the "good" beers and not by "marginal" food and "dingy" digs.

Smith & Wollensky ●   22 20 21 $59

Rittenhouse Hotel, 210 W. Rittenhouse Sq. (bet. Locust &
Walnut Sts.), 215-545-1700; www.smithandwollensky.com
Credit the "testosterone" of the "power-players" crowd along with the "excellent" beef for the appeal of this "standout" chain steakhouse with "attentive, not smothering" service and a "scenic" view of Rittenhouse Square; if a few find the art of the "upsell" alive and well here (yes, it's "pricey"), most know this carnivorium "can't be beat"; P.S. "if you can't close a deal here, go work for a charity."

Snockey's Oyster & Crab House   17 11 16 $27

1020 S. Second St. (Washington Ave.), 215-339-9578;
www.snockeys.com
"Out of the sea into Snockey's" is on the lips of many an afishionado when talking about the "super-fresh" oysters and clams at this South Philly institution doing business since 1912; its "tried-and-true recipes" without the "fancy sauces" and "old-fashioned" service have helped it remain "unscathed by the big boys."

Society Hill Hotel ●   16 16 18 $27

Society Hill Hotel, 301 Chestnut St. (3rd St.), 215-923-3711;
www.societyhillhotel.com
Decor and menu "got fancied up" at this "quaint" and perhaps "underrated" Traditional American "landmark" serving "solid" bar fare downstairs from a 12-room Old City B&B; plenty of "people-watching" goes on at the outdoor tables, where tourists get to "rub elbows with the locals."

Sola   24 16 22 $41

614 W. Lancaster Ave. (Penn St.), Bryn Mawr, 610-526-0123
Main Liners are moved by this "tiny" BYO "Eden" in Bryn Mawr specializing in "warm" service and "delicious" New

American–Eclectic cookery that manages to be "creative" without being "too precious"; oenophiles on the lookout for "quality" stemware like what they see here; N.B. the Food score may not reflect a post-*Survey* chef change.

Solaris Grille   15 16 15 $30

8201 Germantown Ave. (Hartwell St.), 215-242-3400; www.solarisgrille.com

There's "nothing spectacular" going on at this "popular" New American up on the Hill, but that's just fine with "people-watchers" who like the myriad dining areas (i.e. a bar and "lovely" patio) and "good-natured" staff; the "easy", breezy ambiance balances out the "uninspired" vittles.

SoleFood   21 23 19 $46

Loews Philadelphia Hotel, 1200 Market St. (12th St.), 215-231-7300; www.loewshotels.com

"Good experiences" await acolytes of this "high-priced" Loews venue marketing "innovative" fish dishes to the seafood-savvy; even if it's "not so interesting" for skeptics, there's a lot to like here, especially the "hip", "groovy" digs and "excellent" happy hour.

Sotto Varalli   20 20 19 $41

231 S. Broad St. (Locust St.), 215-546-6800; www.varalliusa.com

Theatergoers back the "friendly" staff's brotherly love at this "modern" Avenue of the Arts seafooder (downstairs from its partner, Upstares at Varalli), where the "good" offerings sate before a trip to the Kimmel Center; the weekend jazz is "great", though the fake "gigantic squid hanging over the bar" may not be everyone's cup of sea.

South St. Souvlaki   21 11 19 $20

509 South St. (bet. 5th & 6th Sts.), 215-925-3026

"Yummy" Greek eats at "easy-on-the-credit-card" prices are the norm at this "unpretentious" ("no decor", that is) South Street taverna; if you "don't have time for a sit-down meal", order from the "take-out counter", chat with the cooks and you'll come away "pleased."

Southwark   24 20 21 $42

701 S. Fourth St. (Bainbridge St.), 215-238-1888

Sheri Waide's takes on New American at this "warm" Queen Villager "put many NYC restaurants to shame", while the ambiance (abetted by a "beautiful" mahogany bar) satisfies as a "fine-dining" destination or a "neighborhood haunt"; it also gets points for "helpful" servers and an "affordable" wine list – in other words, it's "super in every way."

Sovalo ⊠   25 22 23 $43

702 N. Second St. (bet. Brown St. & Fairmount Ave.), 215-413-7770; www.sovalo.com

Northern Liberties bursts with pride over this "chic" and "charming" Napa-meets-Italy "up-and-comer" on the

Second Street strip; it's hard not to "come back" considering the "intensely flavorful" dishes (Italian food has "never been better") under the hand of Joseph Scarpone, and factor in "excellent" service and this "bright spot" is likely to stick around awhile.

Sovana Bistro ▽ 25 18 21 $39
696 Unionville Rd. (Rte. 926), Kennett Square, 610-444-5600;
www.sovanabistro.com
Nicholas Farrell has evolved his western Chester County "pizza" shop into a "sexy" French-Med with Django alum Bryan Sikora helping turn out "consistently excellent" food at relatively "reasonable" prices; it's "hard to get into" (no reservations doesn't make it any easier), and it's BYO with a $5 corkage fee.

Spasso 22 18 23 $38
34 S. Front St. (bet. Chestnut & Market Sts.), 215-592-7661;
www.spassoitaliangrill.com
"A quiet dinner for two or a party for 30" go just as smoothly at this "homey" Italian in Old City serving "exceptional", and "affordable", food; the "great" bar and "charming" service make you feel "comfortable", and as far as presentations go, fish filleted tableside is a "beautiful" thing.

Spence Cafe 21 15 19 $39
29-31 E. Gay St. (bet. High & Walnut Sts.), West Chester,
610-738-8844
"College students and profs" check off the merits of this West Chester New American, one of the "best" in the borough for its "interesting" menu served in "dark", if "cavernlike quarters; that it morphs into a "late-night" bar/club scene (with live bands) is cool with the kids.

Spotted Hog 15 15 16 $26
Peddler's Village, Rte. 263 & Street Rd., Lahaska, 215-794-4040;
www.peddlersvillage.com
"Day-trippers" "take a break from shopping" for "quick" lunches and dinners at this "family-friendly", "touristy" Traditional American in Peddler's Village; but wags squeal it's "hogging a prime location" and cry wee, wee, wee all the way home after experiencing "lackluster" fare and "spotty" service.

Spring Mill Café 22 19 20 $43
164 Barren Hill Rd. (bet. Ridge Pike & River Rd.),
Conshohocken, 610-828-2550; www.springmill.com
How about a "Parisian bit of fresh air by way of Conshy" – that's the story of this "quirky", "rustic" country French BYO tucked "out of the way" on Barren Hill Road; owner Michele Haines' food is "worth the caloric hit", and a "knowledgeable" staff maintains the "relaxing" vibe; though a few debate the setting ("tired" or "charming"), most agree this "tiny" place is still perfect for "lovers."

STANDARD TAP ◐　　　24　17　19　$23

901 N. Second St. (Poplar St.), 215-238-0630;
www.standardtap.com

"Not what you'd expect in a bar" is this "dark" Northern
Liberties taphouse and its "fantastic" American fare that
"raises gastropub dining to a new level"; the "perfect"
hangout also features a "killer" jukebox, "stellar" brews
and quintessentially "friendly" service, so it's not a stretch to
conclude there's nothing standard about this place.

Stefano's　　　20　20　19　$40

2519 Huntingdon Pike (Red Lion Rd.), Huntingdon Valley,
215-914-1224; www.stefanos.us

It "holds a special spot" in the hearts of habitués who fre-
quent this "old-fashioned" Italian Huntingdon Valley BYO, a
"friendly" favorite; while the cooking ranges from "average"
to "good", most at least sense the "romance" in the air.

Stella Blu ⊠　　　19　17　19　$38

101 Ford St. (Front St.), West Conshohocken, 610-825-7060;
www.stellablurestaurant.com

"Adorably" "quaint" quarters complement the "good" Italian
food at this "tucked-away" West Conshy crib popular for
"date nights"; expect "noise", "crowds" and "cramped"
conditions, but for what it is, it seldom disappoints.

STRIPED BASS　　　26　26　24　$72

1500 Walnut St. (15th St.), 215-732-4444;
www.stripedbassrestaurant.com

A "Starr's shining" on this "reincarnated" Center City seafooder, Stephen Starr's "grand" yet "sexy", high-ceilinged
"triumph" where the "extraordinary creativity" of chef
Christopher Lee shows in every one of the "cleverly presented", "intensely flavorful" dishes supported by "crisp"
service; it's no surprise then that the room swarms with a
"contented", "beautiful" crowd that willingly pays "top
dollar" (it *is* in a former bank) for the experience.

Sullivan's Steakhouse　　　23　20　21　$50

King of Prussia Mall, 700 W. DeKalb Pike (Mall Blvd.),
King of Prussia, 610-878-9025; www.sullivansteakhouse.com

It seems like "they spray testosterone on you" when you
enter either one of these high-"energy" steakhouse chain
outposts in KoP and Wilmington; manly-sized portions of
"tender" meat means "you don't leave hungry", and
"knockout" martinis and "bouncy" servers help distract
from prices only a "corporate credit card" could cover.

Summer Kitchen　　　22　16　19　$34

Rte. 232 & Penns Park Rd., Penns Park, 215-598-9210;
www.thesummerkitchen.net

Mario Korenstein's "true Cuban colors" show in the "exciting" Eclectic cooking at this casual 40-seat BYO in "the

sticks" of Central Bucks; the inside offers are "lovely", "light and airy", fans are "charmed" by the outdoor patio and bargain-hunters seek out the $17.50 prix fixes on Wednesdays and Thursdays.

SUSANNA FOO | 25 | 24 | 25 | $59 |

1512 Walnut St. (bet. 15th & 16th Sts.), 215-545-2666; www.susannafoo.com

"Food is art" at Philly's best-known and best-"loved" French-Asian "Foo-sion" spot, the "calm and classy" salon of celeb chef Susanna Foo, who turns "any ingredient into a master-piece" on the plate; the staff specializes in "pampering" (perhaps making it easier to swallow the "exorbitant" prices), and while some "aren't sure what all the hype is about", legions of loyalists say this "gold standard for Chinese food" remains "one of the city's treasures."

Sushikazu | ▽ 23 | 13 | 18 | $32 |

920 DeKalb Pike (Skippack Pike), Blue Bell, 610-272-7767; www.sushikazupa.com

Blue Bellers with a yen for the "best" sushi around have discovered this "nondescript" BYO off Route 202; the se-lection of rolls and cooked food are likely to "interest" afi-cionados, and TVs with scenes of Japan are there for those who care.

Swanky Bubbles ● | 21 | 20 | 19 | $37 |

10 S. Front St. (Market St.), 215-928-1200; www.swankybubbles.com

"Hot people lounge around" this Old City champagne bar, taking in the "tiny, tasty" Pan-Asian nibbles, "wonderful" libations and "hip" setting that makes everyone feel like a "jet-setter"; the "cool" and "casual" servers surely fit in, and despite velvety digs that could be "updated", most bubble over with joy when hanging here.

SWANN LOUNGE ● | 26 | 27 | 27 | $55 |

Four Seasons Hotel, 1 Logan Sq. (Benjamin Franklin Pkwy.), 215-963-1500; www.fourseasons.com

"All the best for a little less" than the Fountain, and "less formal" (but still a picture of "luxury"), this New American–New French at the Four Seasons offers "spectacular" food, whether in the cafe, the "great" bar, or at the "amaz-ing" brunch and buffets or during afternoon tea; P.S. some should go here for a "primer" on service, for "every res-taurant should treat its customers this well."

Sweet Lucy's Smokehouse | 22 | 13 | 16 | $17 |

7500 State Rd. (bet. Bleigh Ave. & Rhawn St.), 215-333-9663; www.sweetlucys.com

This BBQ joint in a "weird" spot near I-95's Cottman exit in the Northeast just might be the "best smokehouse in Philly" according to 'cuestronomes (and even "bidness-men") who talk about "swooningly good" "Carolina"-style ribs, pulled pork and "delish" sides dished out by "fast, friendly" folk; now, "this is what barbecue should be."

TACCONELLI'S PIZZERIA ⊄ | 24 | 9 | 15 | $18 |

2604 E. Somerset St. (bet. Almond & Thompson Sts.), 215-425-4983

"Order your dough in advance" or risk going home with nothing advise aficionados of this "legendary" "no-frills" pizzeria in Port Richmond (and more recently South Jersey); it's "well worth the effort" once you taste the "best thin-crust pizza anywhere" (especially the "white with spinach"), though just be prepared to smell "garlicky."

Taco House ⬛⊄ | 15 | 7 | 14 | $11 |

1218 Pine St. (bet. 12th & 13th Sts.), 215-735-1880

"I've never waited more than five minutes or spent more than $4" is the refrain of college kids who rely on this Center City Mexican hut for its "basic" grub ideal for "bulking up on carbs and cheese before a night of drinking"; know before you go that the digs are as "low budget" as the "serviceable" chow, and you should be just fine.

Tai Lake ⬤ | ▽ 23 | 9 | 16 | $23 |

134 N. 10th St. (bet. Cherry & Race Sts.), 215-922-0698; www.tailakerestaurant.com

"Tanks of frogs and fish" greet you at the door of Sam Leung's "fabulous" Chinatown eatery prized for its "superb", "unbelievably fresh" Chinese seafood; for an affordable, undeniably "authentic" experience, "this is the place to go"; P.S. it's open till 3 AM.

Tamarindo's | 23 | 15 | 21 | $30 |

Homemaker's Shopping Plaza, 36 W. Skippack Pike (Butler Pike), Broad Axe, 215-619-2390

Some of the "finest" Mexican you'll find is on the menu at this "upscale" (it "isn't a rice 'n' bean" joint) Yucatán-style BYO "hidden" in a Central Montco strip mall; just about everyone knows about the "comp margaritas", which "soften the long waits for a table" and help turn the place into a "party" every night.

Tampopo | ▽ 20 | 10 | 16 | $13 |

104 S. 21st St. (bet. Chestnut & Walnut Sts.), 215-557-9593 ⬛
719 Sansom St. (bet. S. 7th & S. 8th Sts.), 215-238-9373

"Delicious", "high-quality" food for "so little cash" is the calling card of these Japanese-Korean BYO twins in Center City and off Washington Square; they're touted for takeout, but their "cheerful" vibes may make you want to "eat there", especially at the newer Sansom Street satellite.

Tandoor India | 19 | 11 | 16 | $17 |

106 S. 40th St. (bet. Chestnut & Walnut Sts.), 215-222-7122

Get past the im-penn-etrable "buffet line" and "try a little of everything" at this Indian BYO "standby" on Penn's campus; the all-you-can-eat ($6.95 at lunch, $9.95 at dinner) deals are the main attractions, and the stuff's "tasty" to boot, so chances are you "won't be disappointed."

TANGERINE   24 | 27 | 22 | $50

232 Market St. (bet. 2nd & 3rd Sts.), 215-627-5116;
www.tangerinerestaurant.com

"Come with me to the Casbah" urge "Starr-y eyed" enthusiasts of this "sexy" Moroccan-inspired Med in Old City, the showcase of Todd Fuller's "bold" family-style dishes delivered in a "sultan's den" of a setting complete with "hundreds of flickering candles"; the "cozy" bar is "fabulous" and the staff "focused" – no wonder this place will "never go out of season."

Tango   19 | 20 | 18 | $39

39 Morris Ave. (Lancaster Ave.), Bryn Mawr, 610-526-9500;
www.tastetango.com

Many Main Liners think this "busy", "convivial" New American at the Bryn Mawr train station stays on track with a "diverse" menu and "comfortable" rustic decor in the main room and a more casual, rail-station motif in the other; as long as you can deal with some "noise", you may find it "better than expected."

Taqueria La Michoacana   ∇ 24 | 14 | 17 | $20

301 E. Main St. (Arch St.), Norristown, 610-292-1971

"Authentic" preparations (i.e. "Mexican food as Mexicans know it") of "well-prepared" fare have helped bring this "little-known" "gem" in Norristown a fair share of acclaim; it's wise to disregard the "questionable locale", since the "friendly" folks here "make every effort to please."

Taqueria La Veracruzana   23 | 4 | 13 | $12

908 Washington Ave. (9th St.), 215-465-1440

Whether you "bring your Spanish phrasebook" or not, you'll still fill up on "fantastic" Mexican "soul food" at this BYO "diamond in the rough" in the Italian Market; the value is "incredible", but bring "Pepcid" for the plentiful portions and a pair of shades to blot out the "blinding" fluorescent lights.

Taqueria Moroleon   ∇ 22 | 8 | 14 | $19

15 New Garden Shopping Ctr. (345 Scarlet Rd., Ste. 15),
Kennett Square, 610-444-1210

Sit with "locals" eating "genuine" Mexican food the "way it should be" at this "bare" BYO storefront in western Chester County; it gets "busy" now that it's "gringo"-approved, and don't forget to "take your favorite six-pack of beer" to deal with the "slowest" service north of the Rio Grande.

Taste   – | – | – | E

161 W. Girard Ave. (Hancock St.), 215-634-1008

Mustard Greens alum Billy Wong and chef Jimmy Ng are turning heads at this sophisticated Eclectic BYO bistro on the northern edge of slacker/hipster-heavy Northern Liberties; the huge, bold John Stango paintings on the ceiling reinforce the notion that things here are on the ambitious side.

Tavern on Green
15 | 14 | 16 | $23

2047 Green St. (21st St.), 215-235-6767
Fairmounters "know spring is here" when this "funky" Eclectic "standby" opens its outdoor seating area; the clientele "kick back" over "pub" vittles that are "friendly to all diets, tastes and budgets" (or at least "reliable") and dig the "Ms. Pac-Man" machine, and while "painfully slow" service is to be expected sometimes, this place has appeal, even for a "low-maintenance date."

Teca ●◐⊠
∇ 23 | 19 | 20 | $30

38 E. Gay St. (Walnut St.), West Chester, 610-738-8244
This "cool" "Euro" wine bar/paninoteca in West Chester seduces with its "exceptionally good" Italian sandwiches and other light fare; while the food is "priced right", the best part of being here may be the sidewalk seating area, where you can enjoy a bottle of vino with other "sophisticates."

Ted's Montana Grill
15 | 17 | 17 | $32

260 S. Broad St. (Spruce St.), 215-772-1230;
www.tedsmontanagrill.com
Ted Turner's "family-oriented" steakhouse chain recently roamed to a Center City location space opposite the Kimmel Center on the Avenue of the Arts; though fans applaud the "chirpy" staff and "Old West"–inspired space, debates ensue over the bison and beef-heavy menu – "good" for some and "needs work" to others; P.S. charitable critics want to give them time to sort out "the kinks."

TEIKOKU
23 | 25 | 19 | $41

5492 West Chester Pike (bet. Delchester & Garrett Mill Rds.),
Newtown Square, 610-644-8270; www.teikokurestaurant.com
There's "Zen" and then some at this "amazingly decorated" Japanese-Thai in Newtown Square complete with a "serene" waterfall and soaring bamboo ceiling; the kitchen's "artistry" (patrons can't stop admiring all "the other plates") is an equal partner to the setting, and regulars advise "sit at the sushi bar and watch the pros in action."

Ten Stone
17 | 15 | 17 | $21

2063 South St. (21st St.), 215-735-9939;
www.tenstone.com
As "solid" as "neighborhood" bars go is this "convivial" Center Cityite near the Graduate Hospital purveying a "wide selection" of "fabulous" brews on tap; no, the American food's "not spectacular", but it's "good" and certainly "worth the price", and the setting here is flexible enough for a "casual date" or night out with friends.

Tenth St. Pour House ⌷　　　▽ 21 | 13 | 16 | $13
262 S. 10th St. (Spruce St.), 215-922-5626
The "first-rate" breakfasts and lunches at this "homey" no-dinner Traditional American in Center City are "better than Aspirin" after a "long night"; it's an "inexpensive" standby for many (especially folks from the nearby Jefferson Hospital), so note that even before you "squeeze yourself in" you may have to "wait in the doorway" if you don't go early.

Teresa's Cafe of Wayne　　　22 | 13 | 19 | $29
124 N. Wayne Ave. (Lancaster Ave.), Wayne, 610-293-9909
Some nights, it seems all of Wayne ends up at this "contemporary" Italian BYO where the decibel levels run so high you can't "hear your dinner companion compliment the food"; "crowds" and "no reservations" exacerbate the "wait", and everyone knows "eavesdroppers" appreciate tables thisclose together.

Tex Mex Connection　　　19 | 16 | 20 | $27
201 E. Walnut St. (Sumneytown Pike), North Wales,
215-699-9552; www.texmexconnection.com
"Strong margaritas" (and "so many flavors" of them) connect the dots as to the appeal of this "lively" Central Montco Tex-Mex eatery-cum-"barroom"; some seem to even forget there's food here, but when mentioned, opinions range from "good" to "so-so."

Thai Orchid　　　23 | 18 | 22 | $26
Blue Bell Shopping Ctr., 1748 DeKalb Pike (Township Line Rd.),
Blue Bell, 610-277-9376
These Thai BYOs may now be separately owned, but the line is that "anything on the menu" is still "amazingly good"; word is the "friendly" (and "beautiful") waitresses are as "fascinating" to behold as the decor, and the $7.95 three-course lunch is a "nice" touch.

Thai Pepper　　　16 | 15 | 18 | $27
64 E. Lancaster Ave. (Argyle Rd.), Ardmore,
610-642-5951
Thai standards at "affordable" prices have helped keep this storefront (next to its relative, Mikado) in favor with fans; the critics who sum up the dishes as "unimpressive" and "Americanized" are outvoted by those who conclude the food "solid" and at times "consistently good."

Thai Singha House　　　20 | 13 | 18 | $23
3939 Chestnut St. (39th St.), 215-382-8001
A "student's budget" won't bust at this University City Thai, a Pennsters "favorite" that doles out "generous" servings of "basic" yet "good" foodstuffs from a "long" menu; the "gracious", "customer-friendly" staff helps to offset the "boring" decor.

Thomas'
| 20 | 17 | 19 | $33 |

4201 Main St. (Pensdale St.), 215-483-9075;
www.thomasrestaurant.com

There are few doubting Thomases in the 'Yunk when the subject is this "pleasant surprise" on Main Street, a sound choice whether you're tucking into "good" vittles downstairs at the marble-topped bar or "creative" New American–meets–New French cuisine in the "romantic" room "upstairs"; the "laid-back" vibe makes watching "people stroll by" even more relaxing.

333 Belrose ⊠
| 22 | 19 | 20 | $42 |

333 Belrose Ln. (King of Prussia Rd.), Radnor, 610-293-1000;
www.333belrose.com

"Main Line insiders" and "beautiful people" gather with friends at this "popular" New American "tucked away" in a "funky country house"; "quiet" types and "ladies who lunch" like the "lovely" patio, while "after-work" crowds count on "sophisticated" food ("eclectic" tapas), "martinis" and a "divorcée bazaar" scene at the "noisy" bar.

Tierra Colombiana
| 23 | 15 | 19 | $24 |

4535-39 N. Fifth St. (3 blocks south of Roosevelt Blvd.),
215-324-6086

Though "not in the nicest part" of the upper reaches of North Philly, this Cuban-Colombian mix off Roosevelt Boulevard dishes out "plenty" of "amazing", "hearty" food that's "as vibrant as the patrons"; prices are "*muy bueno*", and a "helpful" staff makes sitting in the "well-appointed" room feel "like home."

Tír na nÓg
| 16 | 17 | 17 | $26 |

1600 Arch St. (N. 16th St.), 267-514-1700;
www.tirnanogphilly.com

"Yuppies" and expats swarm this "party" parlor of a pub opposite City Hall for "standard" if "good", "dressed-up" Irish fare, "excellent" ales and a scene so "packed with eligibles" you can "barely lift your elbow to drink your Guinness"; "friendy" barkeeps and "beautiful" people help keep the liveliness going, and note that weekend nights seem like "frat" boy central.

Tony Luke's Old Philly Style Sandwiches ● ⊠ ⇗
| 24 | 6 | 13 | $11 |

39 E. Oregon Ave. (Front St.), 215-551-5725;
www.tonylukes.com

"The very soul of the city" is in the "unbelievable" cheese steaks and the "trademark" "pork wit' sharp" provolone and broccoli rabe at this "classic" stand off I-95, the stop of "real Philadelphians" who line up after "leaving PHL" or on the way to the stadiums; it's "what South Philly is all about", which easily explains why "you'd sit at a picnic table" amid "no decor."

TOTARO'S Ⓢ | 26 | 13 | 22 | $49 |
729 E. Hector St. (bet. Righter & Walnut Sts.),
Conshohocken, 610-828-9341; www.totaros.com
"Who woulda thunk" something so "plain" on the outside
could produce such "great" food? is the first question
you'll ask yourself after a meal at this "intimate" Conshy
Italian-influenced Eclectic, where "wild game of all sorts"
pops up on the "adventurous" menu; insiders know to
"head for the happy hour" at the bar, but also advise "don't
let the decor fool you – this place isn't cheap."

Trattoria Alberto Ⓢ | ▽ 23 | 20 | 21 | $36 |
116 E. Gay St. (bet. High & Matlack Sts.), West Chester,
610-430-0203; www.trattorialberto.com
Whether you seek the "intimacy of the wine cellar" or dine
with the "bartender", this "comfortable", polished (e.g.
fish filleted tableside) trattoria in college-town West
Chester offers "very good" Italian dishes and "accommodating" service; tip: ask for the "special wine list" com-
prised of Super Tuscans from the owner's winery in Italy.

Trattoria Lucca | ▽ 21 | 16 | 19 | $35 |
1915 E. Passyunk Ave. (bet. McKean & Mifflin Sts.),
215-336-1900; www.trattorialucca.com
If you want to "feel right at home", try Salvatore DiPalma's
"charming" South Philly BYO on Passyunk Avenue's Restaurant Row; though service can be "slow", the "solidly"
good cooking is there to ensure return visits.

Trattoria Primadonna | 19 | 14 | 19 | $37 |
1506 Spruce St. (15th St.), 215-790-0171
Kimmel-goers in search of "good", "straightforward"
Roman-influenced Italian food at a "reasonable" price
would do well to search out this Center City trattoria
whose "gregarious" staff guarantees a "warm reception";
N.B. though they serve wine, feel free to BYO.

Trattoria San Nicola | 22 | 18 | 20 | $36 |
668 Lancaster Ave. (Main Ave.), Berwyn,
610-296-3141 Ⓢ
4 Manor Rd. (W. Lancaster Ave.), Paoli, 610-695-8990;
www.tsannicola.com
The "super value" is part of the lure of these "dependable"
Italians in Berwyn (the original) and Paoli (the roomier
spin-off); the "good" cooking appeals to Main Liners too,
though "crowded", "bustling" digs translate into
"high noise levels."

Trax Café Ⓢ | 21 | 15 | 19 | $37 |
Ambler SEPTA Station, 27 W. Butler Pike (Morris Rd.),
Ambler, 215-591-9777; www.traxcafe.com
This "quaint" "whistle stop" BYO in the old Ambler SEPTA
station offers a "romantic" setting with a side of "train

spotting" and "tasty" Traditional American cooking that's a "nice change of pace from cookie-cutter" chains; even "cold blasts of air" from outside and "tight quarters" ("you better like the people near you") don't derail the experience here.

Tre Scalini
24 | 13 | 20 | $39

1533 S. 11th St. (Tasker St.), 215-551-3870
The name means "three steps", and happy surveyors view this "*tre magnifico*" Italian BYO storefront as many scalini above "typical" South Philly joints; "heavenly" cooking and "homey" airs make it feel like you've "joined the family" for an "amazing meal" at your "grandma's house"; one slight drawback: "parking" can be tough.

Tria ◗
22 | 19 | 21 | $27

123 S. 18th St. (Sansom St.), 215-972-8742;
www.triacafe.com
Foodies and oenophiles "decompress" at this Eclectic, "upscale" Center City wine bar where "knowledgeable" staffers guide fans through a slate of "delicious" light bites and "interesting" wines, cheeses and brews; lauded as a "great addition to the restaurant scene", it's as "tiny" (and "cute") as its name, so expect the place to feel "crowded" sometimes.

Trinacria ⊠
∇ 22 | 19 | 23 | $48

1016 DeKalb Pike (Sumneytown Pike), Center Square,
610-275-0505; www.trinacria-pa.com
This "first-class", white-tablecloth Italian "find" in Center Square ably satisfies on account of its "savory" Sicilian specialties, 400-label wine list and tableside flourishes – i.e. fish filleted right next to you; the "pricey" tabs are offset by an "eager-to-please", "accommodating" corps.

Triumph Brewing Co. ◗
19 | 20 | 19 | $30

400 Union Sq. (Main St.), New Hope, 215-862-8300;
www.triumphbrewing.com
Though the American food is "more interesting than you'd expect", the beer is the "belle of the ball" at this "cavernous" double-decker of a microbrewery in New Hope, an offshoot of the Princeton original; "karaoke" nights are "embarrassingly entertaining", though the "good" live bands help redeem things.

Trolley Car Diner
12 | 14 | 14 | $15

7619 Germantown Ave. (Cresheim Valley Dr.), 215-753-1500;
www.trolleycardiner.com
"Friends and family" meet up at this Mount Airy American diner operating in a "neat" stainless-steel edifice; overall, it "fills a niche" in the neighborhood, and while regulars find it "best for breakfast", the food sparks much debate between fans ("good") and foes ("disappointing"); P.S. "go for the ice cream" in the original trolley car next door.

Twenty Manning   21   22   19 $43
261 S. 20th St. (bet. Locust & Spruce Sts.), 215-731-0900;
www.twentymanning.com
Audrey Claire's "snazzy" relative near Rittenhouse Square
is as "trendy" as ever; you'll still find Kiong Banh's "artfully
prepared" Asian-inflected New American cuisine, "exciting" drinks in the lounge and "plenty of window coverage
for the outdoor parade"; in all, it's easy to "impress a date"
here even if the bill is more accessible for "BMW" owners.

Twenty21 ⌧   20   20   20 $43
2005 Market St. (bet. 20th & 21st Sts.), 215-851-6262;
www.twenty-21.com
Money men and women feel "welcome" at this Commerce
Square New American catering to the "business-lunch"
crowd; adherents insist it "deserves more recognition" for
its "upscale comfort food", "gracious" staff and "dramatic"
floor-to-ceiling bar – but it may be best experienced "if you
have an expense account or are dating a fellow attorney."

Twin Bays Café ⌧   22   20   23 $42
19 S. Whitehorse Rd. (Rte. 23), Phoenixville, 610-415-1300;
www.twinbayscafe.com
"Warm" servers, "lovely" owners and "good" Eclectic
food work their charms on those who've dropped by this
"Victorian" Phoenixville BYO in what was once a point on
the Underground Railroad; while the tabs are "on the expensive side", "cocktails on the deck" help compensate.

211 York ⌧   21   17   20 $43
211 Old York Rd. (bet. Greenwood & Summit Aves.),
Jenkintown, 215-517-5117; www.211york.com
Timothy Papa's "appealing" Jenkintown New American
bistro serves "reliably good", "upscale"-for-the-'hood
fare (i.e. "Center City" aspirations) in a location that's
"easy to miss"; if some want to call 911 over "barren" decor, "consistent" service wins hearts.

UMBRIA ⌧⇥   25   16   22 $39
7131 Germantown Ave. (bet. Mt. Airy & Mt. Pleasant Aves.),
215-242-6470
This "super-small" gold-and-purple "storefront" BYO in "up-
and-coming" Mount Airy is worth the time spent "looking
for a parking space" on Germantown Avenue in light of the
"delicious" Eclectic dishes off an "interesting" menu
backed by "attentive" servers; it's only open Wednesdays–
Saturdays for dinner, and few take umbrage with the cash-
only policy since this place is so "very good."

Upstares at Varalli   20   19   20 $41
1345 Locust St. (Broad St.), 215-546-4200; www.varalliusa.com
The "beautiful view" of the Broad Street "action" and
proximity to theaters are the forces pulling patrons to this

"cosmopolitan" Italian, the upstairs partner of Sotto Varalli; those who return count on the "enjoyable" meals and staff adept at "keeping everything moving" to accommodate curtain time.

U.S. Hotel Bar & Grill   ∇ 17 | 17 | 16 | $28

4439 Main St. (Green Ln.), 215-483-9222
Manayunk's "neighborhood" meet and greetery (aka "old reliable") serves up New American bar bites and just about the "best" mac 'n' cheese around in a "friendly" tavern ambiance suited for "drinks" with chums; P.S. word is that new management is "trying to sort out" service snafus.

Valanni ◗   23 | 20 | 21 | $40

1229 Spruce St. (bet. 12th & 13th Sts.), 215-790-9494;
www.valanni.com
"The suburbanites haven't found out" about this "hip", "buzzy" Wash West Mediterranean boîte and its "excellent" food (and "tasty" tapas-size options) complemented by "courteous" service and "great" barkeeps; the space is "chic" – and "small" – so plan on getting "intimate" with whoever's near you.

Vesuvio ◗   ∇ 17 | 16 | 17 | $34

736-38 S. Eighth St. (Fitzwater St.), 215-922-8380;
www.vesuvio-online.com
A "warm" mood pervades this rustic South Philly Italian enjoyed for its "excellent" bar and staff that "tries hard"; but while some say the food exhibits "good, straightforward" cooking, others judge it "pretty standard" and add the place seems in the midst of an "identity crisis" (is it a "fine dining" spot or a "pool hall"?).

VETRI ⊠   28 | 22 | 27 | $78

1312 Spruce St. (bet. Broad & 13th Sts.), 215-732-3478;
www.vetriristorante.com
"I thought I'd died and gone to Italy" is a common refrain when speaking of "genius" chef Marc Vetri's "rustic" 35-seat Italian in a Center City brownstone; "become the guest who doesn't want to leave" after you sample "wondrous" fare that's the "essence of pleasure" served without "pomp" by the "expert" staff; you'll need to use "speed-dial" on your phone to land a reservation, and sure, it's "costly", but then again, it's a "great use for a home equity loan" since it may be the "best restaurant of its kind in America."

Vickers Tavern ⊠   21 | 22 | 20 | $47

192 E. Welsh Pool Rd. (Gordon Dr.), Exton, 610-363-7998;
www.vickerstavern.com
Some "expect Paul Revere to show up" for dinner at this "romantic" American-Continental housed in an early-18th-century Exton farmhouse; some who report the place is "not the same" (i.e. "inconsistent" food) may take heart in the relatively recent chef change.

Victor Café   18 20 22 $41
1303-05 Dickinson St. (bet. Broad & 13th Sts.), 215-468-3040;
www.victorcafe.com
Those in search of "culture" without time for "a full
evening at the opera" take a seat in this "vintage" South
Philly Italian that's a "classic" in all arias – "singing staff"
and "honest" food in portions as "huge as the voices";
even those who think it a "shtick"-y business say the waiters are "amazing" talents.

Victory Brewing Co. ●   15 10 16 $21
420 Acorn Ln. (Chestnut St.), Downingtown, 610-873-0881;
www.victorybeer.com
"Great beer, really great beer" is sometimes just what you
need, and this "loud" brewpub in Downingtown fits the bill;
expect a "good time and good value", but don't look for
ambiance (is it a "bowling alley"?), and note the food,
though "decent", is "just a side show."

Vientiane Café ⌧⊘   23 16 21 $19
4728 Baltimore Ave. (bet. 47th & 48th Sts.), 215-726-1095
Do what the "locals" do and join "vegetarian anarchists",
"Penn students and their families", and "businesspeople"
at this "tiny" storefront BYO in West Philly for "glorious",
"cheap" Laotian/Thai eats; "don't let appearances fool
you" – the food and "lovely" servers justify a trip here.

VIETNAM   24 20 20 $23
221 N. 11th St. (bet. Race & Vine Sts.), 215-592-1163;
www.eatatvietnam.com
Representing the east side of the cross-street Chinatown
Vietnamese rivalry (think "Army-Navy") is Benny Lai's
"contemporary" eatery known for "unbelievably" good
fare and a scene of weekend fans sipping cocktails at the
"sexy" third-floor lounge; whether for "romantic" dining or
a "casual affair with friends", "it feels like robbery" considering the "extremely low prices" you're paying.

Vietnam Palace   23 17 19 $21
222 N. 11th St. (bet. Race & Vine Sts.), 215-592-9596
It may have a "rival across the street", but Nhon T.
Nguyen's Chinatown Vietnamese more than holds its own
with "quick" service, "delicious" fare off a "diner"-length
menu and "comfortable" quarters; overall, "you can't
complain" – especially when you see the "cheap" check.

Viggiano's   18 18 19 $30
16 E. First Ave. (Fayette St.), Conshohocken, 610-825-3151
"Share a meal" with "family" at this "friendly" "red-
sauce" Conshy feedery comforting clients with "large"
portions of "down-to-earth" fare amid a setting complete
with booths fashioned from carriages; still, "ho-hum" food
and "variable" service upends the experience for some.

Villa di Roma ⌐̸　　　21　10　17　$27

Italian Mkt., 932-36 S. Ninth St. (bet. Christian St. & Washington Ave.), 215-592-1295

The Italian Market's "old", "homey" reliable keeps on churning out "really good" Italiana that's "nonna"-certified; as the "red gravy" adorns the "baseball-size meatballs", "lifers" for waitresses "treat you like family", and though it's cash only, "it's a deal you can't refuse", especially when this spot is as "real as South Philly gets", hon'.

Vincent's ⊠　　　▽　18　16　20　$34

10 E. Gay St. (bet. High & Walnut Sts.), West Chester, 610-696-4262; www.vincentsjazz.com

"Great" jazz and blues steal the show at this West Chester Continental, a "rare find" for the neighborhood that also features a "hot" bar; also playing, albeit on second stage, are the Continental vittles that draw a mixed reaction and lie somewhere between "mediocre" and "good."

Vinny T's of Boston　　　14　14　15　$26

Wynnewood Square Shopping Ctr., 260 E. Lancaster Ave. (bet. Chatham & Old Wynnewood Rds.), Wynnewood, 610-645-5400; www.vinnytsofboston.com

Bring a "doggy bag" for the "lotsa pasta" at this "roomy" Wynnewood Italian chainlet, where the over-*abbondanza* of food is complemented by din akin to a "school lunch room"; the "pleasant" servers are "efficient", which helps keeps the "basic" fare (it "isn't going to win any awards") flowing.

Vintage ◑⊠　　　–　–　–　M

129 S. 13th St. (bet. Chestnut & Walnut Sts.), 215-922-3095

Center City oenophiles have reason to cheer since the arrival of this rustic, slender French bistro/wine bar whose menu (studded with classics such as escargots and steak frites) and 60-by-the-glass offerings are easy to appreciate; welcoming design touches include windows that open out to the street, and a zinc bar topped by a chandelier fashioned from wine bottles.

Warsaw Cafe　　　18　15　19　$34

306 S. 16th St. (Spruce St.), 215-546-0204

Get in touch with your inner "Slav" at this "cheery" Center City mainstay proffering "authentic" Eastern European (read: pierogi and borscht) that both "sticks to your ribs" and is sold at "reasonable" tabs; while some think it "time for a menu change" most maintain the food's "done right."

Washington Crossing Inn　　　19　21　20　$41

Rtes. 32 & 532, Washington Crossing, 215-493-3634; www.washingtoncrossinginn.com

"Understandably touristy" (it's near the site of the legendary boat ride) is this Traditional American situated in a "historical" Washington Crossing inn, where the "charm" is "Colonial", the quarters "comfortable" and the setting "perfect"; foodwise, the food is "consistently good" – so, all told, "generally reliable" sums up the situation here.

Washington Square   20 | 24 | 18 | $50 |
210 W. Washington Sq. (bet. Locust & St. James Sts.),
215-592-7787; www.washingtonsquare-restaurant.com
"Look at all the pretty people" who populate this "ultra-chic" Washington Square New American, part of the Stephen Starr constellation: the "fabulous" Todd Oldham–designed garden is officially "the best setting in town for a drink", while the "interesting" cooking from the kitchen (now under the direction of Christopher Lee) "impress" most of the time but comes with "quite a price tag"; P.S. sightseers get to check out the "Jags and Porsches that clog the street."

WHITE DOG CAFE   22 | 20 | 19 | $36 |
3420 Sansom St. (bet. 34th & 36th Sts.), 215-386-9224;
www.whitedog.com
Judy Wicks' "kitschy" Eclectic "landmark" in a series of University City brownstones is a "favorite with Penn students and their parents" for "reliably good" food (made from primarily locally grown and organic ingredients) that's "good for the body and soul" and for a "great" bar offering a "reasonably" priced menu; overall, you'll "do your part for the environment", even if the "hippie politics" gives some conservatives paws.

White Elephant   21 | 20 | 20 | $30 |
759 Huntingdon Pike (bet. Berkley & San Diego Aves.),
Huntingdon Valley, 215-663-1495
It's hard to ignore the elephants in the room (i.e. the motif) of this "winning" pachyderm-themed Thai BYO in Huntingdon Valley that's a "good second bet" to going to Thailand; count on being "greeted warmly" before sitting down to "delicious" dishes in a place "you'd never expect."

William Penn Inn   23 | 23 | 23 | $43 |
William Penn Inn, 1017 DeKalb Pike (Sumneytown Pike),
Gwynedd, 215-699-9272; www.williampenninn.com
"Make all the old-folks jokes you want", but for "memorable" "special-occasion" repasts "in the lap of luxury" (or just for the $19.95 early-bird specials), Central Montco looks to this circa-1714 American-Continental sporting three "civilized" dining areas; sure, the kitchen "isn't striving for gourmet" – just "classic" fare that it has "down pat" backed by "quality" service – is it any surprise it's "popular"?

Winberie's   15 | 14 | 14 | $28 |
1164 Valley Forge Rd. (bet. Anthony Wayne Dr. & Walker Rd.),
Wayne, 610-293-9333; www.selectrestaurants.com
Though "nothing to write home about", this Wayne mainstay on the edge of Valley Forge National Park does "an

"admirable job" turning out American vittles that pleasantly "surprise" some; for its genre, it may even be a "cut above Fridays, Chili's and the like."

Winnie's Le Bus | 20 | 17 | 18 | $23 |

4266 Main St. (bet. Green & Shurs Lns.), 215-487-2663;
www.lebusmanayunk.com
Manayunk fans "could live on the ["fabulous"] bread alone" at this "lively" "vegetarian" and "kid"-friendly "treasure" offering "excellent" New American fare, namely "great" baked goods and sandwiches, along with "savory" breakfasts and brunches; most maintain this is the kind of "comfort food you could eat" all the time.

Wooden Iron ⌀ | 20 | 19 | 19 | $37 |

118 N. Wayne Ave. (Lancaster Ave.), Wayne,
610-964-7888
"Country club" dining comes "without the membership" fees at this golf-themed, mahogany-embellished Traditional American in Downtown Wayne; once you get past the "enormous bar crowd" studded with "divorcées", you'll sit down to "reliably good" dishes served by "courteous" staffers, while a few duffers try to dismiss the "costly" tabs.

World Café Live | 15 | 19 | 16 | $25 |

3025 Walnut St. (bet. 30th & 31st Sts.), 215-222-1400;
www.worldcafelive.com
This "hip" split-level University City performance venue is the home of Penn's WXPN station and the showcase for "terrific" live acts backed by an "unbelievable sound system"; while some say it's suitable for a "sit-down" meal, the consensus is that the music here far outshines the otherwise "decent" American eats.

YANGMING | 24 | 20 | 22 | $38 |

1051 Conestoga Rd. (Haverford Rd.), Bryn Mawr,
610-527-3200
"Quality never wavers" at Michael Wei's "beautiful" Bryn Mawr Mandarin-Continental where picky Main Liners put aside any "preconceptions about Chinese food" at the first bite of the "heavenly" offerings served by an "attentive" staff that fulfills "whatever request you have with pleasure", even when it's "bustling"; P.S. flip-flop fans should note that this is a "dress-up" affair.

Yardley Inn | 21 | 21 | 22 | $41 |

82 E. Afton Ave. (Delaware Ave.), Yardley, 215-493-3800;
www.yardleyinn.com
This "durable" New American inn place in Bucks is even "better than it used to be" thanks to "well-executed" food abetted by a "lively" bar and "scenic" setting by the Delaware and "friendly" service; it may be the "only game in town" for some, "but it's a good game."

Zakes Cafe   25 | 12 | 20 | $26
444 S. Bethlehem Pike (Lafayette Ave.), Fort Washington,
215-654-7600; www.zakescafe.com
"Don't let the exterior fool you" – this New American BYO
"find" in Fort Washington is the "lifeblood of Montco
moms" on account of its "excellent" breakfasts, lunches
and dinners, and "deliciously decadent" desserts; the
"small" space is always "jam-packed", and what's more,
the "secret" is out, so expect to sit "elbow to elbow" in a
scene akin to a "gossip-filled teahouse."

Zanzibar Blue ●   20 | 21 | 19 | $45
The Bellevue, 200 S. Broad St. (Walnut St.), 215-732-4500;
www.zanzibarblue.com
The Bynum brothers' "fun 'n' funky" Eclectic downstairs in
The Bellevue gives you "exactly what you want from a
great jazz club/restaurant" – "reliable" food, a "friendly"
floor crew, "charming" vibe and "first-rate" music; not to
be overlooked is the "wonderful" Sunday brunch, but then
again, cool cats already know that.

Zesty's   20 | 16 | 19 | $33
4382 Main St. (Levering St.), 215-483-6226; www.zestys.com
"Fresh" fish that's "simply prepared" is to be savored at
this "homey" Greco-Roman outfit on Main Street; while
testy types find it a bit "expensive for what you get", popular opinion swims in a favorable direction (it's a "nice
change from the fussy Manayunk scene").

Zocalo ☒   21 | 17 | 18 | $32
3600 Lancaster Ave. (36th St.), 215-895-0139;
www.zocalophilly.com
"If you love Taco Bell" you won't think much of this "upscale" University City Mex "favorite" that puts a "satisfying twist" on south-of-the-border *comida* and offers
"sunny rooms" and a "great" patio in which to enjoy it;
keep in mind that "gourmet Mexican is not an oxymoron",
and if it seems "pricey", it's possibly because you "can
never stop at one margarita."

Lancaster/ Berks Counties

F	D	S	C

Bird-in-Hand Family Restaurant ⊠ 20 | 15 | 20 | $21
2760 Old Philadelphia Pike (Ronks Rd.), Bird-in-Hand, 717-768-8266; www.bird-in-hand.com/restaurant
It's best to have this "friendly" if "kitschy" Pennsylvania Dutchery in Lancaster County on hand for moments when you need "good, plain" chow and a $13.99 dinner buffet that's "ideal for kids and big families"; it's a must "when you're done shopping" – as many can attest ("it's touristy").

Carr's ∇ 24 | 23 | 23 | $45
50 W. Grant St. (Market St.), Lancaster, 717-299-7090
Tim Carr's "relaxed" New American in the heart of Lancaster's theater district proves you "don't have to go to a major metro area" for "outstanding" food in "upscale" environs; "sophistication" and "good" service are part of its winning profile.

EL SERRANO 21 | 25 | 19 | $25
2151 Columbia Ave. (off Rte. 741 S.), Lancaster, 717-397-6191; www.elserrano.com
Pennsylvania "Dutchmen say *olé!*" and "take a break from their schnitz und knepp" recipes at this Latin-Peruvian that transports fans to a "South America villa" via food with mucho "flair" and "old-world" decor; on weekends, live jazz and rock means the place gets "jammed."

GIBRALTAR 28 | 24 | 23 | $39
931 Harrisburg Pike (Race Ave.), Lancaster, 717-397-2790; www.dhollidays.com
Transport yourself "from Lancaster to the Mediterranean" via this "fabulous", rock-solid seafooder, whose airy,

"contemporary" look featuring an open kitchen pairs nicely with "outstanding" fish dishes (washed down with wines from their 300-label list); in short, it's come a long way from its days as a "cafeteria for Franklin & Marshall College."

Good 'N Plenty ⊠   17 | 13 | 17 | $22
150 Eastbrook Rd. (1 mi. north of Rte. 30), Smoketown, 717-394-7111; www.goodnplenty.com

"Strap on a feedbag" before "bellying up" for a meal with "strangers" at this "classic" all-you-can-eat Smoketown Dutchery where it's wise to ignore the "dining-hall decor" before settling into "massive amounts" of chow; who knew that supping with "tourists" could be so "good"?

GRACIE'S 21ST CENTURY CAFE ⊠   27 | 26 | 24 | $50
1534 Manatawny Rd. (King St.), Pine Forge, 610-323-4004; www.gracies21stcentury.com

"If you can find" this "hip" yet "homey" yet "upscale" Eclectic in Berks, you'll be treated to "creative" "gastronomy", playfully described fare ('consciously caught' striped bass) and decor evocative of the American Southwest; N.B. dinner only, Wednesdays–Saturdays.

GREEN HILLS INN ⊠   24 | 24 | 26 | $57
2444 Morgantown Rd. (9 mi. north of Pennsylvania Tpke., exit 22), Reading, 610-777-9611

There's "quality in the hinterlands" aver admirers of this "friendly" Traditional American near Reading, and fans are divided over whether to indulge in the "classic splendor" of the dining room or in the room overlooking the garden; either way, for "nicely done" standards and a "good" wine list, it's a "bargain by Philadelphia standards."

HAYDN ZUG'S ⊠   24 | 24 | 25 | $43
1987 State St. (Rte. 72), East Petersburg, 717-569-5746; www.haydnzugs.com

So "cozy", you may think you're "at grandma's" is the word on this "Colonial-style" Traditional American haydn in East Petersburg; a "genuinely pleasant" staff ferries "consistently good" dishes to fans who say the fare's on par with some "Downtown Philly" places; the "nice" wine list confirms its rep as a "quietly impressive" operation.

Isaac's Restaurant & Deli   17 | 12 | 16 | $13
Cloister Shopping Ctr., 120 N. Reading Rd. (Martin Ave.), Ephrata, 717-733-7777
Granite Run Sq., 1559 Manheim Pike (Rte. 283), Lancaster, 717-560-7774
25 N. Queen St. (Orange St.), Lancaster, 717-394-5544
Sycamore Ct., 245 Centerville Rd. (Rte. 30), Lancaster, 717-393-1199
The Shoppes at Greenfield, 565 Greenfield Rd. (Rte. 30), Lancaster, 717-393-6067

(continued)

(continued)
Isaac's Restaurant & Deli
4 Trolley Run Rd. (Broad St.), Lititz, 717-625-1181
Shops at Traintown, Rtes. 741 E. & 896, Strasburg, 717-687-7699
Village Sq., 94 Commerce Dr. (bet. Broadcasting &
State Hill Rds.), Wyomissing, 610-376-1717
www.isaacsdeli.com
See review in the Philadelphia Directory.

Lemon Grass Thai
21 16 18 $24
2481 Lincoln Hwy. E. (Eastbrook Rd.), Lancaster, 717-295-1621;
www.thailemongrass.com
See review in the Philadelphia Directory.

Lily's on Main
23 22 24 $36
Brossman Business Complex, 124 E. Main St. (Lake St.),
Ephrata, 717-738-2711; www.lilysonmain.com
It's in the heart of "buggyland", but the "classy", "timeless" ambiance at this "art deco" New American in "quaint" Ephrata makes one think "Philly or New York"; "wonderful", "big-city" cuisine and "leisurely" rural pace mean the "little-town blues just melt away" when you're here.

Log Cabin
20 24 23 $47
11 Lehoy Forest Dr. (Rte. 272), Lancaster, 717-626-1181;
www.logcabinrestaurant.com
"Big eaters" who take the "long, winding drive" up to this 70-plus-year-old, sturdy-as-cedar Traditional American steakhouse in Lancaster get some "quality" red meat with some "high-style" rusticity and "original" works of art in the dining rooms; overall, it's an easy choice "if you can find the place."

Miller's Smorgasbord
17 13 17 $24
2811 Lincoln Hwy. E. (1 mi. east of Rte. 896), Ronks,
717-687-6621; www.millerssmorgasbord.com
"What stretch pants were made for", this Pennsylvania Dutch all-you-can-eat in Lancaster County dishes up "traditional" comfort food capped by "delectable" shoofly pies; it "packs 'em in" quickly, so if you're hungry, you'll have to start lining up early with all the "tourists."

Plain & Fancy Farm
∇ 15 9 14 $20
3121 Old Philadelphia Pike (1 mi. east of Ronks Rd.), Bird-in-Hand,
717-768-4400; www.millerssmorgasbord.com
"Forget intimacy" and dine communally at this 747-size Pennsylvania Dutchery that insiders call "one of the better tour-bus stops" around; "load up" on Amish cookery with the all-you-can-eat meals while you marvel at "more food hurled at you at one time than you can eat."

Qdoba Mexican Grill
16 8 11 $11
Park City, 142 Park City Ctr. (off Rte. 283), Lancaster,
717-299-4766; www.qdoba.com
See review in the Philadelphia Directory.

RESTAURANT AT DONECKERS ⊠ | 25 | 24 | 24 | $51 |

The Doneckers Community, 333 N. State St. (Walnut St.), Ephrata, 717-738-9501; www.doneckers.com

"Center City" slickers searching for "fine dining" in Lancaster County find it in this New French in Ephrata's Donecker Community; Le Bec-Fin grad Greg Gable's "gourmet" food "exceeds expectations", while wife Heidi (the sommelier) "knowledgeably" oversees an "outstanding" wine list; it's pricey, but this "surprise" in the woods is "worth every penny."

Stoudt's Black Angus | 19 | 17 | 20 | $39 |

Rte. 272 & Stoudtburg Rd. (Pennsylvania Tpke., exit 21/286), Adamstown, 717-484-4386; www.stoudtsbeer.com

In "antique" country dwells this Adamstown eatery offering "hearty" German-influenced Traditional American food (and raw bar items), along with "great" microbrews and "good fun"; P.S. "whoever said man can't live on bread alone has never had Ed Stoudt's homemade loaves."

Strawberry Hill | 24 | 21 | 21 | $51 |

128 W. Strawberry St. (bet. Mulberry & Vine Sts.), Lancaster, 717-393-5544; www.strawberryhillrestaurant.com

"Romantic evenings" ("get a table by the fireplace") come easy at this "quaint" and "cozy" Lancaster New American featuring "one of the best wine selections in the state" with "delicious" dishes to match; the "charming" owner and staff infuse the place with even more "warmth."

New Jersey Suburbs

Top Food		Top Service	
26	Sagami	**23**	Giumarello's
	Ritz Seafood		Food for Thought
	Laceno Italian		Siri's Thai French
25	Giumarello's		Rat's
	Mélange Cafe		Catelli

Top Decor		Best Buys	
27	Rat's		Nifty Fifty's
24	Food for Thought		Pop Shop
23	Nunzio		Kibitz Room
	Giumarello's		Tacconelli's Pizzeria
	Catelli		Norma's

	F	D	S	C

Alisa Cafe
22 | 18 | 22 | $39

Barclay Farms Shopping Ctr., 112 Rte. 70 E. (Kings Hwy.), Cherry Hill, 856-354-8807; www.alisacafe.com

Tony Kanjanakorn's Thai-French BYO "still has the touch" even after a move "across the river" from Delco to "strip-mall-chic" digs in Cherry Hill; the "polished food matches the polished wood surfaces" and arrives via "eager-to-please" servers, and even those who quibble about the "expense" admit they still happily "go back."

Anton's at the Swan
22 | 22 | 20 | $47

Swan Hotel, 43 S. Main St. (Swan St.), Lambertville, 609-397-1960; www.antons-at-the-swan.com

The "intimate", "relaxing" atmosphere, "consistent" food and "gracious" service make this "old-money" New American in Lambertville a good bet for a "special occasion"; for those who find it all a "perfect mix", there's even a "charming bar" that makes for "fabulous" nightcaps.

Bahama Breeze
16 | 19 | 16 | $26

Cherry Hill Mall, 2000 Rte. 38 (Haddonfield Rd.), Cherry Hill, 856-317-8317; www.bahamabreeze.com

See review in the Philadelphia Directory.

Barnacle Ben's
20 | 17 | 19 | $30

Acme Shopping Ctr., 300 Young Ave. (bet. Marne Hwy. & Marter Ave.), Moorestown, 856-235-5808; www.barnaclebens.com

This "reliable" fish BYO in Moorestown dishes up both "better food than you'd expect in a strip mall" and slightly "pricey" tabs; the "friendly" staff works its "charm" on patrons while the "pleasant" atmosphere helps hide the fact that "the only thing missing is the ocean."

Barone's
21 | 18 | 20 | $29

Barclay Farms Shopping Ctr., 210 Rte. 70 E. (Kings Hwy.),
Cherry Hill, 856-354-1888
280 Young Ave. (Main St.), Moorestown, 856-234-7900
Villa Barone
753 Haddon Ave. (bet. Frazer & Washington Aves.),
Collingswood, 856-858-2999
www.baronerestaurants.com

"If my family could cook like this, I would have never left home" is the refrain on these "solid" Italian BYO siblings that "single-handedly keep the garlic industry going"; "comfort food" you can "rely" on and a vibe conducive to "congregating" (especially "outside" on "warm evenings") seal the deal.

Beau Rivage
21 | 22 | 21 | $52

128 Taunton Blvd. (Tuckerton Rd.), Medford, 856-983-1999;
www.beaurivage-restaurant.com

The "change to more casual dining" at this "charming" French "favorite" in "rural" Medford has some suggesting the place is "not what it used to be" with its "five-star prices" attached to "hit-or-miss" fare; most, though, say it's "better now that it's not so stuffy" with "wonderful" food and service to boot.

Bell's ⊖
19 | 10 | 19 | $26

183 N. Union St. (bet. Buttonwood & Elm Sts.), Lambertville,
609-397-2226; www.bellstavern.com

"You can't beat the prices" at this "bustling" Lambertville local "favorite" turning out "appealing" preparations of "traditional" Italian-American cooking where the daily blackboard specials are a "joy to read"; though cash only, most welcome the food-"without-the-'tude" vibe.

Big Ed's BBQ
∇ 16 | 9 | 15 | $23

259 Rte. 130 (bet. Jerome St. & Lincoln Ave.), Burlington,
609-387-3611; www.bigedsbbq.com

"Get ready to pig out" in the heart of "suburbia" at this "friendly" Burlington 'cue specialist slinging "fab" ribs and other "messy" fixin's to fans who "can't get enough" of the stuff; protesters who pull it down and single out "BBQ sauce only a factory could make" are outherded.

Blue Eyes
18 | 20 | 19 | $45

139 Egg Harbor Rd. (Delsea Dr.), Sewell, 856-227-5656;
www.blueeyesrestaurant.com

Sinatra gets under "baby boomers'" skin at this "hip" Sewell American steakhouse, a temple to "Frankie" and the "Pack" known for martinis and for the "great", though "loud" ("drowns out conversation") singing that fools you into thinking "Ol' Blue Eyes was sitting next to you"; still, "overpriced" eats and "uneven" food and service make it for some an affair to forget.

Bobby Chez   25 | 10 | 16 | $20
Village Walk Shopping Ctr., 1990 Rte. 70 E. (bet. Old Orchard & Springdale Rds.), Cherry Hill, 856-751-7373 ⑤
33 W. Collings Ave. (bet. Cove Rd. & Norwood Ave.), Collingswood, 856-869-8000 ⑤
Centerton Sq., Marter Ave. & Rte. 38, Mount Laurel, 856-234-4146
Southgate Plaza, 1225 Haddonfield-Berlin Rd. (Lippard Ave.), Voorhees, 856-768-6660 ⑤
www.bobbychezcrabcakes.com
"Maryland, eat your heart out" crow fans of these South Jersey shops where the crab cakes are the "gold standard" and where "you can feel your thighs expanding as you chew"; with limited seating and reps as mostly take-out joints, you may as well bring the goods home and "knock the socks off your houseguests", though for what you pay, the staff should "come over, set the table and serve."

Braddock's Tavern   20 | 22 | 22 | $42
39 S. Main St. (Coates St.), Medford, 609-654-1604;
www.braddocks.com
This "charming" American Colonial tavern in Medford is a favorite for "weddings", a "nice" upstairs porch and a bar where you can "forgo the fancy duds and saddle up with the locals"; still, detractors gripe the fare's "overpriced for the quality" and claim it's grown "long in the tooth."

Buca di Beppo   14 | 17 | 17 | $26
2301 Rte. 38 (Haddonfield Rd.), Cherry Hill, 856-779-3288;
www.bucadibeppo.com
See review in the Philadelphia Directory.

Café Gallery   22 | 22 | 21 | $40
219 High St. (Pearl St.), Burlington, 609-386-6150;
www.cafegalleryburlington.com
This "comfortable", split-level Continental-cum–art gallery in Burlington is a "treat" on account of its "scenic" riverside perch overlooking the Delaware, "consistently good" fare and Sunday brunch; even if your table isn't by the window, the paintings by local artists capture your attention.

Caffe Aldo Lamberti   23 | 21 | 22 | $41
2011 Rte. 70 W. (Haddonfield Rd.), Cherry Hill, 856-663-1747;
www.lambertis.com
Lamberti's "upscale" Italian flagship is a "standard bearer" of "power lunches" and "special occasions" for a "glitzy" Cherry Hill set whose "wallets can take the heat"; overall, expect "fab" food, "superb" wines and "relaxed" vibe.

Casona   – | – | – | M
563 Haddon Ave. (Knight Ave.), Collingswood, 856-854-2874;
www.mycasona.com
Exiles from Philly's Tierra Colombiana and Mixto have ventured into Collingswood's burgeoning BYO scene with a

handsome Havana-themed Latin in a large Victorian-style house; the modestly priced dishes are served in a relaxing setting featuring a coffee bar for lunch snacks and, for fresh-air fans, a wraparound porch.

Catelli   25 23 23 $45

The Plaza, 1000 Main St. (bet. Evesham & Kresson Rds.),
Voorhees, 856-751-6069; www.catellirestaurant.com
Most consider a night at this "memorable" Voorhees Italian "money well spent" as they tout its "superior" (if "expensive") food, a "mind-boggling" number of specials and service "with a smile"; fans like the "enclosed porch" and find the occasional "Sinatra" nights enhance the "elegance."

Cheesecake Factory   19 17 17 $27

931 Haddonfield Rd. (bet. Graham & Severn Aves.), Cherry Hill,
856-665-7567; www.thecheesecakefactory.com
See review in the Philadelphia Directory.

Chez Elena Wu   23 19 21 $31

Ritz Shopping Ctr., 910 Haddonfield-Berlin Rd. (White Horse Rd.),
Voorhees, 856-566-3222
South Jerseyans are wu-ed by this "elegant" BYO next to "the Ritz" shopping center in Voorhees; it's the "benchmark" for "upscale", "contemporary" Asian-French cooking that's "far above the average" and "attentive" service overseen by "splendid hostess" and chef-owner Elena Wu; it all means an "outstanding value."

Coconut Bay Asian Cuisine   19 18 19 $23

Echelon Village Plaza, 1120 White Horse Rd. (Berlin Rd.),
Voorhees, 856-783-8878; www.coconutbayasiancuisine.com
Voorheesians vote that this strip-mall BYO "more than satisfies" in light of an "unbeatable dollar value" and its variety of Asian offerings; the "pretty" setting is conducive to "conversation", and the owner is "always about, tending to his customers like they were family."

Cork   17 17 17 $36

90 Haddon Ave. (bet. Cooper St. & Cuthbert Blvd.),
Westmont, 856-833-9800; www.corknj.com
This Westmont New American "neighborhood retreat" has brought a "welcome city atmosphere" to the "wilds of South Jersey"; though the ratings may suggest it's "nothing special", proponents pop corks over an "enjoyable" meal in a "minimalist" setting; P.S. expect a "crowded" bar and "noise" at prime time.

Creole Cafe   24 16 19 $32

1333 S. Black Horse Pike (Corkery Ln.), Williamstown,
856-262-2334; www.creole-cafe.com
It's "hard to believe" there's "standout" Cajun-Creole cooking coming out of a converted house's kitchen at this BYO in the "Jersey boonies" of Williamstown; while the in-

terior may "need a makeover", many like that the place offers "the Big Easy" without the hassle of going there.

De Anna's | 21 | 19 | 22 | $37 |
54 N. Franklin St. (bet. Church & Coryell Sts.), Lambertville, 609-397-8957
The "improved", slightly larger (yet still "cozy") new location of this "friendly" Lambertville Italian pleases devotees as much as the "fresh", "good" pastas, "transcendent" meatloaf and a welcome liquor license and bar area (though now the tabs are a little "higher").

El Azteca | 17 | 9 | 16 | $18 |
Ramblewood Shopping Ctr., 1155 Rte. 73 N. (Church Rd.), Mount Laurel, 856-914-9302
See review in the Philadelphia Directory.

Elements Café ⊠ | 23 | 15 | 22 | $32 |
517 Station Ave. (White Horse Pike), Haddon Heights, 856-546-8840; www.elementscafe.com
"Inspired" tapas are the draw at this "unpretentious" New American BYO proffering "small plates with huge flavor" that are served with "enthusiasm"; though the little dishes concept may take some "getting use to" in Haddon Heights (this isn't Philly, after all), those who've dined here call it "underappreciated."

Elephant & Castle ◐ | 10 | 11 | 12 | $24 |
Clarion Hotel, 1450 Rte. 70 E. (I-295), Cherry Hill, 856-427-0427; www.elephantcastle.com
See review in the Philadelphia Directory.

Filomena | 21 | 20 | 20 | $33 |
13 Milford Cross Keys Rd. (White Horse Pike), Berlin, 856-753-3540
Commerce Plaza, 1245 Blackwood-Clementon Rd. (Laurel Rd.), Clementon, 856-784-6166
1738 Cooper St. (Almonesson Rd.), Deptford, 856-228-4235
www.filomenalakeview.com
"Where should I start?" ask boosters of these "traditional" South Jersey Italians run by the DiVenturas; fare that's "sure to please" arrives in "big portions" (dessert? "I'm always too full"), and "great" bars make you "feel welcome", especially when live entertainment (Berlin and Deptford) kicks in on most nights; N.B. Berlin is due to move down the road in fall 2006.

FOOD FOR THOUGHT | 24 | 24 | 23 | $39 |
Marlton Crossing Shopping Ctr., 129 Marlton Crossing (Rte. 70), Marlton, 856-797-1126; www.foodforthoughtnj.com
Thoughts turn to this "romantic" Marlton New American BYO for "celebratory" meals and "special occasions"; once inside, you'll be spirited away to an "entirely different world" from its shopping-center surroundings, and expect "excellent" food and "pleasant" service that may have you

wondering why "crowds aren't breaking down the doors to get in."

Full Moon ⌀   18 | 12 | 17 | $23 |
23 Bridge St. (Union St.), Lambertville, 609-397-1096
Luna-tics love the "wonderful" huevos rancheros and omelets at this Eclectic breakfast/lunch Lambertville BYO that comes with a staff as "friendly as your neighbor's kid who mows your lawn" and "hippielike" "luncheonette" digs; check the calendar, as it's open for dinner only once a month during full moons.

GIUMARELLO'S ☒   25 | 23 | 23 | $48 |
329 Haddon Ave. (bet. Cuthbert Blvd. & Kings Hwy.),
Westmont, 856-858-9400; www.giumarellos.com
"Be prepared to spend" – though it'll be "well worth it" – is the dish on this "family"-operated Italian in Westmont associated with "excellent" food and service; the "romantic", "peaceful" patio takes you "far away from the suburbs", but some say the experience is enhanced by sipping "great" martinis at the bar and watching "off-duty lawyers" playing "pickup."

Hamilton's Grill Room   25 | 20 | 22 | $47 |
8 Coryell St. (N. Union St.), Lambertville, 609-397-4343;
www.hamiltonsgrillroom.com
"Outstanding" grilled fare cooked before you, a "charming" courtyard location alongside the Delaware Canal and rustic decor distinguish this Med BYO, a "treasure" in Lambertville; "bring a date" and "eat outside" some advise, or to while away the time, "grab a drink at the nearby Boat House bar."

Inn of the Hawke   15 | 14 | 17 | $29 |
74 S. Union St. (Mount Hope St.), Lambertville, 609-397-9555
If your travels through Lambertville require a stop off for "fish 'n' chips" or to partake in a "beer break", this "friendly" American "watering hole" and hangout should fill the bill; reliable "when you want something better than fast food", it's even more attractive a choice given the "terrific" patio.

Italian Bistro   15 | 14 | 16 | $26 |
1509 Kaighn Ave./Rte. 38 (Chapel Ave.), Cherry Hill,
856-665-6900
590 Delsea Dr. (Holly Dell Dr.), Sewell, 856-589-8883
www.italianbistro.com
See review in the Philadelphia Directory.

Joe's Peking Duck House ⌀   23 | 9 | 20 | $21 |
Marlton Crossing Shopping Ctr., 145 Rte. 73 S. (Rte. 70),
Marlton, 856-985-1551
Fans think the "amazing" Peking duck and won ton soup are signs that this cash-only Marlton BYO is one of the "best" Chinese spots in South Jersey ("who needs to drive

to Philly?"); despite a remodeling, the decor's still "nothing special", though the "nice" tropical fish tank compensates.

KARMA   24 | 16 | 18 | $29
2015 Burlington-Mt. Holly Rd. (Burrs Rd.), Mount Holly, 609-914-0800; www.thekarmarestaurant.com
See review in the Philadelphia Directory.

Kibitz Room   23 | 9 | 14 | $17
Shoppes at Holly Ravine, 100 Springdale Rd. (Evesham Rd.), Cherry Hill, 856-428-7878; www.kibitzroom.net
Those seeking Jewish "soul food" and "deli dining straight out of a Woody Allen film" hit this "crazy-crowded" Cherry Hill strip-maller; noshers get ready to "blow an aorta" with "*Alice-in-Wonderland*"–size portions of "excellent" standards including the "best corned beef west of the Hudson" and marvel over the "pickle bar"; ok, the "fluorescent lighting isn't doing anyone any favors", and if you want friendly, four-star service, go somewhere else.

Kunkel's Seafood & Steakhouse   ▽ 20 | 22 | 24 | $38
920 W. Kings Hwy. (bet. Black Horse & White Horse Pikes), Haddon Heights, 856-547-1225
Haddon Heights' burgeoning dining scene gets a new member with this "welcome" addition, a wood-and-mahogany decorated BYO steakhouse that's off to a fine start by selling "flavorful" cuts and seafood; N.B. they provide a wine closet for customers who bring vino.

La Campagne   25 | 23 | 22 | $52
312 Kresson Rd. (bet. Brace & Marlkress Rds.), Cherry Hill, 856-429-7647; www.lacampagne.com
They "haven't missed a beat" at this "upper-crust" BYO French standby "in the middle of nowhere" (Cherry Hill, actually); the kitchen turns out "quality" cuisine that embodies as much "Gallic spirit" as the "farmhouse" setting; N.B. chef Eric Hall left post-*Survey*.

LACENO ITALIAN GRILL   26 | 17 | 22 | $37
Echelon Village Plaza, 1118 White Horse Rd. (Rte. 561), Voorhees, 856-627-3700
A "miracle" in a shopping mall, this Voorhees BYO specializes in "superb" Italian cooking, especially the seafood preparations that are the "best" around; the "word's out", so it can be "difficult to get a table", but a few may opt to stay away given "attitude" issues among a staff that seems "more attentive to regulars."

La Esperanza   ▽ 28 | 18 | 22 | $20
40 E. Gibbsboro Rd. (Arthur Ave.), Lindenwold, 856-782-7114; www.mexicanhope.com
You'll "never want to visit a chain again" after eating at this Lindenwold Mexican, where adherents sup on "complex", authentic cooking "at its finest" in a "modest" con-

verted home and groove to music from the "jukebox"; that the owners are "always on hand to mingle" is as comforting as the "reasonable" prices.

Lambertville Station　　17 | 19 | 19 | $37
11 Bridge St. (Delaware River), Lambertville, 609-397-8300; www.lambertvillestation.com
"After a day exploring the countryside", pull into this "bustling" Traditional American stop that attracts with a "gorgeous" view of the Delaware River and with its former rail-depot digs; still, despite a "great deal" of a lunch and early-bird dinner, detractors detect "standard" food and note this "train has left the station" awhile ago.

Lilly's on the Canal　　20 | 20 | 18 | $35
2 Canal St. (Bridge St.), Lambertville, 609-397-6242
Lambertville locals and their visitors who shop till they drop drop in for "tasty" fare and "friendly" service at this "hip", bi-level Eclectic operating on two floors in a "funky" "old building" that's pure "industrial chic"; some say upstairs is "quieter", and you get to watch the action in the open kitchen; N.B. though BYO, there's a short list of local wines.

Little Café, A ⊠　　25 | 18 | 22 | $37
Plaza Shoppes, 118 White Horse Rd. E. (Burnt Mill Rd.), Voorhees, 856-784-3344; www.alittlecafe.com
"Date night" becomes "delicious" over Marianne Cuneo Powell's "excellent" Eclectic cooking at her "teensy-weensy" Voorhees strip-mall BYO where you'll not only play footsie with your loved one but "rub elbows with your neighbor"; add "generous" portions and "accommodating" service, and you'll know it's more than a little cafe – it's "a little slice of heaven."

Little Tuna　　22 | 18 | 19 | $34
141 Kings Hwy. (S. Haddon Ave.), Haddonfield, 856-795-0888
If seafood is your weakness, then you'll be happy as a clam at high tide when dining at Marcus Severs' BYO in Haddonfield, an "enjoyable" choice for "delectable", "so-fresh" fish; most feel the move awhile back into larger quarters improves the "chance of getting a reservation" since you're less likely to encounter a "sardine"-can setup.

Manon ⊅　　24 | 20 | 21 | $44
19 N. Union St. (Bridge St.), Lambertville, 609-397-2596
Jean-Michel Dumas' "country" French BYO is a Lambertville "oasis" where you enter through "double French doors" and find "hearty" food "at its best" and *beaucoup* "Provençal" atmosphere (reinforced by a mural of Van Gogh's 'Starry Night' on the ceiling); the seating is "tight", so you'll have to "love thy neighbor, for they share thy space"; N.B. closed Mondays and Tuesdays, and cash only.

Mélange Cafe
25 | 16 | 22 | $35

1601 Chapel Ave. (Rte. 38), Cherry Hill, 856-663-7339;
www.melangecafe.com

"Move over, Emeril", since Joe Brown and company turn out a veritable jambalaya of the "best Creole food north of Nola" fused with Italian accents at his "unique" Cherry Hill BYO; so, come prepared for "flamingly" spicy eats and a vibe that's the "closest thing to Mardi Gras."

Mexican Food Factory
20 | 17 | 18 | $24

601 Rte. 70 W. (Cropwell Rd.), Marlton, 856-983-9222

"New Jersey Mexican restaurant" may be the "scariest four words" you'll see together, but you can expect nice surprises at this "reliable" roadside cantina in Marlton cooking up "good" "old-school" vittles since 1976; the copies of "Frida Kahlo's creepier self-portraits", margaritas and "delightful" outdoor dining mean "you'd never know" this place was on Route 70.

Mikado
25 | 16 | 20 | $29

2320 Rte. 70 W. (S. Union Ave.), Cherry Hill, 856-665-4411
468 S. Lenola Rd. (Kings Hwy.), Maple Shade, 856-638-1801
Elmwood Shopping Center, 793 Rte. 70 E. (Troth Rd.),
Marlton, 856-797-8581

At these "unprepossessing" South Jersey Japanese BYOs, the "newly addicted" are "amazed" at "wonderful" sushi and sashimi so "fresh" it "delights the senses"; in sum, they're "worth the toll" for the majority who "want to keep these places for themselves"; N.B. unrelated to Mikado in Ardmore, PA.

Nifty Fifty's ⬧
19 | 19 | 18 | $13

1310 Blackwood-Clementon Rd. (Laurel Rd.), Clementon,
856-346-1950; www.niftyfiftys.com

See review in the Philadelphia Directory.

No. 9
25 | 13 | 23 | $39

9 Klines Ct. (Bridge St.), Lambertville, 609-397-6380

A "surprise" in Lambertville is Mathew Kane's BYO cooking "fresh", "homesyle" New American bistro eats off a "fantastic" menu; the service is "knowledgeable", and decor debates aside ("cute" vs. "lifeless"), expect you and your neighbors to share thoughts on "how amazing the dishes are."

Norma's Middle Eastern
21 | 13 | 18 | $20

Barclay Farms Shopping Ctr., 132-145 Rte. 70 E. (Kings Hwy.),
Cherry Hill, 856-795-1373; www.normasrestaurant.com

It's "easy to overlook" this family-owned Lebanese BYO attached to a grocery in Barclay Farms, but once you start eating the dependably "good" fare, you "don't want to leave"; it's the "best bargain in town", and what's more, belly dancing enters into the picture on weekends.

Nunzio Ristorante Rustico   23 23 20 $40

706 Haddon Ave. (Collings Ave.), Collingswood,
856-858-9840; www.nunzios.net

"Favorable comparisons to Rome's best" isn't a stretch for
fans of Nunzio Patruno's "beautiful" Collingswood BYO
that's made to look like a "piazza in Italy" and succeeds;
the chef-owner and staff "cook up a storm" of delicious
Italian dishes and "specials that are just that – special"
served by a staff that "makes you feel at home", even if
"high noise levels" jar a bit.

Oasis Grill   – – – M

2431 Church Rd. (bet. Cooper Landing Rd. & Oak Ave.),
Cherry Hill, 856-667-8287;
www.oasisgrillrestaurant.com

Moroccan and Middle Eastern cooking from a former chef
at nearby Norma's helps transform this BYO strip-mall
newcomer in an oasis in a sea of pizzerias and chains;
though the digs may be humble, weekend belly dancing
adds some spice.

Olive   16 20 15 $35

Short Hills Farm, 482 E. Evesham Rd. (Carnie Blvd.),
Cherry Hill, 856-428-4999

There's "lots of activity" at this "cosmopolitan", "see-and-
be-scene" Med-influenced American in Cherry Hill, especially from a "busy" bar scene populated by "singles" in
their "20s and 30s"; it's "more a stop for apps and drinks"
than for full meals, but some attest it still could benefit from
"updating the menu" and shaking up "so-so" service.

Ota-Ya   23 14 19 $31

21 Ferry St. (S. Union St.), Lambertville, 609-397-9228;
www.ota-ya.com

See review in the Philadelphia Directory.

Pacific Grille   20 15 20 $28

Village II Shoppes, 1200 S. Church St. (Academy Dr.),
Mount Laurel, 856-778-0909; www.pacificgrill.com

Despite a fairly recent change of hands, followers still fish
for this "hidden", virtually "unknown" Pacific Rim BYO in a
Mount Laurel strip mall; those who want to keep it to themselves ("hate to let word get out") applaud "good" food,
even if the "dinerlike" digs detract a bit.

P.F. Chang's China Bistro   21 20 19 $29

Promenade at Sagemore, 500 Rte. 73 (Rte. 70), Marlton,
856-396-0818; www.pfchangs.com

See review in the Philadelphia Directory.

Pietro's Coal Oven Pizzeria   19 14 16 $23

140 Rte. 70 W. (Rte. 73), Marlton, 856-596-5500;
www.pietrospizza.com

See review in the Philadelphia Directory.

Pizzicato　　　　20　16　18　$31
Promenade at Sagemore, 500 Rte. 73 (Rte. 70), Marlton, 856-396-0880
See review in the Philadelphia Directory.

Ponzio's ◗　　　　16　12　16　$21
7 Rte. 70 W. (Kings Hwy.), Cherry Hill, 856-428-4808; www.ponzios.com
"The closest thing Camden County has to a social club" is this South Jersey "landmark", the "diner of diners" serving "comforting" coffee-shop specialties including "heavenly" desserts (from an on-site bakery) off an "extensive" menu; and just about everyone, from "housewives" and "politicians", have nothing bad to say about "warm" service, often in the "wha'-cha-want-hon" school.

Pop Shop　　　　19　20　17　$17
729 Haddon Ave. (Collings Ave.), Collingswood, 856-869-0111; www.thepopshopusa.com
"Good ol'-fashioned comfort food" takes on "new twists" at this "noisy", "family-friendly" Collingswood "'50s"-style "soda" shoppe, a "throwback" that appeals to "kids – even the grown-up kind" – with "great" burgers and shakes and the like from an "enormous" menu (including vegan and veggie items) complemented by "small-town" service.

Pub, The　　　　18　13　16　$31
Airport Circle, 7600 Kaighn Ave. (Rte. 130), Pennsauken, 856-665-6440; www.thepubnj.com
If your idea of a hot night is a 600-seat room filled with a "medieval" motif featuring images of knights, you'll love this Pennsauken steakhouse churning out reef 'n' beef since the early '50s; the "reliable" fare sates many souls and the salad bar still "ranks at the top" for fans, but some find things here are just "decent" and add the place "could use updating."

RAT'S　　　　24　27　23　$64
Grounds for Sculpture, 16 Fairgrounds Rd. (Sculptors Way), Hamilton, 609-584-7800; www.ratsrestaurant.org
Look up "beautiful" in Webster's and find a picture of this "destination" Hamilton New French in the "whimsical" and "alluring" Grounds for Sculpture; stroll through the "otherworldly" sculpture gardens before or after settling in to the "gourmet" food complemented by a wine list that "justifies repeat visits"; and even if some find the staff a bit "snooty", the consensus is it's "worth going here at least once."

Red Hot & Blue　　　　18　13　15　$22
Holiday Inn, 2175 Old Marlton Pike (Sayer Ave.), Cherry Hill, 856-665-7427; www.redhotanblue.com
"What's not to like when there's ribs and blues" wonder 'cuennoisseurs of this Cherry Hill BBQ chain link serving up "drinks in jugs", "good" (if just "decent") ribs and

pulled pork, and "super" music on weekends; it's got some "Memphis" soul, though it's time to address "uneven" service and decor that could use a "face-lift"

RITZ SEAFOOD   26 | 16 | 20 | $35 |

Ritz Shopping Ctr., 910 Haddonfield-Berlin Rd. (White Horse Rd.), Voorhees, 856-566-6650; www.ritzseafood.com
There's not much "elbow" room, but there's usually "a crowd" at this BYO Voorhees Asian fusionist specializing in "exciting" seafood prepared "with zest"; it's a "dear" "gem" for its fans, and a wise choice "before or after" a movie at one of the nearby cinemas; N.B. the tea bar features 30 varieties for those looking for some sipping and soothing.

Robin's Nest   ▽ 22 | 21 | 21 | $31 |

2-4 Washington St. (High St.), Mount Holly, 609-261-6149; www.robinsnestmountholly.com
As "quaint as an 1850 parlor of a lady" is this "unpretentious" Mount Holly French-American "treasure" in a culinary "desert" of an area; "wonderful" could equally describe the savories, desserts ("to die for", frankly) and service, not to mention the alfresco accommodations.

SAGAMI   26 | 15 | 21 | $35 |

37 W. Crescent Blvd. (Haddon Ave.), Collingswood, 856-854-9773
Still "heaven in the raw for fans" is the sushi that's "as fresh as you can get on this side of the world" at Collingswood's 32-year-old Japanese BYO; for "flawless" fish, you'll have to settle for "low-ceilinged" quarters, but it's a small concession, since this mainstay continues to bring "joy" to its loyal fans; N.B. before dinner, drop by Moore Brothers Wines.

Sakura Spring   ▽ 22 | 18 | 22 | $27 |

1871 Rte. 70 E. (bet. Greentree Rd. & Wiedo Ln.), Cherry Hill, 856-489-8018
Even those who "aren't fans of Asian food" find something to savor at this BYO Chinese-Japanese hybrid whose "friendly" servers present cuisine that's a "cut above" the norm; the menu is "large" and the tabs relatively "inexpensive."

Sapori   ▽ 25 | 18 | 22 | $36 |

601 Haddon Ave. (Harvard Ave.), Collingswood, 856-858-2288; www.sapori.info
"*Bellissimo!*" sizes up this "romantic", rusticated BYO Collingswood trattoria where the cooking produces "savory" results that take you the "closest you'll get" to Italy in South Jersey; the staff does "everything in its power to please", and pricewise, it's a "terrific value" to Boot.

Siam ⊄   20 | 7 | 15 | $24 |

61 N. Main St. (bet. Coryell & York Sts.), Lambertville, 609-397-8128
The ambiance may be "old shoe" but the food "kicks like a Manolo Blahnik" at this "small" Thai BYO storefront on Lambertville's main drag; while you should expect "slow"

service when they're "crowded", most appreciate the staff's "friendly" vibe and certifiably "rock-bottom" prices.

Siri's Thai French Cuisine 25 | 20 | 23 | $37 |
2117 Old Marlton Pike (Mimosa Dr.), Cherry Hill, 856-663-6781;
www.siris-nj.com
Don't be "fooled" by the strip-mall location, since there's "terrific" fare to spare at this "upscale" BYO Cherry Hill mainstay whose "reasonably" priced food successfully fuses "the best of Thai and French" cuisines; factor in "impeccable" service from "knowledgeable" folks, and you can see why it's been a "special" spot for years.

Somsak 22 | 16 | 21 | $23 |
Echo Shops, 200 White Horse Rd. (Burnt Mill Rd.),
Voorhees, 856-782-1771
"Still the one" is the word in Voorhees about this tiny Thai turning out "terrific" fare in a strip mall; complementing the food are "exceptional" service, "bargain" prices and a variety of "homemade ice creams" that aren't to be missed.

TACCONELLI'S PIZZERIA ≠ 24 | 9 | 15 | $18 |
450 S. Lenola Rd. (Rte. 38), Maple Shade, 856-638-0338
See review in the Philadelphia Directory.

Thai Orchid 23 | 18 | 22 | $26 |
Crossing Plaza, 147-49 Rte. 73 S. (south of Rte. 70), Marlton,
856-985-5300
See review in the Philadelphia Directory.

Tortilla Press 23 | 19 | 20 | $27 |
703 Haddon Ave. (Collings Ave.), Collingswood, 856-869-3345;
www.thetortillapress.com
"Collingswood is going in the right direction", and this "busy", "colorful" Mexican BYO is helping to "lead the way" with "inventive" food and a "personable" staff; P.S. "bring your own tequila" for margaritas that "pack a punch."

Water Lily 21 | 21 | 22 | $37 |
655 Haddon Ave. (Collings Ave.), Collingswood, 856-833-0998;
www.waterlilybistro.com
Seekers of "serenity" like this "sweet", green-and-burgundy hued Collingswood French-Asian BYO for its "very good" fare, whether for lunch or dinner; the lily paintings on one wall ably distract diners from the somewhat "high" tabs.

Word of Mouth 24 | 23 | 20 | $38 |
729 Haddon Ave. (bet. Collings & Washington Aves.),
Collingswood, 856-858-2228
Most have already gotten the news about this "cozy" New American BYO in Collingswood, namely that it serves "superb" food amid a "comfy", "lovely" setting replete with stained glass and tin ceiling; but for "spotty" service, the word is it's "worth every penny."

Wilmington/
Nearby Delaware

Top Food
26 Rest. 821
25 Green Room
    Krazy Kat's
    Moro
    Culinaria

Top Decor
28 Green Room
25 Krazy Kat's
23 Rest. 821
    Moro
    Harry's Seafood

Top Service
25 Green Room
24 Krazy Kat's
23 Moro
22 Culinaria
    Rest. 821

Best Buys
Brew HaHa!
Jake's Hamburgers
Charcoal Pit
La Tolteca
Lamberti's Cucina

F	D	S	C

Back Burner ⊠ | 21 | 17 | 19 | $37 |
425 Hockessin Corner (Old Lancaster Pike), Hockessin,
302-239-2314; www.backburner.com
"Pumpkin mushroom soup" and "casual" airs draw the
northern Delaware's "old-money", "Junior-League lunch
crowd" to this "airy", rustic New American in a Hockessin
strip mall; ok, it could use a "spiff up", but many consider
it "reliable" and hope the "new chef" keeps the "quality"
on the front burner.

Blue Parrot Bar & Grille ◑ | 17 | 17 | 16 | $28 |
1934 W. Sixth St. (Union St.), Wilmington, 302-655-8990;
www.blueparrotgrille.com
You'll "wear your beads with pride" at this N'Awlins house in
the middle of Wilmington's Little Italy, as the "taste of Mardi
Gras" comes through loud and clear ("great" blues and jazz),
and if it seems "booze" and music trump the "authentic"
Cajun cooking, it's a "fun" place to visit "at least once."

Brew HaHa! ⊅ | 16 | 13 | 18 | $10 |
Powder Mill Sq., 3842 Kennett Pike (Buck Rd.), Greenville,
302-658-6336
Branmar Plaza, 1812 Marsh Rd. (Silverside Rd.),
Wilmington, 302-529-1125
Concord Gallery, 3636 Concord Pike (Silverside Rd.),
Wilmington, 302-478-7227
Hotel du Pont, 1007 N. Market St. (10th St.), Wilmington,
302-656-1171 ⊠
835 N. Market St. (bet. 8th & 9th Sts.), Wilmington,
302-777-4499 ⊠

(continued)

(continued)

Brew HaHa!
Rockford Shops, 1420 N. du Pont St. (Delaware Ave.),
Wilmington, 302-778-2656
Shops of Limestone Hills, 5329 Limestone Rd.
(west of Stoney Batter Rd.), Wilmington, 302-234-9600
www.brew-haha.com
See review in the Philadelphia Directory.

Buckley's Tavern   17   17   17 $31
5812 Kennett Pike (south of Rte. 1), Centerville, 302-656-9776
"Preppy", native Wilmingtonians and "Delaware rebels"
alike "kick back" on the "roof deck" or by the fireplace
with "Wasp soul food" at this "popular", long-running
New American tavern in Centerville "château country";
regulars advise grabbing a bottle at the "adjacent wine
shop" and wearing "pajamas at Sunday brunch" to get
"half off" your bucks.

Charcoal Pit   19   10   16 $13
240 Fox Hunt Dr. (off Rte. 40), Bear, 302-834-8000
2600 Concord Pike (Woodrow Ave.), Wilmington,
302-478-2165 ●⇗
714 Greenbank Rd. (Kirkwood Hwy.), Wilmington, 302-998-8853
5200 Pike Creek Center Blvd. (Limestone Rd.), Wilmington,
302-999-7483
www.charcoalpit.com
The "real burger kings" for Delawareans is this quartet of
"institutions" prized for its "cheap" goods, namely "great",
"bodacious" quarter-pounders, "perfect" fries and "terrific"
milkshakes in a "nostalgia"-inducing setting right out of a
"'50s movie"; so as long as "you're not a heart patient", hit
"The Pit" for the perfect "grease" fix – but be sure to "pick
the right times to avoid a wait" and carry some "Pepto."

Chef's Table at the   ▽ 25   22   24 $44
David Finney Inn, The
222 Delaware St. (3rd St.), New Castle, 302-322-6367;
www.chefstablerestaurant.com
"Fresh air for all New Castle" comes via Robert Lhulier's
"promising" yearling, a New American inside the "beautiful"
historic David Finney inn; an "unpretentious" staff serves
"imaginative" food enhanced by a concise wine list high-
lighting some unsung regions; in short, had "William Penn
eaten here, he would have stayed in the neighborhood."

China Royal   ▽ 24   15   23 $20
1845 Marsh Rd. (Silverside Rd.), Wilmington, 302-475-3686
Northern Wilmingtonians know all about this "royally
good", affordably priced Mandarin "hidden" in a strip mall;
look for "fast" service and some of the "best" Chinese
food in the area and a kitchen that "actually listens" if their
patrons have any special requests.

Columbus Inn
21 | 20 | 20 | $41

*2216 Pennsylvania Ave. (Woodlawn Ave.), Wilmington,
302-571-1492; www.columbusinn.com*

"Snag a table by one of the fireplaces" on chilly nights or
go when you get "a babysitter" to this "comfortable"
Traditional American longtimer in Wilmington associated
with Caesar salad "prepared tableside" and "professional" service in "old-world" surroundings; "Sunday
brunch" is "a smash", and the wine list is "great" to boot.

Conley Ward's
19 | 21 | 17 | $48

*110 S. West St. (Martin Luther King Jr. Blvd.), Wilmington,
302-658-6626; www.conleywards.com*

The walk-in wine room housing 1,800 bottles helps set apart
this "upscale", "NYC"-style steakhouse on the Wilmington
waterfront; many cheerfully bring their "expense ac-
counts" for the "right stuff" (that is, "great" beef) and the
chance to dine "outside" in "summer"; alas, for opponents,
"ordinary" eats don't jibe with the "high price" point.

Corner Bistro
19 | 17 | 20 | $26

*Talleyville Towne Shoppes, 3604 Silverside Rd. (Concord Pike),
Wilmington, 302-477-1778; www.mybistro.com*

Not to be overlooked is this "secret" strip-mall Eclectic in
Wilmington whipping up food that "pushes the envelope";
that the wines by the glass are "inexpensive", the service
"quick" and the setting "comfortable" and "modern" all
serve to distinguish it from "Route 202's chains."

CULINARIA ⬙
25 | 20 | 22 | $32

*Branmar Plaza, 1812 Marsh Rd. (Silverside Rd.),
Wilmington, 302-475-4860; www.culinariarestaurant.com*

Those who tuck into Ezio Reynaud's "inventive" New
Americana at this "cosmopolitan" bistro in northern
Wilmington "almost forget" they're in a strip mall; it's "extremely popular" too, so be prepared for "long waits" and
"crowds" partly attributed to "no reservations."

Deep Blue ⬙
23 | 20 | 21 | $44

*111 W. 11th St. (bet. Orange & Tatnall Sts.), Wilmington,
302-777-2040; www.deepbluebarandgrill.com*

"Crawl past the bar" (though things are "happening" there)
and treat yourself to some of the "best" seafood around at
Wilmongton's "top destination" for fish, a blue-hued enclave
near the DuPont Theater drawing "chic" crowds for dinner
and drinks; for penny-pinchers who think the prices will
leave them in deep debt, there's the $30 pre-theater menu.

Domaine Hudson
▽ 25 | 25 | 24 | $37

*1314 N. Washington St. (bet.13th & 14th Sts.), Wilmington,
302-655-9463; www.domainehudson.com*

"Where have you been?" inquire oenophiles and foodies
of this "sophisticated" New American arrival whose wine

bar concept pairs well with the "lovely" little bites for "grazing" and a staff that possesses "knowledge" of what it's pouring; "finally, a place a New Yorker and a Parisian can call home" – best yet, it's in Downtown Wilmington.

Eclipse Bistro
23 | 19 | 21 | $39

1020 N. Union St. (10th St.), Wilmington, 302-658-1588; www.eclipsebistro.com

"A bistro that's a bistro" is the happy refrain on this "casual" American in Wilmington, and locals are over the moon when it comes to "excellent" food and service, an "intimate" setting and "moderate" prices; N.B. all the wines on the list are under $50.

Feby's Fishery
19 | 10 | 16 | $31

3701 Lancaster Pike (bet. Centre & du Pont Rds.), Wilmington, 302-998-9501; www.febysfishery.com

The variety of "fresh" and "simply prepared" seafood offerings reel 'em in to this Wilmington fishery attached to a market; despite relatively recent renovations, the nautical look is still "plain", so the word is "go for the food, not the decor."

GREEN ROOM
25 | 28 | 25 | $57

Hotel du Pont, 11th & Market Sts., Wilmington, 302-594-3154; www.hoteldupont.com

This "grand" French in the Hotel du Pont is "still the best for classically" "elegant" dining in Downtown Wilmington, and "blue-blood" "bankers" come to be "treated" like "kings" thanks to "wonderful" food and "impeccable" service; in other words, it's the "gold standard" when you want to impress someone.

Harry's Savoy Grill ●
21 | 20 | 21 | $44

2020 Naamans Rd. (Foulk Rd.), Wilmington, 302-475-3000; www.harrys-savoy.com

Prime rib and oysters share space on the roster of more "imaginative" items at this "clubby" New American eatery identified as a meeting place for Wilmington's "old guard"; "excellent" wines and "debonair" service make it even more appreciated as a "standby."

HARRY'S SEAFOOD GRILL
23 | 23 | 20 | $43

101 S. Market St. (S. Shipley St.), Wilmington, 302-777-1500; www.harrysseafoodgrill.com

Wilmingtonians "dress trendy" to take clients and out-of-towners to this "gorgeous" seafooder sibling of Harry's Savoy Grill for a "perfect" waterfront scene, "sensational" stuff from the "raw bar" and "cool" ambiance enhanced by big screens above the bar showing "hypnotic" sea-inspired videos.

Hibachi
18 | 16 | 19 | $28

5607 Concord Pike (Naamans Rd.), Wilmington, 302-477-0194
See review in the Philadelphia Directory.

Iron Hill Brewery & Restaurant   17 17 18 $26
Traders Alley, 147 E. Main St. (bet. Chapel & Haines Sts.),
Newark, 302-266-9000
710 S. Madison St. (Beech St.), Wilmington, 302-658-8200
www.ironhillbrewery.com
See review in the Philadelphia Directory.

Jake's Hamburgers   23 5 13 $9
150 S. du Pont Hwy./Rte. 113 (off Rte. 273), New Castle,
302-322-0200
Roselle Ctr., 2405 Kirkwood Hwy. (Rte. 141), Wilmington,
302-994-6800
www.jakeshamburgers.com
Their burgers are "vastly better than what you get from the
fast-food outlets" say backers of this Delaware duo that
makes you order at the counter; wash 'em down with some
shakes, and before you know it you're in "fat heaven."

Jasmine   23 22 21 $32
Concord Gallery, 3618 Concord Pike (Mt. Lebanon Rd.),
Wilmington, 302-479-5618
"Terrific" Pan-Asian including "fresh" sushi encourage
"repeat visits" to this Wilmington spot you "would never
expect to find in a shopping center"; "sleek" decor and
well-"trained" service help give it appeal.

KRAZY KAT'S   25 25 24 $54
Inn at Montchanin Village, Kirk Rd. & Rte. 100, Montchanin,
302-888-4200; www.montchanin.com
"Landed gentry" love to curl up and purr in this "elegant"
New French in the "rolling hills" of Brandywine Valley; it's
got "panache", what with "whimsical", feline-focused decor that "works" complemented by "excellent" food that
can be "cutting-edge" and service that "shines."

Lamberti's Cucina   20 18 20 $26
514 Philadelphia Pike (Marsh Rd.), Wilmington, 302-762-9094
Prices Corner Shopping Ctr., 1300 Centerville Rd.
(Kirkwood Hwy.), Wilmington, 302-995-6955
www.lambertis.com
"Bring a big appetite and a doggy bag" to these affordable
Wilmington Italian twins where they've got the "good" basics down pat and where you'll "never have a bad time"; in
short, the duo "doesn't inspire, but it does satisfy."

La Tolteca   18 11 16 $18
Fairfax Shopping Ctr., 2209 Concord Pike (Rte. 141),
Wilmington, 302-778-4646
Talleyville Shopping Ctr., 4015 Concord Pike
(bet. Brandywine Blvd. & Silverside Rd.), Wilmington,
302-478-9477; www.lastoltecas.com
"*Delicioso*" food that's "not trying to be anything more
than it is" captures the spirit at this "popular" Mexican

mini-chain with outposts in West Chester and Delaware; ok, the low-budget quarters "aren't great on the eyes", and some say the "burritos taste the same as the enchiladas", but for a "cheap date", they'll do just fine.

Luigi Vitrone's Pastabilities ▽ 24 | 18 | 23 | $34

415 N. Lincoln St. (5th St.), Wilmington, 302-656-9822; www.ljv-pastabilities.com
Chef Luigi Vitrone "could teach your Italian grandmother a lesson or two" boast boosters of this "small" brick-walled Wilmington Italian that's "like eating at home with someone else in the kitchen" – actually, you have to walk through the kitchen to get to your table; things are prepared "with love" here, so expect to fall for the place fast.

Mexican Post 18 | 13 | 16 | $22

3100 Naamans Rd. (Shipley Rd.), Wilmington, 302-478-3939; www.mexicanpost.com
See review in the Philadelphia Directory.

Mikimotos Asian Grill & Sushi Bar 25 | 21 | 21 | $38

1212 N. Washington St. (12th St.), Wilmington, 302-656-8638; www.mikimotos.com
"See-and-be-seen" scenesters settle in for "wonderful" sushi and other "inspired" dishes amid "lots of noise" at this "bright" and "modern", "big city"–like Japanese–Pan-Asian that's helping make Downtown Wilmington a "dining destination"; P.S. the sushi happy hour offered at the bar is a "great deal."

Mona Lisa ☒ ▽ 23 | 16 | 22 | $30

607 N. Lincoln St. (6th St.), Wilmington, 302-888-2201
Fans are smiling over "consistently good" specials and standards that "can compete with your grandmother's" at this "intimate", "low-key" Wilmington red-saucer; the staff treats you like part of their "family", so it's not too much of a stretch if folks call this "one of Little Italy's best."

MORO ☒ 25 | 23 | 23 | $52

1307 N. Scott St. (bet. 13th & 14th Sts.), Wilmington, 302-777-1800; www.mororestaurant.net
Wilmingtonians are "proud to take out-of-towners" to Michael DiBianca's "sleek" Downtown New American that offers "an embarrassment of riches" with "deeply satisfying" tastes in "every bite" of food backed by a "huge" wine list and "exemplary" service; it's a "pricey proposition", but worth it for insiders who beg others to "please stay away – I never want to be denied a table."

Mrs. Robino's 14 | 5 | 14 | $19

520 N. Union St. (bet. 5th & 6th Sts.), Wilmington, 302-652-9223
Even if you've been going to this 66-year-old Wilmington landmark forever, you "can't wait to go again" considering

"consistent" "red-gravy" fare "like your grandma used to make" that you enjoy in a setting without "tacky checkered tablecloths"; but naysayers knock the place for "bland" eats and "dark, dreary" digs adding "this one's seen better days."

RESTAURANT 821 ☒ | 26 | 23 | 22 | $52 |

821 N. Market St. (bet. 8th & 9th Sts.), Wilmington, 302-652-8821; www.restaurant821.com
"It would fare well in any major city" is the conclusion of culinary cognoscenti who dine at this "cosmopolitan" Wilmington small-plater that's winning over fans who "keep coming" for "remarkable" compositions of New American cuisine backed by a "good" list of wines; Casanovas croon it's perfect for a "romantic" night at "half the cost of NYC" restaurants.

1717 ☒   ▽ | 21 | 17 | 19 | $37 |

1717 Delaware Ave. (du Pont St.), Wilmington, 302-655-5080; www.1717delave.com
Wilmington's after-work crowd "packs" this "tiny" New American whose "talented" kitchen offers a "diverse" menu strong on small plates; on Fridays and Saturdays "after 10:30 PM", the "subdued" vibe "undergoes a Jekyll-and-Hyde transformation", with the focus being the "edgy" bar scene.

Sugarfoot Fine Foods | – | – | – | I |

Nemours Building, 1007 N. Orange St. (10th St.), Wilmington, 302-654-1600
1014 Lincoln St. (bet. Scott & Union Sts.), Wilmington, 302-655-4800 ☒
www.sugarfootfinefood.com
These casual counter-service cafes proffer a New American roster of light fare (smoothies, sandwiches and such) at breakfast and lunch; the modern Downtowner (which serves cocktails) pulls in the suit-and-tie crowd while the shabby-chic-designed original draws moms and kids; N.B. the company is also renowned for its catering services.

Sullivan's Steakhouse | 23 | 20 | 21 | $50 |

Brandywine Town Ctr., 5525 Concord Pike (Naamans Rd.), Wilmington, 302-479-7970; www.sullivansteakhouse.com
See review in the Philadelphia Directory.

Toscana Kitchen & Bar | 24 | 20 | 21 | $38 |

Rockford Shops, 1412 N. du Pont St. (Delaware Ave.), Wilmington, 302-654-8001; www.toscanakitchen.com
This "trendy" yet "not snobby" Italian "favorite" is not only "the place to be seen in Wilmington", but is touted for "lovingly prepared" food that reportedly tops "most South Philly Italians"; "a "lively" bar, "enthusiastic" service and "reasonable" prices flesh out its winning profile.

Union City Grille ⌧   ▽ 20   15   18 $34
805 N. Union St. (8th St.), Wilmington, 302-654-9780
This Wilmington Traditional American is "beginning to find its
niche" by satisfying fans with its "warm" vibe while satiat-
ing stomachs with "good", if "simple" fare; P.S. "happy-
hour apps" can add up to a "great" small-plates supper.

Utage   ▽ 19   13   19 $29
*Independence Mall, 1601 Concord Pike (Powder Mill Rd.),
Wilmington, 302-652-1230; www.oka-utage.com*
The call for "fresh" sushi and "good" cooked fare is
answered in this long-standing Japanese in Independence Mall; detractors, however", deem the fare "decent"
and brand the setting "bland" enough to make the
"supermarket more fun."

Walter's Steakhouse   21   17   19 $41
*802 N. Union St. (8th St.), Wilmington, 302-652-6780;
www.walterssteakhouse.com*
Their "prime rib must come from the biggest cows on
earth" say adherents of this Downtown Wilmington steakhouse known for "dependable" beef, 300 different wines
and "excellent" service; its "dark", wood-appointed digs
make you "expect Sinatra to walk in."

Washington St. Ale House ◗   16   14   15 $23
*1206 Washington St. (12th St.), Wilmington, 302-658-2537;
www.wsalehouse.com*
"Beer cheese soup" and brews go hand in hand with "ball
games on the TV" at this "lunch" and "happy-hour"
standby in Wilmington; the food is in the "solidly" pub grub
camp, and the scene is decidedly "loud", especially when
the "after-work" "yuppies" come to hang.

Indexes

All restaurants are in the Philadelphia metropolitan area unless otherwise noted (LB=Lancaster/Berks Counties; NJ=New Jersey Suburbs; DE=Wilmington/ Nearby Delaware).

† Locations in multiple regions.

CUISINES

Afghan
Ariana
Kabul

American (New)
Alison/Blue Bell
America B&G
Anton's at Swan/NJ
Back Burner/DE
Basil Bistro
Bistro 7
Black Bass Hotel
Bliss
Blue Horse
Blush
Brick Hotel
Bridget Foy's
Bridgetown Mill
Buckley's Tavern/DE
Carambola
Carr's/LB
Catherine's
Cedar Hollow Inn
Centre Bridge Inn
Chef's Table/David Finney/DE
Chlöe
Christopher's
Coleman
Cork/NJ
Crescent City
Cresheim Cottage
Culinaria/DE
Dark Horse Pub
Derek's
Deuce
Dilworthtown Inn
Domaine Hudson/DE
Drafting Rm.
Elements Café/NJ
Epicurean
EverMay/Delaware
Fayette Street
Food for Thought/NJ
Fork
Four Dogs Tavern
Freight House

Funky Lil' Kitchen
Gables/Chadds Ford
Gayle
Grace Tavern
Grill
Grill Rest.
Gullifty's
Half Moon Saloon
Hamlet Bistro
Happy Rooster
Harry's Savoy/DE
Havana
Horizons
Iron Hill Brewery†
Isaac Newton's
Jake's
Joseph Ambler Inn
Knight House
Landing
La Terrasse
Latest Dish
Lily's on Main/LB
Loie
London Grill
Lula
Mainland Inn
Majolica
Mandoline
Marathon Grill
Marathon on Square
Marigold Kitchen
Matyson
Mendenhall Inn
Moro/DE
Moshulu
Museum Restaurant
New Wave Café
Next
Nineteen
No. 9/NJ
N. 3rd
Orchard
Pace One
Pumpkin
Rest. Alba

Rest. 821/DE
Roller's/Flying Fish
Rose Tattoo
Rouge
Roux 3
Royal Tavern
Salt & Pepper
1717/DE
Simon Pearce
Sola
Solaris Grille
Southwark
Spence Cafe
Strawberry Hill/LB
Sugarfoot Fine Foods/DE
Swann Lounge
Tango
Thomas'
333 Belrose
Twenty Manning
Twenty21
211 York
U.S. Hotel B&G
Vickers Tavern
Washington Square
Winnie's Le Bus
Word of Mouth/NJ
Yardley Inn
Zakes Cafe

American (Traditional)
Avalon
Azalea
Bay Pony Inn
Bell's/NJ
Black Door
Blue Bell Inn
Blue Eyes/NJ
Bonefish Grill
Braddock's Tavern/NJ
Cheeseburger/Paradise
Cheesecake Factory†
Chestnut Grill
Chickie's & Pete's
City Tavern
Cock 'n Bull
Columbus Inn/DE
Copabanana

Copa Too
Cuttalossa Inn
Dave & Buster's
Day by Day
Eclipse Bistro/DE
Fountain Side
Fox & Hound
Friday Sat. Sun.
Gen. Lafayette Inn
General Warren
Green Hills Inn/LB
Hamlet Bistro
Hank's Place
Hard Rock
Haydn Zug's/LB
Independence Brew
Inn/Hawke/NJ
J.B. Dawson's
John Harvard's
Johnny Brenda's
Jonathan's Amer. Grille
Jones
K.C.'s Alley
Kimberton Inn
King George II
Lambertville Station/NJ
Liberties
Log Cabin/LB
L2
Manayunk Brewery
Max & Erma's
McFadden's
Mercato
More Than Ice Cream
Mother's Rest. & Wine Bar
New Tavern
Nodding Head Brew.
North by Northwest
Old Guard Hse. Inn
Olive/NJ
Ortlieb's Jazz
Paradigm
Peacock/Parkway
Plate
Plumsteadville Inn
Ponzio's/NJ
Pop Shop/NJ
Public Hse./Logan Sq.

Pub/Penn Valley
Rembrandt's
Robin's Nest/NJ
Rose Tree Inn
Society Hill Hotel
Spotted Hog
Standard Tap
Stoudt's/LB
Ten Stone
Tenth St. Pour Hse.
Trax Café
Triumph Brewing Co.
Trolley Car
Union City Grille/DE
Washington Crossing
William Penn Inn
Winberie's
Wooden Iron
World Café Live

Asian
Alex Long Asian
Anjou
Buddakan
Bunha Faun
Chez Elena Wu/NJ
Coconut Bay/NJ
Ly Michael's
Nectar
Ritz Seafood/NJ
Roy's
Twenty Manning
Water Lily/NJ

Asian Fusion
Alex Long Asian
Anjou
Buddakan
Duck Sauce
FuziOn
Ly Michael's
Nectar
Roy's
Shangrila

Bakeries
More Than Ice Cream
Pink Rose
Ponzio's/NJ

Barbecue
Abner's BBQ
Big Ed's BBQ/NJ
Bomb Bomb BBQ
Red Hot & Blue/NJ
Rib Crib
Sweet Lucy's

Belgian
Abbaye
Beau Monde
Eulogy Belgian
Monk's Cafe

British
Dark Horse Pub
Elephant & Castle†

Burmese
Rangoon

Cajun
Blue Parrot B&G/DE
Bourbon Blue
Carmine's Creole
Creole Cafe/NJ
High St. Caffé
Ortlieb's Jazz

Californian
California Cafe
Sovalo

Caribbean
Bahama Breeze†
bluezette
Copabanana
Fatou & Fama

Cheese Steaks
Campo's Deli
Dalessandro's
Geno's Steaks
Jim's Steaks
Pat's Steaks
Tony Luke's

Chinese
(* dim sum specialist)
Abacus
Beijing

Blue Pacific
Charles Plaza
Cherry St. Veg.
China Royal/DE
Chun Hing
CinCin
Duck Sauce
Four Rivers
Harmony Veg.*
H.K. Golden Phoenix*
Hunan
Imperial Inn*
Joe's Peking/NJ*
Joy Tsin Lau*
Kingdom of Veg.*
Lai Lai Garden
Lakeside Chinese*
Lee How Fook
Long's Chinese
Mandarin
Mandarin Garden
Margaret Kuo's
Margaret Kuo's Media
Margaret Kuo's Peking
Mustard Greens
Ocean Harbor*
P.F. Chang's†
Ray's Cafe
Sakura Spring/NJ
Sang Kee Asian
Sang Kee Duck Hse.
Shiao Lan Kung
Singapore Kosher
Susanna Foo
Tai Lake
Yangming

Coffeehouses
Bonte
Brew HaHa!†
La Colombe

Coffee Shops/Diners
Ardmore Station
Hank's Place
Little Pete's
Mayfair Diner
Melrose Diner
Morning Glory

Nifty Fifty's†
Ponzio's/NJ
Ruby's
Trolley Car

Colombian
Tierra Colombiana

Continental
Avalon
Bay Pony Inn
Brick Hotel
Bridgetown Mill
Café Gallery/NJ
Chef Charin
Farmicia
Fioravanti
Fountain
Paradigm
Plough & Stars
Seven Stars Inn
Vickers Tavern
Vincent's
William Penn Inn
Yangming

Creole
Bourbon Blue
Carmine's Creole
Creole Cafe/NJ
High St. Caffé
Marsha Brown
Mélange Cafe/NJ

Cuban
Café Habana
Casona/NJ
Cuba Libre
Tierra Colombiana

Delis
Ben & Irv Deli.
Campo's Deli
Famous 4th St. Deli.
Hymie's Deli
Isaac's†
Izzy & Zoe's
Kibitz in City
Kibitz Room/NJ
Murray's Deli

Dessert
Beau Monde
Cheesecake Factory
Dessert
Melting Pot
More Than Ice Cream
Pink Rose
Roselena's

Eclectic
Ansill
Astral Plane
Azure
Beige & Beige
Bridgid's
Cafe Preeya
Cafette
Carman's Country
Citrus
Continental
Continental Mid-town
Corner Bistro/DE
Day by Day
Full Moon/NJ
Georges'
Gracie's/LB
Hamlet Bistro
Johnny Brenda's
Lilly's on Canal/NJ
Little Café/NJ
Maya Bella
Meridith's
Meritage
Mimosa Rest.
Pub/Penn Valley
Reading Term. Mkt.
Red Sky
Roller's/Flying Fish
Rx
Sabrina's Café
Serrano
Sola
SoleFood
Summer Kitchen
Taste
Tavern on Green
Totaro's
Tria

Twin Bays
Umbria
White Dog Cafe
Zanzibar Blue

Eritrean
Dahlak

Ethiopian
Abyssinia

European
Bonte
Django
Duling-Kurtz Hse.
La Pergola
Meritage

Floribbean
Copabanana

Fondue
Melting Pot

French
Alisa Cafe/NJ
Anjou
Beau Monde
Beau Rivage/NJ
Beige & Beige
Birchrunville Store
Cafe Fresko
Chez Elena Wu/NJ
Deux Cheminées
FuziOn
Gilmore's
Golden Pheasant
Green Room/DE
Hotel du Village
Inn at Phillips Mill
La Bonne Auberge
La Campagne/NJ
Lacroix/Rittenhouse
La Terrasse
Loie
Overtures
Paloma
Patou
Robin's Nest/NJ
Savona

Siri's Thai French/NJ
Water Lily/NJ

French (Bistro)
Bistro St. Tropez
Brasserie 73
Caribou Cafe
La Belle Epoque
Le Bar Lyonnais
Le Jardin
Manon/NJ
Pif
Pond/Bistro Cassis
Slate Bleu
Sovana Bistro
Spring Mill Café
Vintage

French (New)
Brasserie Perrier
Bunha Faun
Chez Colette
Fountain
Gourmet
Happy Rooster
Krazy Kat's/DE
La Boheme
La Na
Le Bec-Fin
Nan
Places! Bistro
Pond/Bistro Cassis
Rat's/NJ
Rest. at Doneckers/LB
Rest. Taquet
Siam Cuisine/Black Walnut
Susanna Foo
Swann Lounge
Thomas'

German
Ludwig's Garten
Otto's Brauhaus

Greek
Athena
Dmitri's
Effie's
Estia

Lourdas Greek
Olive Tree Med. Grill
South St. Souvlaki
Zesty's

Hamburgers
Charcoal Pit/DE
Chestnut Grill
Copa Too
Gullifty's
Independence Brew
Jake's Hamburgers/DE
John Harvard's
Manayunk Brewery
McFadden's
Nifty Fifty's†
Pop Shop/NJ
Rembrandt's
Rouge
Ruby's

Hawaiian
Bridgets
Roy's

Ice Cream Parlors
Pop Shop/NJ

Indian
An Indian Affair
Cafe Spice
Karma†
Khajuraho
New Delhi
Palace of Asia
Passage to India
Sitar India
Tandoor India

Indonesian
Indonesia

Irish
Black Sheep Pub
Fadó Irish
Fergie's Pub
Kildare's
Plough & Stars
Shanachie
Tír na nÓg

Israeli
Maccabeam

Italian
(N=Northern; S=Southern)
Abbraccio
Alberto's
August
Ava
Barone's/NJ
Bella Trattoria
Bellini Grill
Bell's/NJ
Bertolini's
Birchrunville Store
Bistro La Baia
Bistro La Viola
Bistro Romano
Bomb Bomb BBQ
Bona Cucina (N)
Branzino
Buca di Beppo†
Butcher's Cafe
Caffe Aldo Lamberti/NJ
Caffe Casta Diva
Caffe Valentino
Catelli/NJ
Core De Roma (S)
Criniti (S)
Cucina Forte (N)
D'Angelo's
Dante & Luigi's
Davio's (N)
De Anna's/NJ
Dolce
Ernesto's 1521
Fellini Cafe (S)
Filomena/NJ (S)
Fish Tank on Main (N)
Fountain Side
Franco's Pastaria (S)
Frederick's
Gioia Mia
Giumarello's/NJ
Gnocchi (N)
Hosteria Da Elio
Il Cantuccio (N)
Illuminare

Il Portico (N)
Il Sol Tuscan (N)
Il Tartufo (N)
Io E Tu
Italian Bistro†
Kristian's
Laceno Italian/NJ
La Collina (N)
La Famiglia
La Fontana
La Locanda/Ghiottone
Lamberti's Cucina/DE
L'Angolo (S)
La Veranda
La Vigna (N)
Le Castagne (N)
Luigi Vitrone's/DE
Maggiano's
Mama Palma's (S)
Mamma Maria
Marco Polo
Maria's/Summit
Marra's (S)
Melograno (N)
Mercato (N)
Mezza Luna
Mimosa (N)
Mio Sogno
Mona Lisa/DE
Monte Carlo
Moonstruck
Mr. Martino's
Mrs. Robino's/DE
Nido
Nunzio/NJ
Paganini Pizza
Paganini Trattoria
Paradiso
Penne
Pepper's Cafe
Picasso
Piccolo Trattoria
Pietro's Pizzeria†
Pizzicato†
Pompeii Cucina
Porcini
Portofino
Positano Coast

Primavera Pizza
Radicchio (N)
Ralph's
Ravenna (N)
Rist. Il Melograno
Rist. La Buca
Rist. Mediterraneo
Rist. Panorama (N)
Rist. Pesto
Rist. Positano (S)
Rist. Primavera
Rist. San Marco
Rist. Verona
Roselena's
Saloon
Sapori/NJ
Savona (N)
Scannicchio's
Shank's & Evelyn's
Sotto Varalli (N)
Sovalo
Spasso
Stefano's
Stella Blu (S)
Teca
Teresa's Cafe
Toscana Kitchen/DE (N)
Trattoria Alberto (N)
Trattoria Lucca
Trattoria Primadonna
Trattoria San Nicola
Tre Scalini
Trinacria (S)
Upstares at Varalli (N)
Vesuvio
Vetri
Victor Café
Viggiano's (S)
Villa di Roma
Vinny T's
Zesty's (S)

Jamaican
Jamaican Jerk Hut

Japanese
(* sushi specialist)
Aoi*
August Moon

Bluefin*
Blue Pacific*
Fuji Mtn.*
Genji*
Goji Tokyo Cuisine*
Haru*
Hibachi†*
Hikaru*
Jasmine/DE*
Kisso Sushi*
Koi*
Lai Lai Garden*
Madame Butterfly*
Manayunk Brewery*
Mandarin*
Margaret Kuo's*
Margaret Kuo's Media*
Margaret Kuo's Peking*
Mikado*
Mikado/NJ*
Mikimotos/DE*
Morimoto
Oishi
Ooka Japanese*
Osaka*
Ota-Ya†*
Raw Sushi Lounge*
Sagami/NJ*
Sakura Spring/NJ
Shiroi Hana*
Sushikazu*
Tampopo
Teikoku
Utage/DE*

Jewish
Ben & Irv Deli.
Famous 4th St. Deli.
Honey's Sit 'n Eat
Hymie's Deli
Izzy & Zoe's
Kibitz in City
Kibitz Room/NJ

Korean
(* barbecue specialist)
August Moon*
Jong Ka Jib

Koi
Oishi
Porky & Porkie*
Tampopo

Kosher
Cherry St. Veg.
Harmony Veg.
Maccabeam
Singapore Kosher

Laotian
Cafe de Laos
Vientiane Café

Lebanese
Cedars
Norma's/NJ

Malaysian
Banana Leaf
Penang

Mediterranean
Al Dar Bistro
Arpeggio
Audrey Claire
Byblos
Cafe Fresko
Cafe San Pietro
Estia
Figs
Gibraltar/LB
Hamilton's Grill/NJ
Le Jardin
Little Marakesh
Meridith's
Mirna's Café
Olive/NJ
Olive Tree Med. Grill
Overtures
Patou
Peacock/Parkway
Pond/Bistro Cassis
Rist. Mediterraneo
Sovana Bistro
Tangerine
Valanni

Mexican
Baja Fresh Mex.
Cantina Los Caballitos
Copabanana
Copa Too
Coyote Crossing
Don Pablo's
El Azteca†
El Sarape
El Sombrero
El Vez
Johnny Mañana's
La Cava
La Esperanza/NJ
La Lupe
Las Cazuelas
La Tolteca/DE
Lolita
Los Catrines
Mexican Food/NJ
Mexican Post†
Paloma
Qdoba Mex.†
Taco House
Tamarindo's
Taq. La Michoacana
Taq. La Veracruzana
Taq. Moroleon
Tortilla Press/NJ
Zocalo

Middle Eastern
Alyan's
Bitar's
La Pergola
Oasis Grill/NJ

Moroccan
Cafe Sud
Casablanca
Fez Moroccan
Little Marakesh
Marrakesh
Oasis Grill/NJ

Noodle Shops
Nan Zhou Noodles
Pho 75
Sang Kee Duck Hse.

Nuevo Latino
Alma de Cuba
El Serrano/LB
¡Pasión!

Pacific Rim
Pacific Grille/NJ

Pakistani
Kabobeesh

Pan-Asian
Bamboo Club
Jasmine/DE
Mantra
Mikimotos/DE
Osaka
Pod
Shangrila
Swanky Bubbles

Pan-Latin
Copabanana
Mixto

Pennsylvania Dutch
Bird-in-Hand Rest./LB
Good 'N Plenty/LB
Miller's Smorgasbord/LB
Plain & Fancy Farm/LB

Persian/Iranian
Persian Grill

Peruvian
El Serrano/LB

Pizza
Arpeggio
Bella Trattoria
Bertolini's
California Pizza
Celebre's
Gullifty's
Illuminare
Mama Palma's
Marra's
Paganini Pizza
Pietro's Pizzeria†
Primavera Pizza
Tacconelli's Pizzeria†

Polish
Warsaw Cafe

Polynesian
Moshulu

Pub Food
Abbaye
America B&G
Black Door
Black Sheep Pub
Chickie's & Pete's
Drafting Rm.
Elephant & Castle†
Fadó Irish
Fergie's Pub
Fox & Hound
Grey Lodge Pub
Independence Brew
Liberties
Manayunk Brewery
McFadden's
McGillin's
Monk's Cafe
Moriarty's
Nodding Head Brew.
N. 3rd
Plough & Stars
Sly Fox Brewery
Standard Tap
Tavern on Green
Victory Brewing
Washington St. Ale/DE

Sandwiches
Ben & Irv Deli.
Campo's Deli
Dalessandro's
Geno's Steaks
Hymie's Deli
Isaac's†
Izzy & Zoe's
Jim's Steaks
Kibitz in City
Pat's Steaks
Pepper's Cafe
Shank's & Evelyn's
Sugarfoot Fine Foods/DE
Teca

Tony Luke's
Winnie's Le Bus

Seafood
Anastasi Seafood
Athena
Barnacle Ben's/NJ
Bobby Chez/NJ
Bona Cucina
Bonefish Grill
Branzino
Bridgets
Chart House
Clam Tavern
Creed's
Deep Blue/DE
Devon Seafood
DiNardo's Seafood
Dmitri's
Feby's Fishery/DE
Fish Tank on Main
Gables/Chadds Ford
Gibraltar/LB
Harry's Seafood/DE
Kunkel's Sea/Steak/NJ
Laceno Italian/NJ
Little Fish
Little Tuna/NJ
Marco Polo
McCormick/Schmick's
Meridith's
Nineteen
Ocean Harbor
Old Orig. Bookbinder's
Palm
Phila. Fish
Philly Crab/Steak
Pub/NJ
Radicchio
Rist. La Buca
Ritz Seafood/NJ
Sansom St. Oyster
Seafood Unlimited
Snockey's Oyster
SoleFood
Sotto Varalli
Striped Bass
Tai Lake

Small Plates
(See also Spanish tapas
specialist)
Ansill (Eclectic)
Continental (Eclectic)
Derek's (New American)
Domaine Hudson/DE (New
  American)
Elements Café/NJ (New
  American)
Lacroix/Rittenhouse (French)
1717/DE (New American)
Teca (Italian)

Soul Food
bluezette
Geechee Girl
Ms. Tootsie's
Public Hse./Logan Sq.

Southern
Abner's BBQ
Carversville Inn
Crescent City
Down Home
Honey's Sit 'n Eat
Jack's Firehse.
Marsha Brown
Ogontz Grill

Southwestern
Adobe Cafe
Agave Grille
Rock Bottom

Spanish
(* tapas specialist)
Amada*
Apamate*
Bar Ferdinand*
Citron Bistro
Continental Mid-town*
Picasso
Valanni*

Steakhouses
Alberto's
Barclay Prime
Blue Eyes/NJ
Bonefish Grill

Bridgets
Capital Grille
Chart House
Chops
Conley Ward's/DE
Creed's
Davio's
Delmonico's
Earl's Prime
Hibachi†
Kunkel's Sea/Steak/NJ
Log Cabin/LB
Morton's
Palm
Philly Crab/Steak
Prime Rib
Pub/NJ
Ruth's Chris
Saloon
Seven Stars Inn
Shula's Steak
Smith & Wollensky
Sullivan's Steak.†
Ted's Montana Grill
Walter's Steak./DE

Taiwanese
Ray's Cafe

Tearooms
Cassatt Tea Room
Ray's Cafe

Tex-Mex
Tex Mex Connect.

Thai
Alisa Cafe/NJ
Cafe de Laos
Chabaa Thai Bistro
Chaleo Thai
Flavor
Gourmet
La Na
Lemon Grass†

My Thai
Nan
Oishi
Pattaya Grill
Pho Xe Lua
Siam/NJ
Siam Cuisine
Siam Cuisine/Black Walnut
Siam Lotus
Silk Cuisine
Siri's Thai French/NJ
Somsak/Taan/NJ
Teikoku
Thai Orchid†
Thai Pepper
Thai Singha
Vientiane Café
White Elephant

Turkish
Divan Turkish Kitchen
Konak

Vegetarian
(* vegan)
Blue Sage Veg.
Cherry St. Veg.
Harmony Veg.*
Horizons*
Kingdom of Veg.*
Singapore Kosher
Winnie's Le Bus

Venezuelan
Sazon

Vietnamese
Nam Phuong
Pho 75
Pho Xe Lua
Vietnam
Vietnam Palace

West African
Fatou & Fama

Philadelphia Area

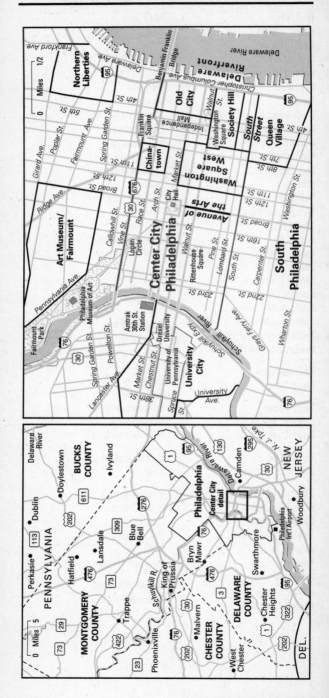

subscribe to zagat.com

LOCATIONS

PHILADELPHIA

Art Museum/Fairmount
Bridgid's
Figs
Goji Tokyo Cuisine
Illuminare
Jack's Firehse.
Little Pete's
London Grill
Long's Chinese
Museum Restaurant
Rembrandt's
Rose Tattoo
Tavern on Green

Avenue of the Arts
Bliss
Capital Grille
Grill
Italian Bistro
McCormick/Schmick's
Nineteen
Palm
Sotto Varalli
Ted's Montana Grill
Upstares at Varalli
Zanzibar Blue

Center City
(East of Broad St.)
Aoi
Bonte
Café Habana
Caribou Cafe
Deux Cheminées
Down Home
Effie's
El Azteca
El Vez
Fergie's Pub
Hard Rock
Independence Brew
Jones
Kibitz in City
La Boheme

Lolita
Ludwig's Garten
Lula
Ly Michael's
Maccabeam
Maggiano's
Marathon Grill
McGillin's
Melting Pot
Mercato
Mixto
More Than Ice Cream
Moriarty's
Morimoto
Ms. Tootsie's
Passage to India
Pompeii Cucina
Portofino
Rangoon
Raw Sushi Lounge
Reading Term. Mkt.
Rist. La Buca
Ruth's Chris
Sang Kee Duck Hse.
Siam Lotus
SoleFood
Taco House
Tampopo
Tenth St. Pour Hse.
Valanni
Vetri
Vintage

Center City
(West of Broad St.)
Alma de Cuba
Apamate
Astral Plane
Audrey Claire
Barclay Prime
Bellini Grill
Bistro La Baia
Bistro La Viola
Bistro St. Tropez

Black Sheep Pub
Bonte
Branzino
Brasserie Perrier
Byblos
Cafe Spice
Caffe Casta Diva
Cassatt Tea Room
Chez Colette
Continental Mid-town
Copabanana
Copa Too
D'Angelo's
Davio's
Day by Day
Devon Seafood
Divan Turkish Kitchen
Dmitri's
Elephant & Castle
Ernesto's 1521
Estia
Fadó Irish
Fellini Cafe
Fountain
Fox & Hound
Friday Sat. Sun.
Fuji Mtn.
Genji
Gioia Mia
Grace Tavern
Grill Rest.
Happy Rooster
Il Portico
Jamaican Jerk Hut
La Colombe
Lacroix/Rittenhouse
La Fontana
Le Bar Lyonnais
Le Bec-Fin
Le Castagne
Le Jardin
Little Pete's
Loie
Los Catrines
L2
Mama Palma's
Mantra

Marathon Grill
Marathon on Square
Matyson
Melograno
Meritage
Monk's Cafe
Morton's
Nodding Head Brew.
¡Pasión!
Peacock/Parkway
Pietro's Pizzeria
Porcini
Prime Rib
Public Hse./Logan Sq.
Pumpkin
Qdoba Mex.
Rouge
Roy's
Sansom St. Oyster
Seafood Unlimited
Shiroi Hana
Shula's Steak
Smith & Wollensky
Striped Bass
Susanna Foo
Swann Lounge
Tampopo
Ten Stone
Tír na nÓg
Trattoria Primadonna
Tria
Twenty Manning
Twenty21
Warsaw Cafe

Chinatown
Banana Leaf
Charles Plaza
Cherry St. Veg.
Four Rivers
Harmony Veg.
H.K. Golden Phoenix
Imperial Inn
Indonesia
Joy Tsin Lau
Kingdom of Veg.
Lakeside Chinese

Lee How Fook
Nan Zhou Noodles
Ocean Harbor
Penang
Pho Xe Lua
Ray's Cafe
Sang Kee Duck Hse.
Shiao Lan Kung
Siam Cuisine
Singapore Kosher
Tai Lake
Vietnam
Vietnam Palace

Delaware Riverfront
Chart House
Dave & Buster's
Hibachi
La Veranda
Moshulu

Manayunk/Roxborough/East Falls
Adobe Cafe
An Indian Affair
Bella Trattoria
Bourbon Blue
Chabaa Thai Bistro
Dalessandro's
Derek's
Fish Tank on Main
Hikaru
Il Tartufo
Jake's
Johnny Mañana's
Kildare's
La Colombe
Manayunk Brewery
Maria's/Summit
Thomas'
U.S. Hotel B&G
Winnie's Le Bus
Zesty's

Northeast Philly
Chickie's & Pete's
Copabanana
El Azteca

Gourmet
Grey Lodge Pub
Italian Bistro
Jim's Steaks
Mayfair Diner
Mexican Post
Moonstruck
Nifty Fifty's
Paloma
Philly Crab/Steak
Pho 75
Sweet Lucy's

Northern Liberties/Port Richmond
Abbaye
Azure
Bar Ferdinand
Deuce
Honey's Sit 'n Eat
Il Cantuccio
Johnny Brenda's
Koi
Las Cazuelas
Liberties
McFadden's
N. 3rd
Ortlieb's Jazz
Sazon
Sovalo
Standard Tap
Tacconelli's Pizzeria
Taste
Washington Square

North Philly
Jong Ka Jib
Tierra Colombiana

Northwest Philly
(Chestnut Hill/Germantown/Mt. Airy)
Abner's BBQ
Cafette
Chestnut Grill
CinCin
Citrus
Cresheim Cottage

Geechee Girl
Hamlet Bistro
Melting Pot
North by Northwest
Osaka
Rib Crib
Roller's/Flying Fish
Solaris Grille
Trolley Car
Umbria

Old City
Amada
Anjou
Ariana
Azalea
Bistro 7
bluezette
Buddakan
Cafe Spice
Campo's Deli
Chlöe
City Tavern
Continental
Cuba Libre
DiNardo's Seafood
Dolce
Eulogy Belgian
Farmicia
Fork
Haru
Kabul
Karma
Kisso Sushi
Konak
La Famiglia
La Locanda/Ghiottone
Mandoline
Mexican Post
Old Orig. Bookbinder's
Paradigm
Patou
Phila. Fish
Pietro's Pizzeria
Pizzicato
Plough & Stars
Radicchio

Red Sky
Rist. Panorama
Serrano
Society Hill Hotel
Spasso
Swanky Bubbles
Tangerine

South Philly
Anastasi Seafood
August
Bitar's
Bomb Bomb BBQ
Butcher's Cafe
Cafe de Laos
Cafe Sud
Caffe Valentino
Cantina Los Caballitos
Carman's Country
Celebre's
Chickie's & Pete's
Criniti
Cucina Forte
Dante & Luigi's
Franco's Pastaria
Geno's Steaks
Io E Tu
Kristian's
La Lupe
L'Angolo
La Vigna
Mamma Maria
Marra's
McFadden's
Melrose Diner
Mezza Luna
Mio Sogno
Morning Glory
Mr. Martino's
Nam Phuong
Nido
Paradiso
Pat's Steaks
Pho 75
Pif
Porky & Porkie
Ralph's

Rist. Pesto
Roselena's
Royal Tavern
Sabrina's Café
Saloon
Scannicchio's
Shank's & Evelyn's
Snockey's Oyster
Taq. La Veracruzana
Tony Luke's
Trattoria Lucca
Tre Scalini
Vesuvio
Victor Café
Villa di Roma

South St./Society Hill/ Queen Village
Alyan's
Ansill
Ava
Beau Monde
Bistro Romano
Black Door
Bridget Foy's
Cedars
Chaleo Thai
Copabanana
Core De Roma
Crescent City
Dark Horse Pub
Dessert
Django
Dmitri's
Famous 4th St. Deli.
Fez Moroccan
Frederick's
Gayle
Gnocchi
Hikaru
Horizons
Hosteria Da Elio
Jim's Steaks
Kildare's
Latest Dish
Little Fish
Marrakesh
Mimosa

Monte Carlo
Mustard Greens
My Thai
New Wave Café
Next
Overtures
Pink Rose
Positano Coast
Rist. Primavera
Salt & Pepper
South St. Souvlaki
Southwark

West Oak Lane
Ogontz Grill

West Philly/University City
Abbraccio
Abyssinia
Beijing
Copabanana
Dahlak
Fatou & Fama
Izzy & Zoe's
Jim's Steaks
Kabobeesh
La Terrasse
Lemon Grass
Marathon Grill
Marigold Kitchen
Nan
New Delhi
Pattaya Grill
Penne
Pod
Qdoba Mex.
Rx
Sitar India
Tandoor India
Thai Singha
Vientiane Café
White Dog Cafe
World Café Live
Zocalo

Wynnefield
Casablanca
Chun Hing
Delmonico's

PHILADELPHIA SUBURBS

Bucks County
Black Bass Hotel
Blue Sage Veg.
Brick Hotel
Bridgetown Mill
Carversville Inn
Casablanca
Centre Bridge Inn
Cheeseburger/Paradise
Cock 'n Bull
Cuttalossa Inn
Don Pablo's
Duck Sauce
Earl's Prime
El Sarape
El Sombrero
EverMay/Delaware
Freight House
Golden Pheasant
Havana
Hotel du Village
Il Sol Tuscan
Inn at Phillips Mill
Isaac Newton's
J.B. Dawson's
King George II
Knight House
La Bonne Auberge
Landing
La Pergola
Madame Butterfly
Marsha Brown
Mother's Rest. & Wine Bar
Nifty Fifty's
Oishi
Ooka Japanese
Ota-Ya
Paganini Pizza
Paganini Trattoria
Philly Crab/Steak
Piccolo Trattoria
Plumsteadville Inn
Rist. Il Melograno
Siam Cuisine
Siam Cuisine/Black Walnut

Slate Bleu
Spotted Hog
Summer Kitchen
Triumph Brewing Co.
Washington Crossing
Yardley Inn

Chester County
America B&G
Avalon
Birchrunville Store
Bonefish Grill
Brew HaHa!
Buca di Beppo
Catherine's
Coyote Crossing
Dilworthtown Inn
Drafting Rm.
Duling-Kurtz Hse.
Epicurean
Four Dogs Tavern
Gilmore's
Half Moon Saloon
High St. Caffé
Iron Hill Brewery
Isaac's
Kildare's
Kimberton Inn
Majolica
Mandarin
Mendenhall Inn
Mimosa Rest.
Orchard
Rist. Verona
Seven Stars Inn
Simon Pearce
Sly Fox Brewery
Sovana Bistro
Spence Cafe
Taq. Moroleon
Teca
Trattoria Alberto
Twin Bays
Vickers Tavern
Vincent's

Clifton Heights
Clam Tavern

Delaware County
Alberto's
America B&G
Baja Fresh Mex.
Bona Cucina
Fellini Cafe
Gables/Chadds Ford
Hank's Place
Hibachi
Iron Hill Brewery
J.B. Dawson's
Jim's Steaks
John Harvard's
Kildare's
La Belle Epoque
La Na
Margaret Kuo's Media
Margaret Kuo's Peking
Nifty Fifty's
Pace One
P.F. Chang's
Picasso
Rose Tree Inn
Roux 3
Ruby's
Teikoku

King of Prussia
Bahama Breeze
Baja Fresh Mex.
Bamboo Club
Bertolini's
Blue Pacific
California Cafe
California Pizza
Cheesecake Factory
Creed's
Fox & Hound
Kildare's
Lemon Grass
Maggiano's
Morton's
Rock Bottom
Ruby's

Ruth's Chris
Sullivan's Steak.

Main Line
Al Dar Bistro
Alex Long Asian
Ardmore Station
August Moon
Basil Bistro
Blush
Bunha Faun
Cafe Fresko
Cafe San Pietro
Carmine's Creole
Cedar Hollow Inn
Chef Charin
Chops
Christopher's
Citron Bistro
Fellini Cafe
Fioravanti
Flavor
General Warren
Georges'
Gullifty's
Hibachi
Hunan
Hymie's Deli
John Harvard's
Khajuraho
La Collina
Lourdas Greek
Margaret Kuo's
Max & Erma's
Meridith's
Mikado
Murray's Deli
Nectar
New Tavern
Old Guard Hse. Inn
Olive Tree Med. Grill
Osaka
Pepper's Cafe
Places! Bistro
Plate
Pond/Bistro Cassis
Primavera Pizza

Pub/Penn Valley
Rest. Alba
Rest. Taquet
Rist. Positano
Rist. Primavera
Ruby's
Sang Kee Asian
Savona
Shangrila
Silk Cuisine
Sola
Tango
Taq. La Michoacana
Teresa's Cafe
Thai Pepper
333 Belrose
Trattoria San Nicola
Victory Brewing
Vinny T's
Winberie's
Wooden Iron
Yangming

Montgomery County
Abacus
Abner's BBQ
Agave Grille
Alison/Blue Bell
Arpeggio
Athena
Baja Fresh Mex.
Bay Pony Inn
Beige & Beige
Ben & Irv Deli.
Blue Bell Inn
Bluefin
Blue Horse
Bonefish Grill
Brasserie 73
Brew HaHa!
Bridgets
Buca di Beppo
Cafe Preeya
Carambola
Coleman
Coyote Crossing
Drafting Rm.
El Sarape

Fayette Street
Fountain Side
Funky Lil' Kitchen
FuziOn
Gen. Lafayette Inn
Hibachi
Iron Hill Brewery
J.B. Dawson's
Jonathan's Amer. Grille
Joseph Ambler Inn
K.C.'s Alley
La Cava
Lai Lai Garden
La Pergola
Little Marakesh
Mainland Inn
Mandarin Garden
Marco Polo
Max & Erma's
Maya Bella
Mirna's Café
Ooka Japanese
Otto's Brauhaus
Palace of Asia
Persian Grill
Ravenna
Rist. Mediterraneo
Rist. San Marco
Shanachie
Sly Fox Brewery
Spring Mill Café
Stefano's
Stella Blu
Sushikazu
Tamarindo's
Tex Mex Connect.
Thai Orchid
Totaro's
Trax Café
Trinacria
211 York
Viggiano's
White Elephant
William Penn Inn
Zakes Cafe

Wyncote
Plate

LANCASTER/BERKS COUNTIES

Adamstown
Stoudt's

Bird-in-Hand
Bird-in-Hand Rest.
Plain & Fancy Farm

East Petersburg
Haydn Zug's

Ephrata
Isaac's
Lily's on Main
Rest. at Doneckers

Lancaster
Carr's
El Serrano
Gibraltar
Isaac's
Lemon Grass
Log Cabin

Qdoba Mex.
Strawberry Hill

Lititz
Isaac's

Pine Forge
Gracie's

Reading
Green Hills Inn

Ronks
Miller's Smorgasbord

Smoketown
Good 'N Plenty

Strasburg
Isaac's

Wyomissing
Isaac's

NEW JERSEY

Berlin
Filomena

Burlington
Big Ed's BBQ
Café Gallery

Cherry Hill
Alisa Cafe
Bahama Breeze
Barone's
Bobby Chez
Buca di Beppo
Caffe Aldo Lamberti
Cheesecake Factory
Elephant & Castle
Italian Bistro
Kibitz Room
La Campagne
Mélange Cafe
Mikado
Norma's
Oasis Grill
Olive
Ponzio's

Red Hot & Blue
Sakura Spring
Siri's Thai French

Clementon
Filomena
Nifty Fifty's

Collingswood
Barone's
Bobby Chez
Casona
Nunzio
Pop Shop
Sagami
Sapori
Tortilla Press
Water Lily
Word of Mouth

Deptford
Filomena

Haddonfield
Little Tuna

Haddon Heights
Elements Café
Kunkel's Sea/Steak

Hamilton
Rat's

Lambertville
Anton's at Swan
Bell's
De Anna's
Full Moon
Hamilton's Grill
Inn/Hawke
Lambertville Station
Lilly's on Canal
Manon
No. 9
Ota-Ya
Siam

Lindenwold
La Esperanza

Maple Shade
Mikado
Tacconelli's Pizzeria

Marlton
Food for Thought
Joe's Peking
Mexican Food
Mikado
P.F. Chang's
Pietro's Pizzeria
Pizzicato
Thai Orchid

Medford
Beau Rivage
Braddock's Tavern

Moorestown
Barnacle Ben's
Barone's

Mount Holly
Karma
Robin's Nest

Mount Laurel
Bobby Chez
El Azteca
Pacific Grille

Pennsauken
Pub

Sewell
Blue Eyes
Italian Bistro

Voorhees
Bobby Chez
Catelli
Chez Elena Wu
Coconut Bay
Laceno Italian
Little Café
Ritz Seafood
Somsak/Taan

Westmont
Cork
Giumarello's

Williamstown
Creole Cafe

DELAWARE

Bear
Charcoal Pit

Centerville
Buckley's Tavern

Greenville
Brew HaHa!

Hockessin
Back Burner

Montchanin
Krazy Kat's

Newark
Iron Hill Brewery

New Castle
Chef's Table/David Finney
Jake's Hamburgers

Wilmington
Blue Parrot B&G
Brew HaHa!
Charcoal Pit
China Royal
Columbus Inn
Conley Ward's
Corner Bistro
Culinaria
Deep Blue
Domaine Hudson
Eclipse Bistro
Feby's Fishery
Green Room
Harry's Savoy
Harry's Seafood
Hibachi
Iron Hill Brewery
Jake's Hamburgers
Jasmine
Lamberti's Cucina
La Tolteca
Luigi Vitrone's
Mexican Post
Mikimotos
Mona Lisa
Moro
Mrs. Robino's
Rest. 821
1717
Sugarfoot Fine Foods
Sullivan's Steak.
Toscana Kitchen
Union City Grille
Utage
Walter's Steak.
Washington St. Ale

SPECIAL FEATURES

(Indexes list the best in each category. Multi-location restaurants' features may vary by branch.)

Breakfast
(See also Hotel Dining)
Ardmore Station
Ben & Irv Deli.
Bird-in-Hand Rest./LB
Carman's Country
Down Home
Famous 4th St. Deli.
Full Moon/NJ
Hank's Place
Honey's Sit 'n Eat
Hymie's Deli
Izzy & Zoe's
La Colombe
La Lupe
Little Pete's
Marathon Grill
Mayfair Diner
Melrose Diner
Morning Glory
Mother's Rest. & Wine Bar
Murray's Deli
Nifty Fifty's
Pink Rose
Ponzio's/NJ
Reading Term. Mkt.
Ruby's
Sabrina's Café
Shank's & Evelyn's
Spotted Hog
Spring Mill Café
Tenth St. Pour Hse.
Tierra Colombiana
Trolley Car

Brunch
Abbraccio
Alberto's
Astral Plane
Bay Pony Inn
Beau Monde
Black Bass Hotel
Black Sheep Pub

Braddock's Tavern/NJ
Brick Hotel
Buckley's Tavern/DE
Café Gallery/NJ
Cafette
Caribou Cafe
Carman's Country
Chart House
Cock 'n Bull
Coleman
Columbus Inn/DE
Continental
Cuba Libre
Dark Horse Pub
Epicurean
Ernesto's 1521
Fadó Irish
Figs
Fork
Fountain
Four Dogs Tavern
Golden Pheasant
Green Room/DE
Gullifty's
Hibachi
Illuminare
Iron Hill Brewery†
Jack's Firehse.
Jake's
Jones
Khajuraho
Kildare's
Kimberton Inn
King George II
La Campagne/NJ
Lacroix/Rittenhouse
Lambertville Station/NJ
Las Cazuelas
Little Pete's
Loie
Mainland Inn
Marathon Grill

Marathon on Square
Mixto
Monk's Cafe
More Than Ice Cream
Morning Glory
Moshulu
Mother's Rest. & Wine Bar
New Wave Café
Next
Nodding Head Brew.
Pace One
Palace of Asia
Patou
Plough & Stars
Plumsteadville Inn
Primavera Pizza
Rat's/NJ
Rembrandt's
Roselena's
Rx
Shangrila
Solaris Grille
Spring Mill Café
Standard Tap
Summer Kitchen
Swann Lounge
Tango
Tenth St. Pour Hse.
Thomas'
Tír na nÓg
Tortilla Press/NJ
Trolley Car
U.S. Hotel B&G
Valanni
Vietnam Palace
Washington Crossing
White Dog Cafe
William Penn Inn
Yardley Inn
Zanzibar Blue
Zesty's

Buffet Served
(Check availability)
Alberto's
America B&G
An Indian Affair
Aoi

Bay Pony Inn
Bird-in-Hand Rest./LB
Black Bass Hotel
Brick Hotel
Café Gallery/NJ
Cock 'n Bull
Columbus Inn/DE
Drafting Rm.
Fatou & Fama
Frederick's
Gen. Lafayette Inn
Green Room/DE
Grill Rest.
Hibachi
Karma†
Khajuraho
Kingdom of Veg.
Manayunk Brewery
Mandarin
Miller's Smorgasbord/LB
Moshulu
Museum Restaurant
New Delhi
Ogontz Grill
Otto's Brauhaus
Palace of Asia
Passage to India
Philly Crab/Steak
Plumsteadville Inn
Porky & Porkie
Primavera Pizza
Rat's/NJ
Roselena's
Sitar India
Swann Lounge
Tandoor India
Trolley Car
Washington Crossing
William Penn Inn
Winberie's

Business Dining
Alberto's
Amada
Bamboo Club
Barclay Prime
Blue Bell Inn
Blush

Bonefish Grill
Brasserie Perrier
Capital Grille
Chops
Columbus Inn/DE
Conley Ward's/DE
Deux Cheminées
Dilworthtown Inn
Domaine Hudson/DE
Earl's Prime
Estia
Fountain
Georges'
Green Room/DE
Grill
Il Portico
Jonathan's Amer. Grille
La Veranda
La Vigna
Le Bec-Fin
Le Castagne
Margaret Kuo's
McCormick/Schmick's
Morton's
Nineteen
Old Orig. Bookbinder's
Palm
Pond/Bistro Cassis
Prime Rib
Rest. Taquet
Rist. Panorama
Roy's
Ruth's Chris
Saloon
Sansom St. Oyster
Savona
Shula's Steak
Smith & Wollensky
Striped Bass
Sullivan's Steak.†
Susanna Foo
Tangerine
Twenty21

BYO
Abacus
Abner's BBQ
Abyssinia

Alex Long Asian
Alisa Cafe/NJ
Alison/Blue Bell
Alyan's
An Indian Affair
Apamate
Ariana
Arpeggio
Athena
Audrey Claire
August
Ava
Avalon
Banana Leaf
Barnacle Ben's/NJ
Barone's/NJ
Beige & Beige
Beijing
Bellini Grill
Ben & Irv Deli.
Birchrunville Store
Bistro La Baia
Bistro La Viola
Bistro 7
Bluefin
Blue Sage Veg.
Bobby Chez/NJ
Bona Cucina
Branzino
Buckley's Tavern/DE
Bunha Faun
Butcher's Cafe
Cafe de Laos
Cafe Fresko
Cafe Preeya
Cafe Sud
Cafette
Caffe Casta Diva
Caffe Valentino
Carambola
Carman's Country
Carmine's Creole
Casablanca
Casona/NJ
Catherine's
Chabaa Thai Bistro
Chaleo Thai
Charles Plaza

Chef Charin
Cherry St. Veg.
Chez Elena Wu/NJ
Chlöe
Chun Hing
Citrus
Coconut Bay/NJ
Copabanana
Core De Roma
Creole Cafe/NJ
Cucina Forte
Day by Day
Dessert
Divan Turkish Kitchen
Django
Dmitri's
Duck Sauce
Effie's
El Azteca†
Elements Café/NJ
El Sombrero
Ernesto's 1521
Farmicia
Fatou & Fama
Fayette Street
Fellini Cafe
Figs
Fioravanti
Fish Tank on Main
Food for Thought/NJ
Fountain Side
Four Rivers
Franco's Pastaria
Full Moon/NJ
Funky Lil' Kitchen
FuziOn
Geechee Girl
Georges'
Gilmore's
Gnocchi
Hamilton's Grill/NJ
Hamlet Bistro
Hank's Place
Harmony Veg.
High St. Caffé
Hosteria Da Elio
Hunan
Il Cantuccio

Inn at Phillips Mill
Isaac's†
Jamaican Jerk Hut
Joe's Peking/NJ
Jong Ka Jib
Kabobeesh
Kabul
Khajuraho
Kibitz in City
Kibitz Room/NJ
Kingdom of Veg.
Kisso Sushi
Kunkel's Sea/Steak/NJ
La Belle Epoque
La Boheme
La Campagne/NJ
La Cava
Laceno Italian/NJ
La Fontana
Lakeside Chinese
La Locanda/Ghiottone
La Lupe
La Na
L'Angolo
La Pergola
Las Cazuelas
Lee How Fook
Lemon Grass†
Lilly's on Canal/NJ
Little Café/NJ
Little Fish
Little Marakesh
Little Tuna/NJ
Lolita
Lourdas Greek
Majolica
Mama Palma's
Mamma Maria
Mandarin
Mandoline
Manon/NJ
Mantra
Marathon Grill
Marigold Kitchen
Matyson
Maya Bella
Mélange Cafe/NJ
Melograno

Mercato
Meridith's
Mikado/NJ
Mimosa
Mimosa Rest.
Mirna's Café
More Than Ice Cream
Mr. Martino's
Ms. Tootsie's
Murray's Deli
Nan
Nan Zhou Noodles
Next
Nido
No. 9/NJ
Norma's/NJ
Nunzio/NJ
Oasis Grill/NJ
Oishi
Olive Tree Med. Grill
Ooka Japanese
Orchard
Ota-Ya†
Overtures
Pacific Grille/NJ
Peacock/Parkway
Pepper's Cafe
Piccolo Trattoria
Pif
Pizzicato/NJ
Pop Shop/NJ
Porcini
Porky & Porkie
Pumpkin
Radicchio
Ravenna
Ray's Cafe
Rest. Alba
Rist. Pesto
Rist. Verona
Ritz Seafood/NJ
Roselena's
Rx
Sabrina's Café
Sagami/NJ
Sakura Spring/NJ
Salt & Pepper
Sang Kee Asian

Sapori/NJ
Sazon
Scannicchio's
Shiao Lan Kung
Siam/NJ
Siam Cuisine
Silk Cuisine
Singapore Kosher
Siri's Thai French/NJ
Sitar India
Sola
Somsak/Taan/NJ
Sovana Bistro
Spring Mill Café
Stefano's
Summer Kitchen
Sushikazu
Sweet Lucy's
Tacconelli's Pizzeria†
Taco House
Tamarindo's
Tampopo
Tandoor India
Taq. La Veracruzana
Taq. Moroleon
Taste
Teresa's Cafe
Thai Orchid†
Tortilla Press/NJ
Trattoria Lucca
Trattoria Primadonna
Trax Café
Tre Scalini
Twin Bays
Umbria
Vientiane Café
Viggiano's
Water Lily/NJ
White Elephant
Word of Mouth/NJ
Zakes Cafe

Catering
Abacus
Abbaye
Abbraccio
Abner's BBQ
Abyssinia

Adobe Cafe
Al Dar Bistro
Alyan's
Aoi
Ardmore Station
Athena
August Moon
Ava
Bamboo Club
Barone's/NJ
Basil Bistro
Beijing
Bellini Grill
Ben & Irv Deli.
Bistro St. Tropez
Bitar's
Black Sheep Pub
Blue Pacific
Blue Sage Veg.
Bobby Chez/NJ
Bomb Bomb BBQ
Bona Cucina
Brasserie Perrier
Brasserie 73
Brick Hotel
Buca di Beppo
Cafe Sud
Cafette
Caffe Aldo Lamberti/NJ
Campo's Deli
Caribou Cafe
Carmine's Creole
Carr's/LB
Catelli/NJ
Cedars
Chez Elena Wu/NJ
Citron Bistro
Copabanana
Creole Cafe/NJ
Cuba Libre
Dahlak
Day by Day
El Azteca
Famous 4th St. Deli.
Fatou & Fama
Fayette Street
Feby's Fishery/DE
Figs

Filomena/NJ
FuziOn
Hamilton's Grill/NJ
Havana
Hibachi
Hunan
Hymie's Deli
Il Sol Tuscan
Isaac's/LB
Izzy & Zoe's
Jack's Firehse.
Jamaican Jerk Hut
Joe's Peking/NJ
Joy Tsin Lau
Kabul
Karma
Khajuraho
Kibitz in City
Kibitz Room/NJ
Kildare's
Kingdom of Veg.
Kisso Sushi
Knight House
Koi
Konak
La Campagne/NJ
Laceno Italian/NJ
Lacroix/Rittenhouse
La Lupe
Lamberti's Cucina/DE
La Pergola
Las Cazuelas
Le Bar Lyonnais
Le Bec-Fin
Lemon Grass/LB
Liberties
Lilly's on Canal/NJ
Little Café/NJ
Little Marakesh
Little Tuna/NJ
Lourdas Greek
L2
Ludwig's Garten
Mamma Maria
Mandarin
Marathon Grill
Marathon on Square
Maria's/Summit

Maya Bella
Mendenhall Inn
Moonstruck
Moriarty's
Morning Glory
Moro/DE
Mrs. Robino's/DE
Murray's Deli
No. 9/NJ
Norma's/NJ
Old Guard Hse. Inn
Ortlieb's Jazz
Otto's Brauhaus
Pace One
Pacific Grille/NJ
Passage to India
Pat's Steaks
Pepper's Cafe
Persian Grill
Phila. Fish
Pho Xe Lua
Pizzicato
Rat's/NJ
Ravenna
Red Hot & Blue/NJ
Roselena's
Rx
Sabrina's Café
Sang Kee Duck Hse.
Seafood Unlimited
Shiroi Hana
Siam Cuisine/Black Walnut
Silk Cuisine
Siri's Thai French/NJ
Sitar India
Sugarfoot Fine Foods/DE
Sushikazu
Tamarindo's
Tandoor India
Tango
Taq. Moroleon
Teca
Tex Mex Connect.
Thai Singha
333 Belrose
Tierra Colombiana
Trax Café
Twin Bays

211 York
Upstares at Varalli
Utage/DE
Vesuvio
Victor Café
Vientiane Café
Washington Crossing
White Elephant
Yardley Inn
Zesty's

Celebrity Chefs

Alma de Cuba, *Douglas Rodriguez*
Amada, *Jose Garces*
Ansill, *David Ansill and Kibett Mengech*
Anton's at Swan/NJ, *Chris Connors*
Birchrunville Store, *Francis Trzeciak*
Bliss, *Francesco Martorella*
Blush, *Nicholas Farina*
Brasserie Perrier, *Georges Perrier*
Buddakan, *Scott Swiderski*
Cantina Los Caballitos, *Miguel Aguilar*
Coleman, *Jim Coleman*
Cuba Libre, *Guillermo Veloso*
Deux Cheminées, *Fritz Blank*
Fountain, *Martin Hamann*
Gayle, *Daniel Stern*
Georges', *Georges Perrier*
Gilmore's, *Peter Gilmore*
Grill, *Terence Feury*
Horizons, *Rich Landau*
Jack's Firehse., *Jack McDavid*
Lacroix/Rittenhouse, *Jean-Marie Lacroix*
La Famiglia, *Gino Sena*
Le Bec-Fin, *Georges Perrier*
London Grill, *Michael McNally*
Mantra, *Albert Paris*
Matyson, *Matt Spector*
Mélange Cafe/NJ, *Joe Brown*
Morimoto, *Masaharu Morimoto*
Moshulu, *Ralph Fernandez*

Nectar, *Patrick Feury*
Nunzio/NJ, *Nunzio Patruno*
¡Pasión!, *Guillermo Pernot*
Pod, *Michael Schulson*
Pond/Bistro Cassis, *Abde Dahrouch*
Southwark, *Ian Moroney*
Striped Bass, *Christopher Lee*
Susanna Foo, *Susanna Foo*
Twenty Manning, *Kiong Banh*
Vetri, *Marc Vetri*
Washington Square, *Christopher Lee*

Child-Friendly

(Alternatives to the usual fast-food places; * children's menu available)
Abbraccio*
Adobe Cafe*
Al Dar Bistro*
Alisa Cafe/NJ
America B&G*
Ardmore Station*
Ariana
Arpeggio*
Athena
Azalea*
Bahama Breeze†*
Barone's/NJ*
Basil Bistro*
Bella Trattoria*
Bell's/NJ
Ben & Irv Deli.*
Bertolini's
Big Ed's BBQ/NJ*
Bird-in-Hand Rest./LB*
Bistro Romano*
Bitar's
Black Sheep Pub
Blue Bell Inn*
Bobby Chez/NJ
Bomb Bomb BBQ*
Bona Cucina
Braddock's Tavern/NJ*
Brick Hotel*
Bridget Foy's*
Bridgid's

Buckley's Tavern/DE*
Cafette*
Caffe Aldo Lamberti/NJ
California Cafe*
California Pizza*
Campo's Deli*
Casablanca*
Catelli/NJ
Charcoal Pit/DE*
Chart House*
Cheesecake Factory*
Chestnut Grill*
Chickie's & Pete's
Christopher's*
City Tavern*
Cock 'n Bull*
Columbus Inn/DE*
Corner Bistro/DE
Cresheim Cottage*
Cucina Forte
Dark Horse Pub
Dave & Buster's*
Day by Day*
Delmonico's*
Devon Seafood*
DiNardo's Seafood*
Down Home
Drafting Rm.*
Duling-Kurtz Hse.*
Effie's
El Azteca†*
Elements Café/NJ
Elephant & Castle†*
El Sombrero*
Epicurean*
Famous 4th St. Deli.
Fatou & Fama
Feby's Fishery/DE*
Fellini Cafe*
Fez Moroccan
Filomena/NJ*
Food for Thought/NJ
Fountain*
Four Dogs Tavern*
Frederick's*
Fuji Mtn.
FuziOn
Geechee Girl

Gen. Lafayette Inn*
Geno's Steaks
Gibraltar/LB*
Good 'N Plenty/LB*
Gracie's/LB*
Green Room/DE*
Grill*
Grill Rest.*
Gullifty's*
Hank's Place
Hard Rock*
Harry's Savoy/DE*
Harry's Seafood/DE*
Havana*
Haydn Zug's/LB*
Hibachi†*
Honey's Sit 'n Eat*
Hymie's Deli*
Il Portico*
Il Sol Tuscan*
Independence Brew*
Inn/Hawke/NJ*
Iron Hill Brewery†*
Isaac Newton's*
Isaac's†*
Italian Bistro†*
Izzy & Zoe's*
Jack's Firehse.*
Jake's Hamburgers/DE
J.B. Dawson's*
Jim's Steaks*
John Harvard's*
Johnny Mañana's*
Jones
Kabobeesh*
Kabul
Kibitz Room/NJ*
Kildare's*
Kimberton Inn*
Konak*
La Campagne/NJ
Laceno Italian/NJ
La Esperanza/NJ*
La Locanda/Ghiottone
La Lupe
Landing*
La Pergola
Las Cazuelas

La Tolteca/DE*
Little Pete's
Little Tuna/NJ
Log Cabin/LB*
Maggiano's*
Mama Palma's
Mamma Maria*
Manayunk Brewery*
Mandarin
Mandarin Garden
Marathon Grill*
Marathon on Square*
Maria's/Summit*
Marrakesh
Marra's*
Max & Erma's*
Mayfair Diner*
McGillin's*
Mélange Cafe/NJ
Melrose Diner*
Mercato
Mexican Food/NJ*
Mexican Post†*
Mikado
Mikado/NJ
Miller's Smorgasbord/LB*
Mirna's Café*
Mixto*
Moonstruck*
Moriarty's*
Moshulu*
Mrs. Robino's/DE*
New Tavern*
Nifty Fifty's†
No. 9/NJ
Norma's/NJ*
North by Northwest*
Nunzio/NJ
Old Guard Hse. Inn*
Ooka Japanese*
Ota-Ya/NJ
Otto's Brauhaus*
Pace One*
Pacific Grille/NJ*
Penne*
Persian Grill*
P.F. Chang's†
Phila. Fish*

Philly Crab/Steak*
Pietro's Pizzeria†*
Pizzicato†*
Plate*
Plough & Stars*
Plumsteadville Inn*
Ponzio's/NJ*
Pop Shop/NJ*
Primavera Pizza*
Pub/NJ*
Qdoba Mex.†*
Ralph's
Rangoon
Rat's/NJ
Ravenna
Red Hot & Blue/NJ*
Rembrandt's
Rist. Panorama
Rist. Pesto
Rist. Positano
Rist. Primavera*
Ritz Seafood/NJ
Rock Bottom*
Roselena's
Rose Tattoo
Roy's*
Ruby's*
Sabrina's Café
Sagami/NJ
Scannicchio's
Serrano
Seven Stars Inn*
Shank's & Evelyn's
Shiao Lan Kung
Shiroi Hana
Siam Cuisine
Simon Pearce*
Siri's Thai French/NJ
Sitar India
Snockey's Oyster*
Solaris Grille*
Somsak/Taan/NJ
South St. Souvlaki
Spasso
Spotted Hog*
Stoudt's/LB*
Sushikazu
Sweet Lucy's

Tamarindo's
Tango*
Taq. Moroleon*
Teca
Tex Mex Connect.*
Tierra Colombiana*
Tortilla Press/NJ*
Toscana Kitchen/DE
Totaro's
Tre Scalini
Trinacria
Trolley Car*
Twenty21
Vesuvio*
Victory Brewing*
Vietnam
Vietnam Palace
Viggiano's*
Villa di Roma
Vincent's
Vinny T's*
Washington Crossing*
Washington St. Ale/DE*
White Dog Cafe*
White Elephant
William Penn Inn*
Winberie's*
Winnie's Le Bus*
Word of Mouth/NJ
Yangming
Zanzibar Blue
Zesty's*
Zocalo*

Critic-Proof
(Gets lots of business despite
so-so food)
Buca di Beppo†
Dave & Buster's
Elephant & Castle†
Fox & Hound
Hard Rock
John Harvard's

Delivery/Takeout
(D=delivery, T=takeout)
Abacus (D)
Abbaye (D)
Alisa Cafe/NJ (T)

America B&G (D)
Anjou (D)
Ardmore Station (D)
August Moon (D)
Azalea (D)
Bahama Breeze/NJ (T)
Beijing (D)
Bell's/NJ (T)
Ben & Irv Deli. (D)
Big Ed's BBQ/NJ (T)
Bobby Chez/NJ (T)
Brick Hotel (D)
Byblos (D)
Cafe Spice (D)
Campo's Deli (D)
Carr's/LB (D)
Cedars (D)
Celebre's (D)
Charcoal Pit/DE (D)
Charles Plaza (D)
Cherry St. Veg. (D)
CinCin (D)
Copabanana (D)
Davio's (D)
Day by Day (D)
Effie's (D)
Fez Moroccan (D)
Filomena/NJ (T)
Franco's Pastaria (D)
Fuji Mtn. (D)
Full Moon/NJ (T)
Harmony Veg. (D)
Hymie's Deli (D)
Isaac's/LB (D)
Italian Bistro (D)
Izzy & Zoe's (D)
Joe's Peking/NJ (T)
Kingdom of Veg. (D)
La Lupe (D)
Little Café/NJ (D)
Little Pete's (D)
Long's Chinese (D)
Maccabeam (D)
Mandarin Garden (D)
Marathon Grill (D)
Marathon on Square (D)
Marra's (D)
Maya Bella (D)

Mayfair Diner (D)
Mikado (D)
Mikado/NJ (T)
Murray's Deli (D)
New Delhi (D)
Norma's/NJ (T)
Ota-Ya/NJ (T)
Passage to India (D)
P.F. Chang's/NJ (T)
Pink Rose (D)
Seafood Unlimited (D)
Shiroi Hana (D)
Siam/NJ (T)
Siam Cuisine (D)
Singapore Kosher (D)
Sitar India (D)
Stella Blu (D)
Taco House (D)
Tandoor India (D)
Taq. La Veracruzana (D)
Tenth St. Pour Hse. (D)
Thai Pepper (D)
Vesuvio (D)

Dining Alone

(Other than hotels and places with counter service)
Abner's BBQ
Aoi
Ardmore Station
Beau Monde
Ben & Irv Deli.
Bitar's
Black Sheep Pub
Bonte
Brew HaHa!†
Cafette
Caribou Cafe
Cheeseburger/Paradise
Copabanana
Criniti
Dalessandro's
Deuce
Devon Seafood
Down Home
Effie's
Famous 4th St. Deli.
Farmicia

Honey's Sit 'n Eat
Horizons
Izzy & Zoe's
Jake's Hamburgers/DE
Jim's Steaks
Jonathan's Amer. Grille
K.C.'s Alley
Kildare's
La Pergola
Ly Michael's
Maccabeam
Marathon Grill
Mayfair Diner
Mexican Post
Monk's Cafe
Morning Glory
Nifty Fifty's
Pat's Steaks
Pop Shop/NJ
Positano Coast
Raw Sushi Lounge
Reading Term. Mkt.
Sang Kee Duck Hse.
Seafood Unlimited
Shank's & Evelyn's
Tango
Ted's Montana Grill
Tony Luke's
Trolley Car

Entertainment

(Call for days and times of
performances)
Abbraccio (varies)
Alberto's (piano/band)
Alma de Cuba (Cuban jazz)
America B&G (band/vocals)
Anjou (DJ)
Bahama Breeze† (Caribbean)
Bay Pony Inn (guitar/vocals)
Beau Monde (cabaret/DJ)
Bistro Romano (piano)
Black Bass Hotel (piano/vocals)
Blue Bell Inn (bands)
Blue Eyes/NJ (singer)
Blue Horse (Latin bands/jazz)
bluezette (jazz)
Bourbon Blue (varies)
Brick Hotel (jazz)

Buckley's Tavern/DE (varies)
Café Habana (varies)
Cafe Spice (DJ/Indian)
Caffe Aldo Lamberti/NJ
   (accordion)
Casablanca (belly dancing)
Catelli/NJ (jazz)
Chickie's & Pete's (varies)
Christopher's (varies)
City Tavern (harpsichord)
Cock 'n Bull (dinner theater)
Coleman (jazz duo/piano)
Creed's (varies)
Cuba Libre (DJ/salsa)
Cuttalossa Inn (varies)
Dahlak (open mike/vocals)
D'Angelo's (DJ)
Deep Blue/DE (jazz/rock)
Dilworthtown Inn (jazz)
Epicurean (varies)
Eulogy Belgian (bands)
Fadó Irish (Irish bands/DJ)
Fergie's Pub (bands)
Fez Moroccan (belly dancing)
Filomena/NJ (varies)
Food for Thought/NJ (piano)
Fountain (bands)
Four Dogs Tavern (acoustic)
Franco's Pastaria (open mic)
Frederick's (band/piano/vocals)
Freight House (varies)
Gables/Chadds Ford (jazz)
Gen. Lafayette Inn (folk/rock)
Gracie's/LB (varies)
Green Room/DE (varies)
Grill Rest. (piano)
Gullifty's (varies)
Half Moon Saloon (varies)
Happy Rooster (karaoke)
Harry's Savoy/DE (varies)
Havana (live music)
High St. Caffé (guitar/jazz)
Il Sol Tuscan (jazz)
Independence Brew (varies)
Iron Hill Brewery† (varies)
Jack's Firehse. (varies)
Jamaican Jerk Hut (varies)
Johnny Mañana's (mariachi)

Special Features

Joseph Ambler Inn (piano)
Joy Tsin Lau (karaoke)
Kabul (Afghani music)
Kildare's (bands/DJ)
Kimberton Inn (varies)
King George II (piano)
Konak (varies)
La Collina (piano/jazz)
La Locanda/Ghiottone (guitar)
La Tolteca/DE (mariachi)
Little Marakesh (belly dancing)
Log Cabin/LB (piano)
Loie (DJ)
L2 (jazz)
Ludwig's Garten (jazz)
Maggiano's (piano/jazz)
Mamma Maria (accordion)
Manayunk Brewery (varies)
Marathon Grill (varies)
Marrakesh (belly dancing)
McFadden's (DJ)
McGillin's (bands)
Mendenhall Inn (varies)
Norma's/NJ (belly dancing)
North by Northwest (salsa)
Olive/NJ (DJ)
Ortlieb's Jazz (jazz)
Paradiso (jazz)
Patou (jazz)
Plough & Stars (Irish band)
Plumsteadville Inn (piano)
Portofino (varies)
Prime Rib (piano/bass)
Pub/NJ (jazz)
Rat's/NJ (piano/jazz)
Reading Term. Mkt. (jazz band)
Red Hot & Blue/NJ (blues)
Rembrandt's (varies)
Rest. at Doneckers/LB (piano)
Rist. Mediterraneo (varies)
Rist. San Marco (piano)
Rose Tree Inn (piano)
Serrano (varies)
Siam Lotus (DJ)
Singapore Kosher (karaoke)
Sotto Varalli (jazz)
Spence Cafe (jazz/rock)
Stoudt's/LB (German)

Sullivan's Steak.† (jazz)
Swanky Bubbles (DJ)
Swann Lounge (jazz)
Tai Lake (karaoke)
Taq. La Veracruzana (varies)
Taq. Moroleon (Mexican band)
Tex Mex Connect. (varies)
Tierra Colombiana (salsa)
Tír na nÓg (Irish/trivia)
Tortilla Press/NJ (guitar)
Toscana Kitchen/DE (jazz)
Trattoria Alberto (varies)
Trattoria Primadonna (guitar)
Trinacria (guitar)
Twenty21 (jazz trio)
Valanni (DJ)
Vickers Tavern (piano)
Victor Café (opera)
Vincent's (blues/jazz/piano)
White Dog Cafe (piano)
William Penn Inn (jazz)
World Café Live (varies)
Zanzibar Blue (jazz)

Family-Style

Bellini Grill
Bird-in-Hand Rest./LB
Buca di Beppo
Fez Moroccan
Frederick's
Gnocchi
Good 'N Plenty/LB
Indonesia
Isaac's/LB
Italian Bistro†
La Veranda
Maggiano's
Mandarin Garden
Margaret Kuo's
Miller's Smorgasbord/LB
P.F. Chang's†
Pho Xe Lua
Pietro's Pizzeria
Plain & Fancy Farm/LB
Sang Kee Duck Hse.
Swanky Bubbles
Viggiano's
Vinny T's

Fireplaces
Abbraccio
Alberto's
America B&G
An Indian Affair
Avalon
Back Burner/DE
Bay Pony Inn
Beau Monde
Beau Rivage/NJ
Black Bass Hotel
Black Door
Black Sheep Pub
Braddock's Tavern/NJ
Branzino
Brick Hotel
Bridgetown Mill
Bridgid's
Buckley's Tavern/DE
Garversville Inn
Casona/NJ
Centre Bridge Inn
Chef's Table/David Finney/DE
Cock 'n Bull
Columbus Inn/DE
Coyote Crossing
Creed's
Cresheim Cottage
Cuttalossa Inn
Delmonico's
Deux Cheminées
Dilworthtown Inn
Duling-Kurtz Hse.
Effie's
Elephant & Castle†
Epicurean
EverMay/Delaware
Fadó Irish
Filomena/NJ
Four Dogs Tavern
Gables/Chadds Ford
Gen. Lafayette Inn
Georges'
Giumarello's/NJ
Golden Pheasant
Grace Tavern
Gracie's/LB
Green Hills Inn/LB

Harry's Savoy/DE
Harry's Seafood/DE
Havana
Hibachi
Hotel du Village
Inn at Phillips Mill
Inn/Hawke/NJ
Jones
Kildare's
Kimberton Inn
King George II
Krazy Kat's/DE
La Bonne Auberge
La Campagne/NJ
Landing
Log Cabin/LB
McGillin's
Mendenhall Inn
Mexican Post/DE
Monte Carlo
Moriarty's
Old Guard Hse. Inn
Pace One
Plough & Stars
Plumsteadville Inn
Pub/NJ
Rat's/NJ
Ravenna
Rest. at Doneckers/LB
Rose Tree Inn
Saloon
Serrano
Shanachie
Standard Tap
Swann Lounge
Union City Grille/DE
Vesuvio
Vickers Tavern
Vincent's
Washington Crossing
Washington St. Ale/DE
Yardley Inn
Zesty's

Historic Places
(Year opened; * building)
1681 King George II
1702 La Bonne Auberge*

Special Features

1706 Cresheim Cottage*	1870 Marsha Brown*
1714 William Penn Inn*	1875 Deux Cheminées*
1717 Bay Pony Inn*	1890 Jack's Firehse.*
1726 La Famiglia*	1892 Reading Term. Mkt.*
1734 Joseph Ambler Inn*	1896 Rx*
1736 Seven Stars Inn	1897 Gables/Chadds Ford*
1740 Pace One*	1900 Ralph's
1743 Blue Bell Inn*	1900 Robin's Nest/NJ*
1745 Black Bass Hotel*	1900 Winnie's Le Bus*
1745 General Warren*	1903 U.S. Hotel B&G*
1751 Plumsteadville Inn	1905 Casona/NJ*
1756 Inn at Phillips Mill*	1907 Hotel du Village*
1758 Cuttalossa Inn*	1907 Marigold Kitchen*
1758 Dilworthtown Inn*	1910 Victor Café
1764 Brick Hotel*	1913 Green Room/DE
1776 DiNardo's Seafood*	1920 Susanna Foo*
1780 Places! Bistro*	1923 Famous 4th St. Deli.
1790 EverMay/Delaware*	1927 Marra's
1790 Mainland Inn*	1929 Miller's Smorgasbord/LB
1790 Twin Bays*	1930 Log Cabin/LB*
1791 Bridgetown Mill*	1930 Otto's Brauhaus
1796 Kimberton Inn*	1930 Pat's Steaks
1800 Bistro Romano*	1932 Mayfair Diner
1800 Bourbon Blue*	1935 Melrose Diner
1800 Old Guard Hse. Inn*	1936 Buckley's Tavern/DE
1801 London Grill*	1938 Anastasi Seafood
1806 Snockey's Oyster*	1939 Bell's/NJ
1810 Carversville Inn*	1939 Jim's Steaks
1823 Braddock's Tavern/NJ*	1940 Mrs. Robino's/DE
1830 Duling-Kurtz Hse.*	1940 Pub/Penn Valley*
1832 Yardley Inn*	1945 Murray's Deli
1833 New Tavern*	1948 Tacconelli's Pizzeria
1846 Knight House*	1950 Ben & Irv Deli.
1849 Dante & Luigi's*	1950 Rose Tree Inn
1850 Roselena's*	1951 Pub/NJ
1850 Washington Crossing	1953 Columbus Inn/DE
1851 Catherine's*	1955 Hymie's Deli
1852 Haydn Zug's/LB*	1956 Charcoal Pit/DE
1854 Los Catrines*	
1854 Tavern on Green*	**Hotel Dining**
1855 Mendenhall Inn*	Bellevue, The
1860 Inn/Hawke/NJ*	Zanzibar Blue
1860 Little Fish*	Best Western Inn
1860 McGillin's	Palace of Asia
1863 Lambertville Station/NJ*	Black Bass Hotel
1864 Slate Bleu*	Black Bass Hotel
1865 Old Orig. Bookbinder's*	Brick Hotel
1870 Ernesto's 1521*	Brick Hotel

Centre Bridge Inn
  Centre Bridge Inn
Chestnut Hill Hotel
  Chestnut Grill
Clarion Hotel
  Elephant & Castle/NJ
Clarion Inn at Mendenhall
  Mendenhall Inn
Crowne Plaza Philadelphia
  Center City
  Elephant & Castle
Duling-Kurtz House
  Duling-Kurtz Hse.
EverMay On The Delaware
  EverMay/Delaware
Four Seasons Hotel
  Fountain
  Swann Lounge
Gen. Lafayette Inn
  Gen. Lafayette Inn
General Warren Inne
  General Warren
Golden Pheasant Inn
  Golden Pheasant
Hilton Philadelphia City Ave.
  Delmonico's
Holiday Inn
  Red Hot & Blue/NJ
Hotel du Pont
  Brew HaHa!/DE
  Green Room/DE
Hotel du Village
  Hotel du Village
Inn at Montchanin Village
  Krazy Kat's/DE
Inn at Penn
  Penne
  Pod
Inn at Phillips Mill
  Inn at Phillips Mill
Joseph Ambler Inn
  Joseph Ambler Inn
Loews Philadelphia Hotel
  SoleFood
Omni Hotel
  Azalea
Pace One Country Inn
  Pace One

Park Hyatt at the Bellevue
  Nineteen
  Palm
Penn's View Hotel
  Rist. Panorama
Plumsteadville Inn
  Plumsteadville Inn
Radisson Plaza Warwick Hotel
  Prime Rib
Rittenhouse Hotel
  Cassatt Tea Room
  Lacroix/Rittenhouse
  Smith & Wollensky
Ritz-Carlton Philadelphia
  Grill
Sheraton Philadelphia City Ctr.
  Shula's Steak
Society Hill Hotel
  Society Hill Hotel
Sofitel Philadelphia
  Chez Colette
Swan Hotel
  Anton's at Swan/NJ
Wayne Hotel
  Rest. Taquet
Westin Philadelphia
  Grill Rest.
William Penn Inn
  William Penn Inn

Jacket Required
Dilworthtown Inn
Fountain
Lacroix/Rittenhouse
La Famiglia
Le Bec-Fin

Late Dining
(Weekday closing hour)
Abbaye (1 AM)
Abyssinia (1 AM)
Bahama Breeze (varies)
Banana Leaf (2 AM)
Bar Ferdinand (12 AM)
Black Door (2 AM)
Black Sheep Pub (12 AM)
Blue Parrot B&G/DE (1 AM)
Bridget Foy's (12 AM)
Byblos (2 AM)

Special Features

Cantina Los Caballitos (1 AM)
Charcoal Pit/DE (varies)
Chickie's & Pete's (varies)
Christopher's (1 AM)
Copabanana (varies)
Copa Too (12:45 AM)
Crescent City (12 AM)
Dahlak (2 AM)
Dalessandro's (12 AM)
D'Angelo's (12 AM)
Dark Horse Pub (12 AM)
Deuce (1 AM)
Elephant & Castle† (varies)
Eulogy Belgian (1:30 AM)
Fadó Irish (12 AM)
Fergie's Pub (12 AM)
Fox & Hound (varies)
Freight House (12 AM)
Geno's Steaks (24 hrs.)
Grace Tavern (2 AM)
Grey Lodge Pub (2 AM)
Hard Rock (12 AM)
Harry's Savoy/DE (1 AM)
H.K. Golden Phoenix (12 AM)
Imperial Inn (12 AM)
Independence Brew (varies)
Iron Hill Brewery (varies)
Jim's Steaks (varies)
Johnny Brenda's (1 AM)
Jones (12 AM)
K.C.'s Alley (12 AM)
Kildare's (12 AM)
La Lupe (12 AM)
Little Pete's (varies)
Mantra (1 AM)
Mayfair Diner (24 hrs.)
McFadden's (2 AM)
McGillin's (1 AM)
Melrose Diner (24 hrs.)
Mexican Post (varies)
Monk's Cafe (1 AM)
Moriarty's (1 AM)
New Wave Café (1 AM)
Nodding Head Brew. (12 AM)
N. 3rd (1 AM)
Ortlieb's Jazz (12 AM)
Pat's Steaks (24 hrs.)
Penang (1 AM)

Ponzio's/NJ (1 AM)
Pub/Penn Valley (2 AM)
Rembrandt's (1 AM)
Rock Bottom (varies)
Royal Tavern (1 AM)
Shiao Lan Kung (12:30 AM)
Smith & Wollensky (1:30 AM)
Society Hill Hotel (12 AM)
Standard Tap (1 AM)
Swanky Bubbles (1 AM)
Swann Lounge (12 AM)
Tai Lake (3 AM)
Teca (2 AM)
Tony Luke's (varies)
Tria (1 AM)
Triumph Brewing Co. (varies)
Valanni (1 AM)
Vesuvio (12 AM)
Victory Brewing (12 AM)
Vintage (2 AM)
Washington St. Ale/DE (1 AM)
Zanzibar Blue (varies)

Meet for a Drink

Abbaye
Alberto's
Al Dar Bistro
Alma de Cuba
Bamboo Club
Bar Ferdinand
Beau Monde
Bell's/NJ
Black Sheep Pub
bluezette
Blush
Bonefish Grill
Brasserie Perrier
Cantina Los Caballitos
Capital Grille
Caribou Cafe
Cheeseburger/Paradise
Chops
Citron Bistro
Continental
Continental Mid-town
Copa Too
Coyote Crossing
Crescent City

Cuba Libre
Dark Horse Pub
Davio's
Delmonico's
Derek's
Deuce
Earl's Prime
Eulogy Belgian
Fadó Irish
Fergie's Pub
Georges'
Grey Lodge Pub
Happy Rooster
Horizons
Independence Brew
Inn/Hawke/NJ
Iron Hill Brewery†
Jonathan's Amer. Grille
Jones
Kildare's
Loie
London Grill
Los Catrines
L2
Manayunk Brewery
Mantra
McCormick/Schmick's
McFadden's
Mexican Post
Mixto
Monk's Cafe
Moriarty's
New Wave Café
Nineteen
Penne
Plough & Stars
Pond/Bistro Cassis
Prime Rib
Rist. Panorama
Royal Tavern
Shanachie
Sly Fox Brewery
Society Hill Hotel
Standard Tap
Swann Lounge
Tango
Ted's Montana Grill
Tír na nÓg

Triumph Brewing Co.
Twenty Manning
Twenty21
Valanni
Vintage
Wooden Iron

Microbreweries
Gen. Lafayette Inn
Independence Brew
Iron Hill Brewery†
John Harvard's
Manayunk Brewery
Nodding Head Brew.
Rock Bottom
Sly Fox Brewery
Stoudt's/LB
Triumph Brewing Co.
Victory Brewing

Natural/Organic
(These restaurants often
or always use organic,
local ingredients)
Alisa Cafe/NJ
Apamate
Baja Fresh Mex.
Barnacle Ben's/NJ
Barone's/NJ
Bistro La Baia
Carr's/LB
Charles Plaza
Cherry St. Veg.
Chlöe
Citrus
Coleman
Continental
Corner Bistro/DE
Cresheim Cottage
D'Angelo's
Farmicia
Fish Tank on Main
Little Fish
Loie
Lolita
Marathon Grill
Marco Polo
Maya Bella
Meritage

Palm
Pattaya Grill
Phila. Fish
Pif
Portofino
Pumpkin
Rest. Alba
Roller's/Flying Fish
Rouge
Royal Tavern
Rx
Salt & Pepper
Simon Pearce
Sovalo
White Dog Cafe

Noteworthy Newcomers
Amada
Ansill
Banana Leaf
Bar Ferdinand
Black Door
Blush
Casona/NJ
Crescent City
Derek's
Deuce
Divan Turkish Kitchen
Estia
Funky Lil' Kitchen
Gayle
Gioia Mia
Hamlet Bistro
Horizons
Jonathan's Amer. Grille
La Fontana
Majolica
Mantra
Nineteen
Pond/Bistro Cassis
Slate Bleu
Sovana Bistro
Taste
Ted's Montana Grill
Vintage

Offbeat
Abner's BBQ
Ansill

Astral Plane
Bamboo Club
Bitar's
Bonte
Buca di Beppo†
Butcher's Cafe
Carman's Country
Continental Mid-town
El Vez
Farmicia
Gracie's/LB
Honey's Sit 'n Eat
Jake's Hamburgers/DE
Jones
La Esperanza/NJ
La Lupe
Little Café/NJ
Little Pete's
Maggiano's
Manon/NJ
Melrose Diner
Morimoto
Morning Glory
Moshulu
Norma's/NJ
Ota-Ya†
Penang
Pod
Pop Shop/NJ
Rat's/NJ
Shanachie
Shank's & Evelyn's
Siam/NJ
Simon Pearce
Siri's Thai French/NJ
Somsak/Taan/NJ
Tacconelli's Pizzeria
Trolley Car
Water Lily/NJ

Open Kitchen
Alison/Blue Bell
Amada
Apamate
Audrey Claire
Basil Bistro
Beijing
Bistro 7

California Cafe
Carambola
Carmine's Creole
Delmonico's
Dilworthtown Inn
Dmitri's
Estia
Fayette Street
Fioravanti
Funky Lil' Kitchen
Gibraltar/LB
Lilly's on Canal/NJ
Little Fish
Lolita
Luigi Vitrone's/DE
Mandoline
Mercato
Old Orig. Bookbinder's
Pumpkin
Rest. Alba
Roy's
Striped Bass
Sullivan's Steak.†

Outdoor Dining
(G=garden; P=patio;
S=sidewalk; T=terrace)
Abbaye (S)
Adobe Cafe (P)
Alberto's (P)
Alma de Cuba (S)
Anjou (S)
Anton's at Swan/NJ (P)
Arpeggio (S)
Astral Plane (S)
Athena (P)
Audrey Claire (S)
Bahama Breeze† (T)
Barone's/NJ (P,S)
Bay Pony Inn (T)
Beau Monde (T)
Bertolini's (P)
Birchrunville Store (T)
Bistro La Baia (S)
Bistro La Viola (S)
Bliss (S)
Blue Parrot B&G/DE (P)
Bobby Chez/NJ (S)

Branzino (P)
Brasserie Perrier (S)
Brasserie 73 (P)
Brick Hotel (G)
Bridget Foy's (S)
Bridgetown Mill (P)
Buckley's Tavern/DE (T)
Byblos (P)
Café Gallery/NJ (T)
Cafe San Pietro (S)
Cafe Sud (P)
Cafette (G)
Caffe Aldo Lamberti/NJ (P)
Caribou Cafe (T)
Cassatt Tea Room (G)
Catherine's (P)
Centre Bridge Inn (T)
Chart House (T)
Chestnut Grill (P,S)
City Tavern (G)
Columbus Inn/DE (P)
Continental (S)
Continental Mid-town (P,S)
Coyote Crossing (P)
Cresheim Cottage (P)
Cuba Libre (S)
Cuttalossa Inn (T)
Derek's (P,S)
Devon Seafood (P)
Dilworthtown Inn (P)
Drafting Rm. (P)
Elephant & Castle (S)
El Serrano/LB (P)
Ernesto's 1521 (G)
Figs (S)
Filomena/NJ (P)
Fork (S)
Four Dogs Tavern (P)
Frederick's (S)
Freight House (T)
FuziOn (S)
Gables/Chadds Ford (P)
Gibraltar/LB (G,P)
Giumarello's/NJ (P)
Golden Pheasant (G,T)
Gracie's/LB (G,P)
Harry's Savoy/DE (P,T)
Havana (P)

Hosteria Da Elio (P)
Illuminare (G,T)
Il Sol Tuscan (P)
Inn at Phillips Mill (G)
Inn/Hawke/NJ (P)
Isaac Newton's (G)
Isaac's† (P)
Izzy & Zoe's (S)
Jack's Firehse. (P,S)
Jamaican Jerk Hut (G)
Johnny Mañana's (S)
Joseph Ambler Inn (P)
Karma (S)
Kildare's (P)
La Boheme (S)
La Campagne/NJ (G,T)
La Colombe (S)
La Lupe (S)
Landing (G,T)
La Veranda (T)
La Vigna (P)
Le Jardin (G,S)
Lemon Grass/LB (P)
Lilly's on Canal/NJ (P)
Lolita (S)
Maggiano's (P)
Manayunk Brewery (T)
Maya Bella (P)
Mélange Cafe/NJ (P)
Melograno (S)
Mexican Food/NJ (P)
Mimosa (P)
Mimosa Rest. (P)
Monte Carlo (P)
More Than Ice Cream (S)
Morning Glory (G,P)
Moshulu (T)
Mother's Rest. & Wine Bar (S)
New Tavern (P)
New Wave Café (S)
North by Northwest (P)
Ogontz Grill (P)
Otto's Brauhaus (G)
Pace One (G)
Pat's Steaks (S)
Pattaya Grill (P,S)
Pepper's Cafe (P)
Phila. Fish (P)

Pietro's Pizzeria (P,S,T)
Pizzicato (S)
Places! Bistro (G,P)
Plate (P)
Plough & Stars (S)
Pompeii Cucina (G)
Pond/Bistro Cassis (G)
Positano Coast (P)
Primavera Pizza (P)
Radicchio (S)
Rat's/NJ (T)
Ravenna (P)
Red Sky (S)
Rembrandt's (S)
Rest. Taquet (P)
Robin's Nest/NJ (P)
Rouge (P)
Roux 3 (P)
Rx (S)
Savona (T)
Serrano (S)
Society Hill Hotel (S)
Solaris Grille (G,P)
Spasso (P)
Spring Mill Café (P)
Summer Kitchen (P)
Swanky Bubbles (S)
Swann Lounge (G)
Tango (P)
Taq. La Veracruzana (S)
Tavern on Green (S)
Teca (S)
Thomas' (S)
333 Belrose (P)
Tír na nÓg (P)
Toscana Kitchen/DE (P)
Trattoria Alberto (G,S)
Trattoria Primadonna (S)
Tria (S)
Twenty Manning (S)
Twenty21 (G)
Vesuvio (S)
Vincent's (P)
Washington Crossing (P)
Washington Square (P,S)
Washington St. Ale/DE (P)
Winberie's (P)
Word of Mouth/NJ (P)

Zesty's (S)
Zocalo (P)

Parking
(V=valet, *=validated)
Alberto's (V)
Alma de Cuba (V)
Amada (V)
An Indian Affair*
Apamate*
Ariana (V)
Azalea (V)
Bahama Breeze (V)
Black Bass Hotel (V)
Bliss*
bluezette (V)
Bourbon Blue (V)
Brasserie Perrier (V)
Bridgets (V)
Buddakan (V)
Caffe Aldo Lamberti/NJ (V)
Capital Grille (V)
Cassatt Tea Room (V)
Centre Bridge Inn (V)
Chart House (V)
Chez Colette (V)
Chops (V)
Columbus Inn/DE (V)
Conley Ward's/DE (V)
Copabanana*
Crescent City (V)
Cuba Libre (V)
D'Angelo's*
Dave & Buster's*
Davio's (V)
Delmonico's (V)
Derek's*
DiNardo's Seafood*
Dolce (V)
El Vez*
Estia*
Fountain (V)
Fox & Hound*
Frederick's (V)
Freight House (V)
Gioia Mia (V)
Giumarello's/NJ (V)
Green Room/DE (V)

Grill (V)
Grill Rest. (V)
Hibachi (V)
H.K. Golden Phoenix*
Il Portico (V)
Jake's (V)
Jones (V)
Joy Tsin Lau*
Kabul*
Kildare's (V)
King George II (V)
Kristian's (V)
La Collina (V)
Lacroix/Rittenhouse (V)
La Famiglia (V)
Lakeside Chinese*
La Veranda (V)
Le Bar Lyonnais (V)
Le Bec-Fin (V)
Los Catrines (V)
Maggiano's (V)*
Manayunk Brewery (V)
Marsha Brown (V)
Matyson*
McCormick/Schmick's (V)
Monte Carlo (V)
Morimoto (V)
Morton's (V)
Moshulu (V)
Palm (V)*
Paradigm (V)
¡Pasión!*
Patou (V)
Penne (V)
Pho Xe Lua*
Pod (V)
Pompeii Cucina*
Porcini*
Portofino*
Positano Coast (V)
Prime Rib (V)
Pumpkin*
Red Sky (V)
Rest. 821/DE (V)
Rist. La Buca*
Rist. Panorama (V)*
Rist. Primavera (V)
Roy's (V)

Ruth's Chris (V)
Sansom St. Oyster*
Savona (V)
Shiroi Hana*
Shula's Steak (V)*
Smith & Wollensky (V)
Solaris Grille*
Striped Bass (V)
Sullivan's Steak. (V)
Susanna Foo (V)
Swanky Bubbles (V)
Swann Lounge (V)
Tai Lake*
Tangerine (V)
Ted's Montana Grill (V)
Tír na nÓg (V)
Trattoria Alberto (V)
Twenty21*
Upstares at Varalli*
Vesuvio (V)
Washington Square (V)
William Penn Inn (V)
Winnie's Le Bus*
Zanzibar Blue (V)*
Zesty's (V)

People-Watching

Alma de Cuba
Amada
America B&G
Audrey Claire
Bamboo Club
Banana Leaf
Barclay Prime
Bar Ferdinand
Blue Pacific
bluezette
Blush
Bourbon Blue
Brasserie Perrier
Bridget Foy's
Buddakan
Caffe Aldo Lamberti/NJ
Cantina Los Caballitos
Capital Grille
Catelli/NJ
Chickie's & Pete's
Chops

Citron Bistro
Continental
Continental Mid-town
Copabanana
Creed's
Crescent City
Cuba Libre
Derek's
Divan Turkish Kitchen
Dmitri's
Eulogy Belgian
Fadó Irish
Famous 4th St. Deli.
Fork
Geno's Steaks
Georges'
Grill
Hymie's Deli
Jake's
Jake's Hamburgers/DE
Jones
Kildare's
Lacroix/Rittenhouse
Latest Dish
Le Castagne
Loie
London Grill
Los Catrines
Maggiano's
Mantra
McCormick/Schmick's
McFadden's
Melrose Diner
Mexican Post
Mirna's Café
Mixto
Morimoto
Moro/DE
Moshulu
New Tavern
Palm
¡Pasión!
Pat's Steaks
Pif
Plate
Pod
Pond/Bistro Cassis
Ponzio's/NJ

Pop Shop/NJ
Prime Rib
Public Hse./Logan Sq.
Radicchio
Raw Sushi Lounge
Rist. Panorama
Rouge
Roux 3
Royal Tavern
Roy's
Shanachie
Smith & Wollensky
Striped Bass
Sullivan's Steak.†
Tangerine
Tango
Teikoku
Tír na nÓg
Tony Luke's
Twenty Manning
Union City Grille/DE
Upstares at Varalli
Valanni
Vesuvio
Vinny T's
Vintage
Zanzibar Blue

Power Scenes

Alma de Cuba
Amada
Barclay Prime
Blush
Brasserie Perrier
Buddakan
Caffe Aldo Lamberti/NJ
Capital Grille
Catelli/NJ
Chops
Continental Mid-town
Earl's Prime
Estia
Famous 4th St. Deli.
Fountain
Gayle
Georges'
Green Room/DE
Grill Rest.

Lacroix/Rittenhouse
La Veranda
Le Bec-Fin
Le Castagne
McCormick/Schmick's
Mexican Post
Morimoto
Morton's
Palm
Pond/Bistro Cassis
Ponzio's/NJ
Prime Rib
Rouge
Roy's
Ruth's Chris
Saloon
Shula's Steak
Smith & Wollensky
Striped Bass
Sullivan's Steak.†
Susanna Foo
Wooden Iron

Pre-Theater Dining
(Call for prices and times)
Bay Pony Inn
Deep Blue/DE
Deux Cheminées
Pompeii Cucina
Toscana Kitchen/DE
Valanni
Vesuvio

Private Rooms
(Restaurants charge less at
off times; call for capacity)
Abbraccio
Adobe Cafe
Alberto's
Alma de Cuba
Alyan's
America B&G
Arpeggio
August Moon
Avalon
Back Burner/DE
Barone's/NJ
Basil Bistro
Bay Pony Inn

Bistro Romano
Bistro St. Tropez
Black Sheep Pub
Blue Bell Inn
Blue Horse
bluezette
Bourbon Blue
Brasserie Perrier
Brick Hotel
Bridgetown Mill
Buca di Beppo
Byblos
Caffe Aldo Lamberti/NJ
California Cafe
Capital Grille
Casablanca
Catelli/NJ
Centre Bridge Inn
Chart House
Chez Elena Wu/NJ
Chickie's & Pete's
Chops
CinCin
City Tavern
Coleman
Continental Mid-town
Copabanana
Coyote Crossing
Creed's
Cresheim Cottage
Cuba Libre
Dark Horse Pub
Dave & Buster's
Davio's
Derek's
Devon Seafood
Dilworthtown Inn
DiNardo's Seafood
Drafting Rm.
Duling-Kurtz Hse.
Effie's
Epicurean
EverMay/Delaware
Feby's Fishery/DE
Fergie's Pub
Fez Moroccan
Food for Thought/NJ
Fountain Side

Four Dogs Tavern
Freight House
Gen. Lafayette Inn
General Warren
Giumarello's/NJ
Gracie's/LB
Green Hills Inn/LB
Gullifty's
Hamilton's Grill/NJ
Hard Rock
Harry's Savoy/DE
H.K. Golden Phoenix
Il Portico
Iron Hill Brewery†
Italian Bistro†
Jack's Firehse.
John Harvard's
Joseph Ambler Inn
King George II
La Bonne Auberge
La Collina
Lacroix/Rittenhouse
Lai Lai Garden
Lamberti's Cucina/DE
La Veranda
Le Bec-Fin
Liberties
Lily's on Main/LB
Los Catrines
Ludwig's Garten
Luigi Vitrone's/DE
Maggiano's
Mainland Inn
Mamma Maria
Margaret Kuo's Peking
Maya Bella
McCormick/Schmick's
McGillin's
Melting Pot
Mendenhall Inn
Meritage
Mikado
Mio Sogno
Mixto
Moriarty's
Morton's
Moshulu
Mrs. Robino's/DE

Nectar
New Tavern
Old Orig. Bookbinder's
Olive/NJ
Osaka
Pace One
Pacific Grille/NJ
Palace of Asia
Patou
Pho Xe Lua
Pietro's Pizzeria
Pif
Places! Bistro
Plate
Plumsteadville Inn
Pod
Pompeii Cucina
Portofino
Primavera Pizza
Prime Rib
Pub/NJ
Ralph's
Rat's/NJ
Rest. 821/DE
Rest. Taquet
Rist. Positano
Rist. San Marco
Roselena's
Rose Tree Inn
Roux 3
Roy's
Ruth's Chris
Saloon
Savona
Serrano
Seven Stars Inn
Shangrila
Shiroi Hana
Shula's Steak
Simon Pearce
Siri's Thai French/NJ
Smith & Wollensky
Solaris Grille
SoleFood
Spasso
Spring Mill Café
Stefano's
Sullivan's Steak./DE

Susanna Foo
Tai Lake
Tangerine
Tango
Teikoku
Ten Stone
Thomas'
333 Belrose
Tierra Colombiana
Totaro's
Trattoria Alberto
Trattoria Lucca
Trattoria Primadonna
Trinacria
Twenty21
Twin Bays
Upstares at Varalli
Utage/DE
Vesuvio
Vickers Tavern
Vietnam
Viggiano's
Vincent's
Washington Crossing
White Dog Cafe
World Café Live
Yardley Inn
Zanzibar Blue

Prix Fixe Menus

(Call for prices and times)
America B&G
Aoi
Bay Pony Inn
Birchrunville Store
Black Bass Hotel
Bridgetown Mill
Café Gallery/NJ
Caribou Cafe
Carmine's Creole
Casablanca
Cassatt Tea Room
Chez Colette
Chun Hing
Cuba Libre
Deux Cheminées
Devon Seafood
Dilworthtown Inn

Drafting Rm.
EverMay/Delaware
Fayette Street
Fez Moroccan
Fountain
Gen. Lafayette Inn
Gnocchi
Golden Pheasant
Good 'N Plenty/LB
Green Hills Inn/LB
Haydn Zug's/LB
Indonesia
Kabobeesh
Kimberton Inn
Kingdom of Veg.
Koi
La Bonne Auberge
La Campagne/NJ
Lacroix/Rittenhouse
La Locanda/Ghiottone
Le Bec-Fin
Lemon Grass/LB
Little Marakesh
Mainland Inn
Mamma Maria
Manon/NJ
Marrakesh
Mendenhall Inn
Meritage
Miller's Smorgasbord/LB
Monte Carlo
Morimoto
Moro/DE
My Thai
Norma's/NJ
Nunzio/NJ
Orchard
Pace One
Paradigm
Pattaya Grill
Peacock/Parkway
Pif
Rat's/NJ
Rest. at Doneckers/LB
Rest. 821/DE
Rest. Taquet
Roy's
Sansom St. Oyster

Savona
Shangrila
Spring Mill Café
Striped Bass
Summer Kitchen
Susanna Foo
Thai Orchid
Thai Singha
Thomas'
Twenty Manning
Twenty21
Vetri
William Penn Inn
Zocalo

Quick Bites
Abner's BBQ
Alyan's
Apamate
Ardmore Station
Banana Leaf
Bar Ferdinand
Bitar's
Bonte
Brew HaHa!†
Campo's Deli
Cantina Los Caballitos
Cheeseburger/Paradise
Full Moon/NJ
Grey Lodge Pub
Indonesia
Isaac's/LB
Jake's Hamburgers/DE
Jim's Steaks
Kildare's
La Lupe
Little Pete's
Mayfair Diner
McFadden's
Melrose Diner
Monk's Cafe
Pat's Steaks
Ponzio's/NJ
Pop Shop/NJ
Reading Term. Mkt.
Royal Tavern
Shanachie
South St. Souvlaki

Tierra Colombiana
Tony Luke's
Trolley Car

Quiet Conversation
Birchrunville Store
Bistro 7
Braddock's Tavern/NJ
Caffe Casta Diva
Deux Cheminées
Dilworthtown Inn
Estia
Food for Thought/NJ
Fountain
Gilmore's
Gioia Mia
Hamlet Bistro
Inn at Phillips Mill
La Bonne Auberge
Lacroix/Rittenhouse
La Famiglia
Le Castagne
Le Jardin
Nineteen
Overtures
Rat's/NJ
Roselena's
Simon Pearce
Singapore Kosher
Slate Bleu
Susanna Foo
Swann Lounge
Umbria
Yardley Inn

Raw Bars
Bamboo Club
Blue Eyes/NJ
Blue Horse
Caffe Aldo Lamberti/NJ
Creed's
Earl's Prime
Feby's Fishery/DE
Freight House
Harry's Seafood/DE
Johnny Brenda's
Koi
Kunkel's Sea/Steak/NJ

Little Tuna/NJ
Marsha Brown
Meritage
Mikimotos/DE
Nineteen
Olive/NJ
Osaka
Pace One
Phila. Fish
Sansom St. Oyster
Snockey's Oyster
SoleFood
Sotto Varalli
Stoudt's/LB
Striped Bass
Trax Café
Walter's Steak./DE
Washington Square

Romantic Places
Anton's at Swan/NJ
Apamate
Astral Plane
Beau Monde
Beau Rivage/NJ
Birchrunville Store
Bistro Romano
Bistro 7
Blush
Caffe Casta Diva
Carversville Inn
Catelli/NJ
Chlöe
Creole Cafe/NJ
Dessert
Deux Cheminées
Dilworthtown Inn
Divan Turkish Kitchen
Duling-Kurtz Hse.
Earl's Prime
Estia
EverMay/Delaware
Fountain
Frederick's
Gayle
Gilmore's
Gioia Mia
Giumarello's/NJ

Golden Pheasant
Hamlet Bistro
Horizons
Hotel du Village
Inn at Phillips Mill
La Bonne Auberge
Le Bar Lyonnais
Le Bec-Fin
Le Jardin
Lilly's on Canal/NJ
Log Cabin/LB
Majolica
Marigold Kitchen
Mendenhall Inn
Monte Carlo
Mr. Martino's
Nineteen
Overtures
Paradiso
¡Pasión!
Pond/Bistro Cassis
Rat's/NJ
Roselena's
Rose Tattoo
Simon Pearce
Slate Bleu
Southwark
Spring Mill Café
Striped Bass
Summer Kitchen
Susanna Foo
Tangerine
Taste
Twenty Manning
Umbria
Valanni
Vetri
Vickers Tavern
Water Lily/NJ
Yardley Inn

Senior Appeal

Abacus
Bay Pony Inn
Ben & Irv Deli.
Bird-in-Hand Rest./LB
Blush
Buca di Beppo/NJ

Cafe Preeya
Caffe Casta Diva
Cedar Hollow Inn
Dessert
Divan Turkish Kitchen
Earl's Prime
Ernesto's 1521
Estia
Frederick's
Gen. Lafayette Inn
Georges'
Gioia Mia
Good 'N Plenty/LB
Hank's Place
Honey's Sit 'n Eat
Horizons
Isaac's/LB
Italian Bistro†
Jonathan's Amer. Grille
La Fontana
La Pergola
Little Pete's
Little Tuna/NJ
Majolica
Margaret Kuo's
Marigold Kitchen
Mayfair Diner
Melrose Diner
Miller's Smorgasbord/LB
Moonstruck
Murray's Deli
Nineteen
Old Guard Hse. Inn
Otto's Brauhaus
Plain & Fancy Farm/LB
Plate
Pond/Bistro Cassis
Pop Shop/NJ
Radicchio
Rist. Il Melograno
Roller's/Flying Fish
Simon Pearce
Taste
Vesuvio
Viggiano's
Vinny T's
Water Lily/NJ
White Elephant

William Penn Inn
Yardley Inn

Singles Scenes
Alma de Cuba
Amada
Ansill
Bar Ferdinand
Big Ed's BBQ/NJ
Black Sheep Pub
Bourbon Blue
Café Habana
Cantina Los Caballitos
Continental Mid-town
Coyote Crossing
Cuba Libre
Derek's
Deuce
Eulogy Belgian
Fadó Irish
Fergie's Pub
Independence Brew
Jones
Kildare's
Kisso Sushi
Latest Dish
Loie
Los Catrines
L2
Manayunk Brewery
Mantra
Marathon on Square
McFadden's
Mixto
North by Northwest
N. 3rd
Ortlieb's Jazz
Plough & Stars
Pod
Pond/Bistro Cassis
Public Hse./Logan Sq.
Raw Sushi Lounge
Sly Fox Brewery
Standard Tap
Swanky Bubbles
Tír na nÓg
Twenty Manning
Valanni

Sleepers
(Good to excellent food,
but little known)
Abyssinia
Ansill
Bona Cucina
Cafe Sud
Caffe Valentino
Carr's/LB
Cassatt Tea Room
Cedars
Chabaa Thai Bistro
Chaleo Thai
Chef's Table/David Finney/DE
China Royal/DE
Chun Hing
Creole Cafe/NJ
Delmonico's
Domaine Hudson/DE
Elements Café/NJ
Fioravanti
Flavor
Four Rivers
Geechee Girl
Gibraltar/LB
Golden Pheasant
Gourmet
Gracie's/LB
Green Hills Inn/LB
Haydn Zug's/LB
Horizons
Hotel du Village
Jake's Hamburgers/DE
Jong Ka Jib
La Esperanza/NJ
Lily's on Main/LB
Luigi Vitrone's/DE
Maria's/Summit
Mimosa Rest.
Mio Sogno
Mona Lisa/DE
Ms. Tootsie's
Nan Zhou Noodles
Olive Tree Med. Grill
Orchard
Pepper's Cafe
Pho Xe Lua
Rist. Il Melograno

Rist. Verona
Robin's Nest/NJ
Sakura Spring/NJ
Sapori/NJ
Siam Cuisine/Black Walnut
Siam Lotus
Silk Cuisine
Somsak/Taan/NJ
Sovana Bistro
Strawberry Hill/LB
Sushikazu
Tai Lake
Taq. La Michoacana
Taq. Moroleon
Teca
Tierra Colombiana
Trattoria Alberto
Trinacria

Tasting Menus

Amada
Birchrunville Store
Bridgetown Mill
Carmine's Creole
Cuba Libre
Dilworthtown Inn
Fountain
Gibraltar/LB
Gilmore's
Grill Rest.
Koi
Krazy Kat's/DE
La Bonne Auberge
La Campagne/NJ
Lacroix/Rittenhouse
Le Bec-Fin
Le Jardin
Marigold Kitchen
Matyson
Mélange Cafe/NJ
Melting Pot
Mercato
Meritage
Monte Carlo
Morimoto
Moro/DE
Norma's/NJ
Nunzio/NJ

Orchard
Pif
Rat's/NJ
Rest. at Doneckers/LB
Rest. 821/DE
Rest. Taquet
Savona
Shiroi Hana
Spence Cafe
Spring Mill Café
Striped Bass
Susanna Foo
Trattoria Alberto
Twenty21
Vetri

Transporting Experiences

Anton's at Swan/NJ
Astral Plane
Bamboo Club
Birchrunville Store
Fatou & Fama
Gilmore's
Hamilton's Grill/NJ
Illuminare
Jamaican Jerk Hut
Kabul
Krazy Kat's/DE
La Campagne/NJ
Lacroix/Rittenhouse
Le Bec-Fin
Le Castagne
Little Marakesh
Ludwig's Garten
Manon/NJ
Margaret Kuo's
Marrakesh
Morimoto
Moro/DE
Moshulu
Paloma
Penang
Pif
Rat's/NJ
Rest. at Doneckers/LB
Siri's Thai French/NJ
Tangerine
Taq. Moroleon

Vetri
Zanzibar Blue

Trendy
Alma de Cuba
Amada
Ansill
Apamate
Audrey Claire
Banana Leaf
Barclay Prime
Bar Ferdinand
bluezette
Blush
Buddakan
Cafe Spice
Cantina Los Caballitos
Capital Grille
Casona/NJ
Continental
Continental Mid-town
Cuba Libre
Deuce
Django
Domaine Hudson/DE
Eulogy Belgian
Fadó Irish
Funky Lil' Kitchen
Krazy Kat's/DE
Latest Dish
Loie
London Grill
Los Catrines
L2
Mantra
Mélange Cafe/NJ
Mixto
Morimoto
No. 9/NJ
North by Northwest
Nunzio/NJ
Paradigm
¡Pasión!
Pod
Rat's/NJ
Rest. at Doneckers/LB
Rouge
Royal Tavern

Sagami/NJ
Siam/NJ
Siri's Thai French/NJ
Swanky Bubbles
Tangerine
Tír na nÓg
Twenty Manning
Valanni
Vetri
Wooden Iron
Yangming

Views
Ardmore Station
Azalea
Bay Pony Inn
Bistro St. Tropez
Black Bass Hotel
Café Gallery/NJ
Chart House
Conley Ward's/DE
Cuttalossa Inn
Dave & Buster's
Devon Seafood
DiNardo's Seafood
EverMay/Delaware
Fountain
Hamilton's Grill/NJ
Harry's Seafood/DE
Hibachi
Jake's
King George II
Krazy Kat's/DE
La Bonne Auberge
Lacroix/Rittenhouse
Lambertville Station/NJ
Landing
La Veranda
Lilly's on Canal/NJ
Moshulu
Mother's Rest. & Wine Bar
Nineteen
Pond/Bistro Cassis
Rat's/NJ
Robin's Nest/NJ
Rouge
Simon Pearce
Society Hill Hotel

Swann Lounge
Trax Café
Upstares at Varalli
Yardley Inn

Visitors on Expense Account
Barclay Prime
Blush
Brasserie Perrier
Capital Grille
Chops
Deux Cheminées
Dilworthtown Inn
Estia
Fountain
Grill
Il Portico
Le Bec-Fin
McCormick/Schmick's
Monte Carlo
Morimoto
Morton's
Nineteen
Old Orig. Bookbinder's
Pond/Bistro Cassis
Prime Rib
Roy's
Ruth's Chris
Shula's Steak
Smith & Wollensky
Striped Bass
Sullivan's Steak.†
Susanna Foo
Tangerine

Waterside
Black Bass Hotel
Bourbon Blue
Café Gallery/NJ
Centre Bridge Inn
Chart House
Cuttalossa Inn
Dave & Buster's
EverMay/Delaware
Golden Pheasant
Hamilton's Grill/NJ
Harry's Seafood/DE
King George II

Lambertville Station/NJ
Landing
La Veranda
Lilly's on Canal/NJ
Manayunk Brewery
Moshulu
Robin's Nest/NJ
Simon Pearce

Wine Bars
Bar Ferdinand
Domaine Hudson/DE
Horizons
Rist. Panorama
Teca
Tria
Vintage

Winning Wine Lists
Amada
Ansill
Back Burner/DE
Bamboo Club
Beau Rivage/NJ
Blue Bell Inn
Blush
Capital Grille
Caribou Cafe
Chops
Deux Cheminées
Dilworthtown Inn
Domaine Hudson/DE
Fountain
Georges'
Green Hills Inn/LB
Grill
Harry's Savoy/DE
Haydn Zug's/LB
Jake's
La Bonne Auberge
Lacroix/Rittenhouse
La Famiglia
Le Bar Lyonnais
Le Bec-Fin
Le Castagne
Mainland Inn
Meritage
Monte Carlo
Morton's

Penne
Pond/Bistro Cassis
Prime Rib
Rat's/NJ
Rest. 821/DE
Rest. Taquet
Rist. Panorama
Rist. Positano
Roux 3
Saloon
Savona
Shula's Steak
Striped Bass
Sullivan's Steak.†
Trinacria
Twenty21
Vetri
Vintage
Yardley Inn

Worth a Trip

Birchrunville
  Birchrunville Store
Blue Bell
  Alison/Blue Bell
Carversville
  Carversville Inn
Cherry Hill
  La Campagne/NJ
Collingswood
  Nunzio/NJ
  Sagami/NJ
Dresher
  Carambola
Ephrata
  Rest. at Doneckers/LB
Exton
  Duling-Kurtz Hse.
Hamilton
  Rat's/NJ
Hockessin
  Back Burner/DE

Kennett Square
  Sovana Bistro
  Taq. Moroleon
Kimberton
  Kimberton Inn
Lambertville
  Hamilton's Grill/NJ
Lancaster
  Log Cabin/LB
Lansdale
  Ravenna
Mainland
  Mainland Inn
Marlton
  Food for Thought/NJ
  Joe's Peking/NJ
Mendenhall
  Mendenhall Inn
Mount Holly
  Robin's Nest/NJ
Narberth
  Carmine's Creole
New Hope
  Hotel du Village
  Inn at Phillips Mill
  La Bonne Auberge
Pine Forge
  Gracie's/LB
Reading
  Green Hills Inn/LB
Southampton
  Blue Sage Veg.
Voorhees
  Little Café/NJ
West Chester
  Gilmore's
  Simon Pearce
Wilmington
  Moro/DE
  Toscana Kitchen/DE
Yardley
  Yardley Inn

Wine Vintage Chart

This chart is designed to help you select wine to go with your meal. It is based on the same 0 to 30 scale used throughout this *Survey*. The ratings (prepared by our friend **Howard Stravitz,** a law professor at the University of South Carolina) reflect both the quality of the vintage and the wine's readiness for present consumption. Thus, if a wine is not fully mature or is over the hill, its rating has been reduced. We do not include 1987, 1991–1993 vintages because they are not especially recommended for most areas. A dash indicates that a wine is either past its peak or too young to rate.

	'85	'86	'88	'89	'90	'94	'95	'96	'97	'98	'99	'00	'01	'02	'03	'04
WHITES																
French:																
Alsace	24	–	22	27	27	26	25	25	24	26	23	26	27	25	22	–
Burgundy	26	25	–	24	22	–	28	29	24	23	26	25	24	27	23	24
Loire Valley	–	–	–	–	–	20	23	22	–	24	25	26	27	25	23	–
Champagne	28	25	24	26	29	–	26	27	24	23	24	24	22	26	–	–
Sauternes	21	28	29	25	27	–	21	23	25	23	24	24	28	25	26	–
German	–	–	25	26	27	25	24	27	26	25	25	23	29	27	25	25
California (Napa, Sonoma, Mendocino):																
Chardonnay	–	–	–	–	–	–	–	–	–	–	24	25	28	27	26	–
Sauvignon Blanc/Sémillon	–	–	–	–	–	–	–	–	–	–	–	–	27	28	26	–
REDS																
French:																
Bordeaux	24	25	24	26	29	22	26	25	23	25	24	28	26	23	25	23
Burgundy	23	–	21	24	26	–	26	28	25	22	27	22	25	27	24	–
Rhône	–	–	26	29	29	24	25	22	24	28	27	27	26	–	25	–
Beaujolais	–	–	–	–	–	–	–	–	–	–	–	24	–	25	28	25
California (Napa, Sonoma, Mendocino):																
Cab./Merlot	27	26	–	–	28	29	27	25	28	23	26	22	27	25	24	–
Pinot Noir	–	–	–	–	–	–	–	–	24	24	25	24	27	28	26	–
Zinfandel	–	–	–	–	–	–	–	–	–	–	–	–	26	26	28	–
Italian:																
Tuscany	–	–	–	25	22	25	20	29	24	28	24	26	24	–	–	–
Piedmont	–	–	24	26	28	–	23	26	27	25	25	28	26	18	–	–
Spanish:																
Rioja	–	–	–	–	–	26	26	24	25	22	25	25	27	20	–	–
Ribera del Duero/Priorat	–	–	–	–	–	26	26	27	25	24	26	26	27	20	–	–